BEST of the BEST
from
OKLAHOMA
COOKBOOK

Selected Recipes from Oklahoma's
FAVORITE COOKBOOKS

Bison roam free on the 39,000-acre Tallgrass Prairie Preserve in northern Oklahoma. Once spanning portions of 14 states, the preserve is now the largest protected remnant of tallgrass prairie left on earth. As its name suggests, the most obvious features of this native North American ecosystem are tall grasses which average between five and six feet tall.

BEST of the BEST
from
OKLAHOMA
COOKBOOK

Selected Recipes from Oklahoma's
FAVORITE COOKBOOKS

Edited by
Gwen McKee
and
Barbara Moseley

Illustrated by Tupper England

QUAIL RIDGE PRESS
Preserving America's Food Heritage

Recipe Collection ©1996 Quail Ridge Press, Inc.

Reprinted with permission and all rights reserved under the name
of the cookbooks, organizations, or individuals listed below.

Applause! Oklahoma's Best Performing Recipes ©1995 Oklahoma's City Orchestra League; *Cafe Oklahoma* ©1994 Junior Service League, Midwest City; *Cleora's Kitchens* ©1985 Council Oaks Books, Ltd.; *Discover Oklahoma Cookin'* ©1993 Oklahoma 4-H Foundation, Inc.; *15-Minute, Lowfat Meals* ©1996 Jayne Benkendorf; Fat Free & Ultra Lowfat Recipes ©1995 Doris Cross, Prima Publishing; *Fat Free 2* ©1996 Doris Cross, Prima Publishing; *Gourmet Our Way* ©1995 Cascia Parent Faculty Assn.; *Long Lost Recipes of Aunt Susan* ©1989 Patricia V. MacDonald; *Mary's Recipe Box* ©1996 Mary Gubser, Council Oak Books, Ltd.; *National Cowboy Hall of Fame Cookbook* ©1995 National Cowboy Hall of Fame: Hearst Books, NY, imprint of William Morrow and Company, Inc.; *Oklahoma Cookin'* ©1995 Barnard Elementary School; *The Oklahoma Celebrity Cookbook* ©1991 Executive Coffee Service; *Our Country Cookin'* ©1984 Junior Social Workers; *Pioneer Chef* ©1991 Telephone Pioneers of America, Oklahoma Chapter 41; *Pow Wow Chow* ©1984 Five Civilized Tribes Museum; *Quick Breads, Soups & Stews* ©1991 Mary Gubser, Council Oak Books, Ltd.; *Recipes and Remembrances* ©1994 Northfork Electric Cooperative, Inc.; *The Route 66 Cookbook* ©1993 Marian Clark, Council Oak Books, Ltd; *Sooner Sampler* ©1987 Junior League of Norman, Inc.; *Sounds Delicious!* ©1986 Volunteer Council of the Tulsa Philharmonic Society, Inc.; *Spiced with Wit* ©1992 Patricia V. MacDonald; *Stir-Ups* ©Junior Welfare League of Enid; *Thunderbird Cookers of AT&T* ©1986 Telephone Pioneers of America, Oklahoma Chapter 94; *When a Man's Fancy Turns to Cooking* ©1996 G. Wesley Rice

Library of Congress Cataloging-in-Publication Data

Best of the best from Oklahoma cookbook : selected recipes from Oklahoma's
    favorite cookbooks / edited by Gwen McKee and Barbara Moseley;
    illustrated by Tupper England.
        p. cm. – (Best of the best state cookbook series)
Includes index.
ISBN-13: 978-0-937552-65-0
ISBN-10: 0-937552-65-8
1. Cookery, American—Southwestern style. 2. Cookery—Oklahoma.
I. McKee, Gwen. II. Moseley, Barbara.
TX715.2.S698467 1996
641.59766—dc20   96-19063
                                                        CIP

ISBN-13: 978-0-937552-65-0 • ISBN-10: 0-937552-65-8

First printing, July 1996 • Second, October 1999 • Third, July 2001
Fourth, January 2005 • Fifth, February 2010

Printed by Tara TPS in South Korea

Cover photo by Pauline Fahle, Oklahoma Wildlife & Prairie Heritage Alliance
Back cover photo by Greg Campbell

QUAIL RIDGE PRESS
P. O. Box 123 • Brandon, MS 39043 • 1-800-343-1583
info@quailridge.com • www.quailridge.com

Contents

Preface...7

List of Contributors.............................9

Appetizers and Beverages.................................11

Bread and Breakfast...25

Soups...53

Salads...63

Pasta, Pizza, Rice, Etc.......................................83

Vegetables...99

Poultry...129

Meats...147

Cakes...175

Cookies and Candies.......................................199

Pies and Other Desserts.................................221

Catalog of Contributing Cookbooks.................255

Index...262

Best of the Best Cookbook Series.................272

COURTESY OF OKLAHOMA TOURISM

Known as Oklahoma's favorite son, Will Rogers (Nov. 4, 1879–Aug. 15, 1935) was a Cherokee-American cowboy, comedian, humorist, social commentator, vaudeville performer, and actor. The Will Rogers Memorial Museum in Claremore stands on the site purchased by Rogers in 1911 for his retirement home.

Preface

Just saying the word Oklahoma brings to mind buffalo-speckled plains, colorful Indian artifacts, fields of waving wheat, stretches of ancient granite mountains.... Add to that cosmopolitan big cities and charming small towns, sparkling blue waters and evergreen timbered mountains, and you have a kaleidoscope backdrop for this intriguing state.

"Oklahoma is the heart, it's the vital organ of our national existence," Will Rogers bragged about his native state in 1926. It's still true that what is best about America can be found in Oklahoma...and that certainly holds true for its food.

Chicken-fried steak and barbecue may be thought of as Oklahoma's state foods, and yes, Sooners serve those dishes up deliciously; but that is only the beginning. Judging from the wonderful recipes contributed to this cookbook from fifty-nine of the leading cookbooks from throughout the state, we are convinced that Oklahomans know what good food is all about. Some recipes are totally new, while others are centuries old. And some are old favorites with a new twist. There are even some fancy chef creations; but most are good-old home cookin' that anybody can duplicate deliciously in their own kitchen. It seems that the secrets from those "box lunches" that used to be creatively prepared by the early settler women to win the hearts of many a farmer and cowboy are revealed in this book.

It would not be possible for us to put such a comprehensive book as this together without the cooperation of a lot of friendly, delightful people who we have had the privilege of working with throughout the process. State, county, and city employees proudly provided us with pictures and information about their communities. Food editors, media personnel, and book and gift store managers helped us find cookbooks—and please forgive us if we inadvertently omitted any in our arduous research.

Specifically, we want to thank Waynell Harris for gathering photographs (she and Paul sometimes had to roam where the buffalo roam); and Tupper England for capturing the essence of Oklahoma in her charming drawings; and our office pals, Sheila Williams, Annette Goode, Madonna White, and Shawn McKee for assisting in so much of the phoning, copying, computerizing, encouraging, and just general foot-working that is involved in putting it all together.

We are proud to share the samplings of Oklahoma's delicious food from proud pioneer women to city-slicker chefs, from chuck wagon cooks to modern-day homemakers all across the land. After spending a delicious time in the Sooner State, we concur that "You're doing fine, Oklahoma." This book surely proves that.

Gwen McKee and Barbara Moseley

Contributing Cookbooks

Applause!
Cafe Oklahoma
Centennial Cookbook
Cleora's Kitchens
Come Grow with Us
Company Fare I
Company Fare II
Cookbook of Treasured Recipes
Cooking A+ Recipes
Country Cooking
Court Clerk's Bar and Grill
Dine with the Angels
Discover Oklahoma Cookin'
Fat Free & Ultra Lowfat Recipes
Fat Free 2
Feast in Fellowship
Feeding Our Flock
15 Minute, Lowfat Meals
Four Generations of Johnson Family Favorites
Gourmet Our Way
Gourmet: The Quick and Easy Way
Healthy America
Helen's Southwest Specialties
Here's What's Cookin' at Zion
Home Cookin' Is a Family Affair
The Homeplace Cookbook
Kitchen Klatter Keepsakes
Long Lost Recipes of Aunt Susan
Mary's Recipe Box
National Cowboy Hall of Fame Chuck Wagon Cookbook

Contributing Cookbooks

The Oklahoma Celebrity Cookbook
Oklahoma Cookin'
Old and New
100 Years of Cooking
Our Country Cookin'
The Pioneer Chef
Pow Wow Chow
Quick Breads, Soups & Stews
Recipes & Remembrances
The Route 66 Cookbook
Seasoned with Love
Seems Like I Done It This A-Way
Seems Like I Done It This A-Way II
Seems Like I Done It This A-Way III
Sequoyah's Cookin'
Shattuck Community Cookbook
Sisters Two and Family Too
Something Special Cookbook
Sooner Sampler
Sounds Delicious!
Spiced with Wit
Spring Creek Club
Stir-Ups
Thank Heaven for Home Made Cooks
Thunderbird Cookers of AT&T
United Methodist Cookbook 1993
Watonga Cheese Festival Cookbook 17th Edition
What's Cooking in Okarche?
When a Man's Fancy Turns to Cooking

Appetizers and Beverages

PHOTO BY DUSTIN M. RAMSEY

Philbrook Museum of Art in Tulsa is distinguished by nationally recognized facilities, gardens, exhibitions, quality collections, and innovative educational programming. Set within a twenty-three acre site just three miles from downtown Tulsa, the seventy-two room villa is the former home of Oklahoma oil pioneer Waite Phillips and his wife. It was built in 1927 and donated to the city in 1938.

Layered Dip

1 (8-ounce) carton sour cream
1 tablespoon taco seasoning mix (½ package)
1 (16-ounce) can refried beans
1 (6-ounce) carton avocado dip
1 (4½-ounce) can chopped ripe olives
2 large tomatoes, diced
1 onion or 1 bunch green onions
1 (4-ounce) can chopped green chiles
1½ cups (or more) shredded cheese

Combine sour cream and taco seasoning mix, then layer in 9x13-inch pan in order given. Needs to set overnight or several hours. Remove from refrigerator about 30 minutes before serving. Serve with corn chips.

Thank Heaven for Home Made Cooks

Oklahoma Caviar Dip

2 (16-ounce) cans black-eyed peas, drained
1 (16-ounce) can white hominy, drained
2 medium tomatoes, chopped
3 green onions, chopped
2 jalapeño peppers, chopped
1¼ cups chopped onions
1 cup finely chopped parsley
1 clove garlic, minced
1 (8-ounce) bottle of Italian salad dressing

Combine peas, hominy, tomatoes, green onions, jalapeño peppers, onions, parsley, and garlic in bowl; mix well. Combine with salad dressing in serving bowl; mix well. Chill in refrigerator for 2 hours. Serve with large corn chips. May process half the pea mixture in blender for smoother consistency if desired. Yields 12 servings.

Approx Per Serving: Cal 180; T Fat 12g; Cal from Fat 52%; Prot 5g; Carbo 20g; Fiber 6g; Chol 0mg; Sod 432mg.

The Pioneer Chef

The name "Oklahoma" comes from the Choctaw language; okla meaning "people" and homma, or humma, meaning "red."

Vegetable Dip

1 pint mayonnaise
1 pint sour cream
3 tablespoons parsley flakes
3 teaspoons seasoning salt

3 tablespoons onion flakes
3 teaspoons dill weed
(⅛ teaspoon powdered dill
may be used)

Mix all ingredients together. Serve with various fresh vegetables such as carrots, celery, cauliflower, green peppers, etc.

Seems Like I Done It This A-Way III

Too Easy Tamale Dip

2 (15-ounce) cans tamales
1 (16-ounce) can chili
without beans
1 (8-ounce) jar picante sauce

2 (5-ounce) jars Old English
cheese
1 onion, chopped

Chop the tamales and add rest of ingredients and blend. Put in fondue or crock and keep warm. Serve with anything "dipable." Easy and very good. Serves 20 with other hors d'oeuvres.

Stir Ups

Pumpkin Dip

A *"must try" recipe for fall!*

4 cups powdered sugar
2 (8-ounce) packages cream
cheese, softened
1 (30-ounce) can solid pack
pumpkin

2 teaspoons ground
cinnamon
1 teaspoon ground ginger
Gingersnap cookies

In a large mixing bowl, combine powdered sugar and cream cheese, beating with mixer until well-blended. Beat in remaining ingredients (except cookies). Store in airtight container in refrigerator. Serve as a dip with gingersnap cookies.

Note: Beautiful served in pumpkin that has been hollowed out with fall leaves at the base. Yields 7 cups.

Cafe Oklahoma

Shrimp Dip

1 (8-ounce) package cream
cheese, softened
⅔ cup real mayonnaise
(not Miracle Whip)
1½ cups chopped green
onions

1½ cups chopped celery
(fine)
2 tablespoons lemon juice
1 can small shrimp

Mix all ingredients and refrigerate.

100 Years of Cooking

Annie's Mexicorn Dip

1 small can Mexicorn,
drained
1 small can white corn,
drained
1 cup grated, sharp Cheddar
cheese
½ cup sour cream

½ cup mayonnaise
½ cup chopped green onions
1 (4-ounce) can chopped
green chiles
1 teaspoon Lawry's seasoned
salt
Garlic salt to taste

Mix the above ingredients well. Chill in the refrigerator 1 hour.
Before serving, sprinkle on a little chili powder for decoration.
Serve with big corn chips for dipping.

Gourmet: The Quick and Easy Way

Curry Chicken Spread

1 (8-ounce) package cream
cheese, softened
½ cup mayonnaise
2 teaspoons lemon juice
½ teaspoon salt
¼ teaspoon curry powder

⅛ teaspoon pepper
2 cups finely minced cooked
chicken
½ cup mango chutney
¼ cup chopped green onions

Blend first 7 ingredients and spread in a serving dish. Layer the
mango chutney over the top. Garnish with chopped green
onions. Serve with crackers. Makes 8 servings.

Applause!

Sooner Salsa

A quick and easy salsa!

1 (16-ounce) can stewed
tomatoes
4 medium tomatoes, chopped
3 small jalapeño peppers,
chopped and seeded

⅓ cup chopped onion
½ teaspoon salt
½ teaspoon cayenne pepper

Combine tomatoes, peppers, and onion in food processor and process until desired consistency. Add salt and cayenne pepper; process again to mix. Store in refrigerator.

Note: With jalapeños—keep as many or as few seeds as you wish; the more seeds, the hotter the salsa. Yields 4 cups.

Cafe Oklahoma

Blender Salsa

6 medium tomatoes, peeled
½ cup chopped green
chiles
⅓ cup chopped onion

1 teaspoon salt
3 jalapeño peppers
1 clove garlic

Combine all ingredients in blender container. Process to desired consistency. Freezes well. Yields 2 cups.

100 Years of Cooking

Holiday Cheese Roll

1 pound processed cheese
  spread, softened
8 ounces cream cheese,
  softened
1 (4-ounce) can chopped
  green chiles
2 ounces diced pimentos,
  drained
3 green onions, chopped
1 teaspoon chopped
  jalapeños, optional
1 cup chopped pecans

Carefully roll the processed cheese spread between two pieces of wax paper to a rectangle 11x17 inches; remove top layer. Beat cream cheese until consistency to spread evenly on top of cheese spread. Sprinkle remaining ingredients evenly on top of cream cheese. Roll jelly-roll style, removing wax paper with each quarter turn until mixture is enclosed. Place seam-side-down in dish. Refrigerate until well chilled. Serve with Melba toast or other thin crisp crackers.

Watonga Cheese Festival Cookbook 17th Edition

Chutney Cream Cheese Ball

1 (8-ounce) package cream
  cheese, softened
1½ cups grated Cheddar
½ teaspoon curry powder
½ teaspoon garlic powder
¼ teaspoon salt
4 teaspoons sherry
½–1 jar Major Grey's
  Mango Chutney
Chopped green onions
2 hard-boiled eggs, chopped
½ pound bacon, crumbled
Chopped pecans or peanuts

Mix first 6 ingredients in food processor. On serving plate, form in a mound; chill. Spread with chutney. Layer onions, eggs, bacon, and nuts. Serve with crackers. Serves 8–10.

Four Generations of Johnson Family Favorites

Pepperoni Cheese Ball

2 (8-ounce) packages cream cheese, softened
2 tablespoons dry minced onion
½ cup diced green pepper
¼ cup bacon bits
3½ ounces pepperoni, finely chopped
1 (8-ounce) can crushed pineapple, drained
1 tablespoon seasoned salt
1 cup chopped pecans

Mix all ingredients, reserving ¼ cup pecans. Shape into ball. Cover with remaining pecans.

Our Country Cookin'

Tortilla Wagonwheels

2 (8-ounce) packages cream cheese, softened
3 tablespoons sour cream
1 (4-ounce) can mild chopped green chiles, drained
1 cup finely diced bell pepper
3 tablespoons chopped pimiento
4 green onions, finely chopped
4 slices bacon, cooked and crumbled (can substitute real bacon bits)
Seasoning salt and garlic to taste
6–8 large flour tortillas

Mix cream cheese and sour cream until smooth. Add remaining ingredients, except tortillas; combine well. Spread mixture ⅛-inch thick on each flat tortilla. Tightly roll each tortilla, jelly-roll style. Chill. Cut in ½-inch slices and serve. Yields 7–8 dozen.

Cafe Oklahoma

Pankey's Easy Hors D'Oeuvres

1 package flour tortillas
1 (8-ounce) package cream cheese, softened
1 small jar picante sauce
1 small can black olives
Sliced jalapeño peppers

Spread cream cheese on tortillas, then layer with remaining ingredients. Roll and slice into bite-size pieces. Best if chilled before serving.

100 Years of Cooking

Fun Veggies

Kids love them.

1 cup instant potato flakes
½ cup grated Parmesan
  cheese
½ teaspoon celery salt
¼ cup melted margarine or
  butter buds

¼ teaspoon garlic powder
Raw zucchini, green peppers,
  broccoli, cauliflower,
  mushrooms
2 eggs, or egg beaters

Combine first 5 ingredients. Dip vegetables in egg; coat with potato flakes mixture. Bake at 400° for 25 minutes. Serve with Ranch style dip.

Cooking A+ Recipes

Ranch Seasoned Bagel Chips

2 bagels
2 egg whites, slightly beaten
1 (1-ounce) package dry
  ranch dressing mix

Butter flavor nonstick
  cooking spray

Preheat oven to 400°. Stand a bagel on its edge and carefully slice ¼-inch slices horizontally. Each bagel should make 5–6 slices. Spray a large baking sheet with butter-flavor nonstick cooking spray. Using a pastry brush, paint both sides of each bagel slice lightly with egg white; do not soak. Place slices on baking sheet and sprinkle with dry ranch dressing mix. Spray lightly with nonstick cooking spray and bake at 400° for 4–5 minutes. Turn each slice and bake another 5–6 minutes or until golden brown. Allow to cool and store in airtight container. Try different kinds of seasonings using the same method. Makes 4 servings.

Grams of Fat Per Serving 1. Calories Per Serving 86.

Other Suggested Seasonings: Molly McButter Sour Cream; Molly McButter Bacon Flavor; salt and dill weed; salt and garlic.

Fat Free & Ultra Lowfat Recipes

Grandma Amy's Meatballs

1 pound ground chuck or
beef
1 teaspoon salt
¼ teaspoon pepper
¼ cup ketchup or chili
sauce

1 tablespoon Worcestershire
¼ cup finely chopped onions
½ cup crushed cornflakes or
crackers
½ cup evaporated milk

Mix well. Shape into meatballs. Put on pan (cookie sheet) and bake in 400° oven for 12–15 minutes. Serve with hot sauce or plain. Delicious appetizer.

SAUCE:

1 cup ketchup

2 teaspoons horseradish

Mix together ketchup and horseradish; adjust amounts to taste.

Centennial Cookbook

Swedish Pecans

1 pound pecans
2 egg whites
1 cup sugar

¼ teaspoon salt
½ cup butter, melted

Toast pecans in a 325° oven for 10 minutes. Beat egg whites to stiff peaks; fold in sugar and salt. Beat to stiff peaks; fold in pecans. Melt butter in big cookie sheet. Pour pecan mixture in cookie sheet. Bake at 325° for 30 minutes, stirring every 10 minutes. Makes 4 cups.

Feeding Our Flock

Sausage Balls

1 pound sausage
1 small onion, chopped fine
1 green pepper, chopped fine
1 pound cheese, grated
3–4 cups Bisquick

Combine sausage, onion, pepper and cheese. Mix until not sticky, adding Bisquick gradually. Knead then roll into balls. Place on ungreased cookie sheet and bake at 350° for approximately 6 minutes. Turn over and bake on other side for approximately 3 minutes.

Dine with the Angels

Sausage-Cheese Balls

1 pound sausage
¼ cup onion
16 ounces sweet sauerkraut,
    drained well
4 ounces cream cheese,
    softened
2 tablespoons bread crumbs
Parsley flakes
½ cup flour
1 cup bread crumbs
2 eggs
¼ cup milk

SAUCE:
1 cup mayonnaise
1 teaspoon mustard
Tabasco, if desired

Cook sausage and onion; drain and cool. Combine sauerkraut, cream cheese, bread crumbs, and parsley flakes. Add sausage to this; mix and refrigerate for 1 hour. Shape into 1- to 1½-inch balls. Roll balls in ½ cup flour and 1 cup bread crumbs. Dip balls in mixture of 2 eggs and ¼ cup milk. Then dip back in flour mixture. Deep fat fry for 2–3 minutes. Serve with sauce.

Watonga Cheese Festival Cookbook 17th Edition

The Watonga Cheese Festival is held the first Friday and Saturday of October. It includes the Great Rat Race, the Great Mouse Walk, plus crafts, entertainment, food and fun. The Watonga Cheese Factory is open year-round for visitors to observe the cheese-making process firsthand.

Savory Stuffed Mushrooms

A hit at the "A Few of Our Favorite Things" cocktail party.

1 pound fresh mushrooms
4 slices bacon, diced
¾ cup chopped onion
2 tablespoons minced green
  bell pepper

1 teaspoon salt
Dash of freshly ground pepper
3 ounces cream cheese,
  softened

Remove stems from mushrooms; chop. Sauté bacon until partially cooked. Add onion, bell pepper, salt, pepper, and stems. Cook until tender; cool. Remove to bowl; add cream cheese and mix well. Press into mushroom caps, mounding slightly. Preheat oven to 375°. Place in jelly roll pan; add ¼ cup hot water to bottom of pan and bake 20 minutes. Yields 25–30 pieces.

Sounds Delicious!

Salmon Party Log

1 (14¾-ounce) can Honey
  Boy Red Salmon
1 (8-ounce) package cream
  cheese, softened
1 tablespoon lemon juice
2 teaspoons grated onion
2 teaspoons horseradish

¼ teaspoon liquid smoke
  (optional)
¼ teaspoon salt
3 drops of bottled hot pepper
  sauce (optional)
⅓ cup chopped pecans
1 cup parsley flakes

Drain and flake salmon. If desired, remove skin and bones. Combine salmon, cream cheese, lemon juice, onion, horseradish, liquid smoke, salt, and hot pepper sauce. Mix well. Chill. Shape into log and roll in mixture of pecans and parsley flakes. Serve as a spread with crisp crackers. Makes 2½ cups.

Shattuck Community Cookbook

Suzanne's Crab Appetizer

12 ounces cream cheese
2 tablespoons Worcestershire
1 tablespoon lemon juice
2 tablespoons mayonnaise
1 small onion, grated

Dash of garlic salt
1 bottle Heinz Chili Sauce
1 (6½-ounce) can crab,
    drained
Parsley

Mix cream cheese, Worcestershire, lemon juice, mayonnaise, onion, and garlic salt; spread on shallow plate. Pour chili sauce over this mixture. Spread crab over chili sauce. Garnish with parsley. Serve with snack crackers.

Sooner Sampler

A partial listing of
Famous Oklahomans

Johnny Bench, baseball player, Oklahoma City

John Berryman, poet, McAlester

Garth Brooks, singer, Tulsa

Jeremy Castle, singer, Blanchard

Iron Eyes Cody, Cherokee actor

Gordon Cooper, astronaut, Shawnee

Ralph Ellison, writer, Oklahoma City

James Garner, actor, Norman

Owen K. Garriott, astronaut, Enid

Vince Gill, singer, Norman

Chester Gould, cartoonist, Pawnee

Woody Guthrie, singer, composer, Okemah

Roy Harris, composer, Lincoln Cty

Paul Harvey, broadcaster, Tulsa

Van Heflin, actor, Walters

Tony Hillerman, author, Sacred Heart

Ron Howard, actor, director, Duncan

Ben Johnson, actor, Pawhuska

Jennifer Jones, actress, Tulsa

Jeane Kirkpatrick, diplomat, Duncan

Shannon Lucid, astronaut, Bethany

Mickey Mantle, baseball player, Spavinaw

Reba McEntire, singer, McAlester

Shannon Miller, Olympic gymnast, Enmond

Bill Moyers, journalist, Hugo

Daniel Patrick Moynihan, N.Y. senator, Tulsa

Patti Page, singer, Clarence

Brad Pitt, actor, Shawnee

Tony Randall, actor, Tulsa

Oral Roberts, evangelist, Ada

Dale Robertson, actor, Oklahoma City

Will Rogers, humorist, Oologah

Dan Rowan, comedian, Beggs

Maria Tallchief, ballerina, Fairfax

Jim Thorpe, athlete, Prague

Ted Shakleford, actor, Tulsa

Herbal Tea

5 cups water
½ cup chopped fresh mint
1 tablespoon dried sage
leaves
1 tablespoon lemon verbena
or 1 teaspoon dried
tarragon leaves

4 teaspoons light honey
4 teaspoons lemon juice
4 lemon wedges (optional)
4 mint sprigs (optional)

In a saucepan, bring the water to boiling. Pour the boiling water into a warmed teapot and add the mint, sage, and tarragon. Cover and steep for 5 minutes. Strain the tea mixture into 4 cups. Stir 1 teaspoon honey and 1 teaspoon lemon juice into each cup. Garnish with a lemon wedge and mint sprig.

The Homeplace Cookbook

Lemon-Lime Punch

1 packages lime Kool-Aid
(add water according to
directions)
3 small packages lime Jell-O
2 cups boiling water (to
dissolve Jell-O)
2 large cans pineapple juice

2 (12-ounce) cans frozen
lemonade (add water
according to directions)
1 cup sugar
2 quarts (1 [2-liter] bottle)
ginger ale
3 quarts (1 [3-liter] bottle) 7-Up

Mix together first 6 ingredients. Add ginger ale and 7-Up just before serving. Makes close to 5 gallons.

Note: Other flavors can be used too. Use the same flavor Jell-O and Kool-Aid.

Here's What's Cookin' at Zion

A port in Oklahoma? That's right. In fact, the Tulsa Port of Catoosa is one of the largest, most inland river-ports in the United States. Primarily following the Arkansas River, it offers year-round, ice-free barge service with river flow levels controlled by the U.S. Army Corps of Engineers. Located in a 2,000-acre industrial park and employing more than 2,500 people, products can travel easily and efficiently from America's heartland to the rest of the globe.

Orange Mint

It is my honest conviction that having this recipe should be a requirement, and that it should be issued when your social security number is given.

2½ cups water
2 cups sugar
Juice of 2 oranges and
grated rind of both

Juice of 6 lemons and grated
rind of 2
2 handfuls fresh mint leaves

Make a simple syrup of the sugar and water by boiling them together for 10 minutes. Add the juice of the fruits and the grated rind of the oranges and lemons. Pour this over the mint leaves, which have been well-washed. I like to bruise a few of the leaves so that the flavor is more pronounced. Cover tightly and let this brew for several hours. Strain through a sieve, then through one thickness of cheesecloth.

This makes one quart of rich juice, which may be kept in the refrigerator indefinitely.

To serve, fill tall glasses with finely powdered ice and pour ¼ cup (4 tablespoons) of this juice over the snow-like ice, then finish filling the glass with either ginger ale or cold water.

Long Lost Recipes of Aunt Susan

Slush Punch

3 small packages Kool-Aid
3 cups sugar
6 cups warm water

1 large can pineapple juice
1 (2-liter) bottle 7-Up

Mix Kool-Aid and sugar into warm water until dissolved. Add pineapple juice. Freeze, stirring occasionally as slush forms. Add pop to frozen slush and serve!

Sequoyah's Cookin'

Bread and Breakfast

COURTESY OF OKLAHOMA TOURISM

Nearly eight percent of all Oklahomans are Native Americans—more than any other state. Part of the Native American culture is preserved through dances such as the men's Fancy Dance featuring vivid regalia with dramatic movement, including spins and leaps. Of the many types of dances performed at a pow-wow, the Fancy Dance is often the biggest crowd-pleasing competition.

Jalapeño Corn Bread

"Muy caliente!" they say in Spanish. This dish is hot, hot, hot! But great, if you're an aficionado of Mexican cuisine or just like super spicy foods. Whether you're planning a fiesta or simply want something to wake up a plate of pinto beans, try this zesty corn bread.

3 cups yellow cornmeal
1 cup cream-style corn
1 teaspoon sugar
2 teaspoons salt
1 cup chopped onion
1½ teaspoons baking
   powder

1 cup vegetable oil
3 eggs
1¾ cups sweet milk
½ cup chopped jalapeño
   peppers
1⅓ cups grated cheese

Mix all and pour into a 9x13-inch ungreased pan and bake in a preheated 350° oven for one hour.

Note: If you're not familiar with the jalapeño pepper, be forewarned: These hot green peppers are not for people with timid taste buds. And don't be fooled by a can marked "mild" jalapeño peppers. Even the "mild" variety can make your eyes water.

Pow Wow Chow

Broccoli Bread

1 package cornbread mix
½ cup melted margarine
½ cup cottage cheese
1 small onion, chopped finely

2 eggs, beaten
1 teaspoon salt
1 small package frozen
   chopped broccoli

Spray 9x13-inch pan with oil. Mix ingredients and pour into pan. Bake in 400° oven for 30–35 minutes.

Feast in Fellowship

©CALEB LONG

The Myriad Botanical Gardens is a lush, tropical oasis nestled in the heart of downtown Oklahoma City. The Crystal Bridge, Oklahoma City's most distinctive landmark, is a glittering, 224-foot tropical paradise and a photographer's dream.

Squaw Bread

1 pint sour milk	1 teaspoon salt
1 tablespoon shortening	½ teaspoon soda
3 heaping teaspoons baking powder	Flour

Add enough flour to first 5 ingredients to make dough easy to handle. Knead it smooth and roll out until your dough is about ½ inch thick. Cut this into portions about the size of a quart jar lid, or make into strips; make some slits in it. Now cook in deep fat, just like doughnuts.

Sequoyah's Cookin'

Southern Spoon Bread

2 cups white corn meal	1½ teaspoons salt
2½ cups boiling water	3 eggs
¼ cup butter	1½ cups buttermilk
1 teaspoon sugar	½ teaspoon baking soda

Pour boiling water over meal; stir until thick and smooth. Cool to lukewarm. Add butter, sugar, and salt, and mix well. Beat eggs separately. Add yolks, then buttermilk in which baking soda has been added. Add egg whites last. Pour into deep buttered baking dish. Bake at 350° for 45 minutes.

Company Fare I

White Bread

5 cups water	4 tablespoons yeast
3 cups milk	4 eggs
1½ cups sugar	2 tablespoons instant mashed
1½ cups oil	potatoes
3½ tablespoons salt	Flour

Mix in order. Knead 10 minutes. Let rise 30 minutes. Punch down; let rise second time until double in bulk. Put in pans. Enough for 12 loaves. Bake at 350° for approximately ½ hour.

Here's What's Cookin' at Zion

Speedy Rolls and Bread

This recipe is from St. Mary's School Hot Lunch recipe book. These were baked during the 1950s, '60s, and '70s.

2 (1-ounce) cakes or 2
  packages dry yeast
1 pint water, lukewarm
½ cup sugar
¾ cup butter, shortening or
  oil, softened or melted

1¾ quarts flour
½ cup dry milk
1 tablespoon salt

Put yeast and lukewarm water in mixing bowl; add sugar. Let set until dissolved, then add melted butter. Add combined flour, dry milk, and salt, using dough hook (if by hand, knead well). Let dough rise once and knead before shaping. Shape into rolls or loaves and let rise double. Bake rolls at 425° for 7–12 minutes. Bake bread at 325° for 30–45 minutes.

Note: For cinnamon rolls, roll dough into a rectangle. Brush with melted butter. Sprinkle with sugar and cinnamon. Roll and slice. Let rise double. Bake and add a glaze.

Cooking A+ Recipes

Easy No-Knead Refrigerator Rolls

2 packages dry yeast
2 cups warm water
½ cup sugar
2 teaspoons salt

¼ cup oil
2 eggs, beaten
6½ cups flour

Dissolve yeast in warm water in large bowl. Add sugar, salt, oil, and eggs; mix well. Add flour; mix well. Place in greased bowl. Chill, covered, for 2 hours or longer. Shape into rolls. Place on greased baking sheet. Let rise for 1½–2 hours or until doubled in bulk. Bake at 375° for 15–20 minutes or until golden brown. May store dough in refrigerator for up to 5 days. Yields 36 servings.

Approx per serving: Cal 112; Prot 3g; Carbo 20g; Fiber 1g; T Fat 2g; 17% Cal from Fat; Chol 12mg; Sod 123mg.

Discover Oklahoma Cookin'

Biscuits

5 cups self-rising flour	1 cup warm water
1 teaspoon soda, optional	Milk, enough to make dough
6 tablespoons sugar	2 cups buttermilk
1 cup Crisco or its like	
2 packages dry yeast or 2 squares cake yeast	

If soda is used with buttermilk, sift soda with flour. Mix flour and sugar in mixing bowl. Cut shortening into mixture. Dissolve yeast in warm water; pour into flour mixture, then add milk. Mix, roll and cut ¼- to ½-inch thick. Put in refrigerator and use as needed. Let rise 2 hours and cook. Bake at 450° for 15–20 minutes or until done.

Note: If you desire to have quick biscuits, use lukewarm milk as well as water if you want them to rise quicker.

Seems Like I Done It This A-Way II

Mile-High Biscuits

3 cups all-purpose flour	¾ teaspoon salt
2 tablespoons sugar	¾ cup shortening
1 tablespoon plus 1½ teaspoons baking powder	1 egg, beaten
¾ teaspoon cream of tartar	¾ cup milk

Combine first 5 ingredients, mixing well; cut in shortening with a pastry blender until mixture resembles coarse meal. Combine egg and milk; add to flour mixture, stirring until dry ingredients are moistened. Turn dough out onto a lightly floured surface; knead 8 or 10 times. Roll dough to 1-inch thickness; cut with a 2½-inch biscuit cutter. Place biscuits on an ungreased baking sheet. Bake at 450° for 15 minutes or until golden brown. Yields 15 biscuits.

100 Years of Cooking

Pinch Cake

4 cans biscuits
1½ cups brown sugar

½ cup butter
2 tablespoons cinnamon

Cut each of the uncooked biscuits into fourths and place in well greased Bundt pan. Heat and bring to a boil brown sugar, butter, and cinnamon. Pour over the biscuits and bake in a 350° oven 25–30 minutes. Let cool 10 minutes. Turn out onto serving platter and serve. May use half of recipe in a loaf pan.

Kitchen Klatter Keepsakes

Herb Biscuits

¼ cup shortening
1 cup white flour
1 cup whole-wheat flour
2 teaspoons dried basil
3 teaspoons baking powder

½ teaspoon salt
1 teaspoon freshly ground
 pepper
¾ cup milk
1 tablespoon sugar (optional)

Preheat oven to 450°. Cut shortening into the flour until mixture is fine crumbs. Add remaining ingredients, except milk. Continue to cut mixture until thoroughly mixed. Stir in just enough milk for dough to form a ball. Place dough on floured surface and roll in flour to coat. Knead bread 25 times. Roll to ½-inch thick. Cut with floured biscuit cutter. Place on ungreased cookie sheet, leaving about 1 inch between biscuits. Bake 12 minutes. Serve warm. Yields 10 biscuits.

The Homeplace Cookbook

Hot Pull-Apart Biscuits

1 (10-biscuit) package
refrigerated biscuits
3 tablespoons margarine,
melted
½ teaspoon chili powder

½ cup shredded Cheddar
cheese
¼ cup chopped jalapeño
peppers

Cut biscuits into quarters. Combine margarine and chili powder in a 9-inch pie plate. Place biscuit pieces in pie plate and toss to coat each piece with margarine mixture. Sprinkle cheese and peppers on top. Bake at 350° for 15 minutes or until brown.

Shattuck Community Cookbook

Raspberry Cream Cheese Coffeecake

1 (3-ounce) package cream
cheese
4 tablespoons softened butter

2 cups Bisquick
⅓ cup milk
½ cup raspberry preserves

GLAZE:

1 cup powdered sugar
1½ tablespoons milk

½ teaspoon vanilla

Cut cream cheese and butter into Bisquick until crumbly. Blend in milk. Turn onto floured surface and knead 8–10 times. Place on wax paper and roll to 12x8-inch rectangle. Turn onto greased jelly roll pan and remove paper. Spread preserves down center of dough. Make two ½-inch cuts at 1-inch intervals along both long edges of rectangle. Fold strips over filling, sealing sides with fingers to prevent preserves from leaking out. Bake at 425° for 12–15 minutes. Combine ingredients for Glaze and drizzle over coffeecake. Makes 8 servings.

Come Grow with Us

Sour Cream Coffee Cake

Sour Cream Coffee Cake has been a delight for bakers both at home and in commercial establishments long enough to give it classical status. Lighter sour cream with less fat content works just as well as regular sour cream.

FILLING:

½ cup brown sugar, packed
⅓ cup all-purpose flour
2 teaspoons ground
  cinnamon

¼ cup cold butter, cut in
  pieces
1 cup coarsely chopped
  walnuts or pecans

Combine the brown sugar, flour, and cinnamon in a food processor. With the steel blade in place, pulse several times to mix ingredients. Add the cold butter, whirling until the mixture resembles coarse cornmeal. Transfer to a small bowl, stir in the nuts and set aside. Preheat oven to 350°. Brush a Bundt pan with melted butter or coat with vegetable spray.

CAKE:

2 cups all-purpose flour
1½ teaspoons baking
  powder
1 teaspoon baking soda
½ teaspoon salt

½ cup butter or margarine
1 cup sugar
2 large eggs
1 cup sour cream
1 teaspoon vanilla extract

Sift the flour, baking powder, baking soda, and salt together and set aside. In the large bowl of an electric mixer, cream the butter and sugar together until light and fluffy. Add the eggs one at a time, beating well after each addition. Alternately add the dry ingredients and the sour cream to the butter mixture, beginning and ending with the flour mixture. Scrape down the sides and beat until creamy. Stir in the vanilla and mix well. Pour half the batter into a prepared Bundt pan, spreading evenly. Sprinkle the filling over the batter. Spread remaining batter over the filling. Bake approximately 40 minutes, test for doneness, and if necessary bake 10 minutes longer. Remove the cake to a wire rack and cool 10 minutes before turning out of the pan. Serves 10–12.

Quick Breads, Soups & Stews

Cream Cheese Braid

PASTRY:

1 cup sour cream
½ cup sugar
1 teaspoon salt
½ cup margarine, melted

½ cup warm water
2 packages dry yeast
2 eggs, beaten
4 cups flour

Heat sour cream over low heat. Stir in sugar, salt, and margarine. Cool to lukewarm. Dissolve yeast in warm water. Combine sour cream mixture, yeast mixture, eggs, and flour. Mix this well. Cover and refrigerate overnight.

FILLING:

16 ounces cream cheese,
    softened
¾ cup sugar

1 egg, beaten
⅛ teaspoon salt
2 teaspoons vanilla

GLAZE:

4 tablespoons milk

2 teaspoons vanilla

The next day combine cream cheese and sugar. Then add egg, salt, and vanilla. Divide dough into fourths. Roll one of the fourths into a 12x8-inch rectangle. Spread ¼ of the cream cheese filling over this dough. Roll up jelly-roll style, pinching the edges to seal it. Place seam-side-down on a greased baking sheet and make slits ⅔ of the way down at 2-inch intervals to resemble braids. Cover and let rise till double (approximately 1 hour). Bake at 375° for 12–15 minutes. Pour Glaze over braid while warm.

Sooner Sampler

Pumpkin Cheese Bread

2½ cups sugar
1 (8-ounce) package cream
  cheese, softened
½ cup margarine
4 eggs
1 (16-ounce) can pumpkin
3½ cups flour
2 teaspoons baking soda

1 teaspoon salt
1 teaspoon cinnamon
½ teaspoon baking powder
¼ teaspoon ground cloves
1 cup chopped nuts
2 cups powdered sugar
3 tablespoons milk

Preheat oven to 350°. Mix sugar, cream cheese and margarine at medium speed on electric mixer until well blended. Add eggs, one at a time, mixing well after each addition. Blend in pumpkin. Add combined dry ingredients, mixing just until moistened. Fold in nuts. Pour into two greased and floured 9 x 5-inch loaf pans. Bake 1 hour or until wooden pick inserted in center comes out clean. Cool 5 minutes; remove from pans. Glaze with combined powdered sugar and milk. Garnish with pecan halves and maraschino cherry halves, if desired. Makes 2 loaves.

Watonga Cheese Festival Cookbook 17th Edition

Kolaches

2 packages yeast
¼ cup lukewarm water
1 teaspoon sugar
2 cups scalded half-and-half,
  cooled to lukewarm
½ cup sugar
2 teaspoons salt

1 teaspoon nutmeg
½ cup butter, melted and
  cooled
6–7 cups flour
3 eggs, beaten
1½ teaspoons grated lemon
  peel

Dissolve yeast in lukewarm water with the 1 teaspoon sugar in a cup. In large mixing bowl, combine half-and-half, ½ cup sugar, salt, nutmeg, butter, and about half the flour. Beat with mixer 3 or 4 minutes. Mix in eggs. Using a wooden spoon, mix in lemon peel and gradually add flour until dough is too stiff to mix, then turn out on floured surface and knead about 5 minutes. Dough should be smooth. Place in large greased bowl to

(continued)

(Kolaches continued)

rise. Cover with foil. When double in size, punch down and let rise again to double size.

Make dough into balls about the size of a blue prune plum and place on greased baking sheets. Let rise again, then make indentation in center with fingers; put in about 1 tablespoon filling and top with 1 teaspoon topping. Let rise again slightly. Bake to golden brown at 400° for about 12–15 minutes. Grease sides of rolls with Crisco while hot. Makes about 50.

APRICOT FILLING:

1 pound dried apricots	Sugar to taste
1 (12- to 16-ounce) jar apricot preserves	

Grind apricots. Put in small saucepan and cover with water. Simmer until water is absorbed. Add preserves and a little sugar and cook a little more. Cool. Makes about 3 dozen.

COTTAGE CHEESE FILLING:

24 ounces cottage cheese	½ teaspoon nutmeg
1 teaspoon grated lemon peel	3 beaten egg yolks
½ cup sugar	1 cup raisins

Drain cottage cheese (or use dry cottage cheese). Put through food grinder on medium. Add remaining ingredients. If mixture seems dry, add just a little cream. Filling needs to be thick enough so it doesn't run. Makes about 3 dozen.

PRUNE FILLING:

1 pound pitted prunes	Grated lemon peel to taste
Cinnamon and sugar to taste	

Cook prunes in just enough water to cover. Put through food grinder on medium. Add cinnamon, sugar, and grated lemon peel to taste.

TOPPING:

½ cup flour	¼ cup margarine
½ cup sugar	

Using pie blender, blend together until well mixed and slightly crumbly. Put teaspoon on top of Kolache filling.

Spring Creek Club

Apricot Date Loaf

½ cup butter, softened
⅔ cup light brown sugar, firmly packed
¼ teaspoon grated orange rind
¼ teaspoon grated lemon rind
2 eggs

1½ cups cottage cheese
3 cups flour
1 tablespoon baking powder
1 teaspoon baking soda
1 teaspoon salt
1 cup diced, dried apricots
1 cup diced dates

Cream together butter, sugar, and rinds until light and fluffy. Beat in eggs and cottage cheese thoroughly. Sift together flour, baking powder, soda, and salt. Mix in fruits, coating pieces to prevent sticking together. Add dry ingredients to cottage cheese mixture; blend well. Pack into loaf pan; bake 50–55 minutes at 350°. Remove from pan; cool on wire rack.

Recipes and Remembrances

Strawberry Bread

2 cups frozen, unsweetened whole strawberries
2¼ cups sugar, divided
3 cups plus 2 tablespoons flour
1 tablespoon cinnamon

1 teaspoon salt
1 teaspoon baking soda
1¼ cups oil
4 eggs, beaten
1¼ cups chopped pecans

Preheat oven to 350°. Place strawberries in medium bowl and sprinkle with ¼ cup sugar. Toss to coat and let stand until strawberries are thawed, then slice. Combine flour, remaining sugar, cinnamon, salt, and baking soda in large bowl; mix well. Stir oil and eggs into strawberries; add strawberry mixture to flour mixture. Add in pecans and blend until dry ingredients are just moistened (do not over mix). Divide batter between 2 (4½x8½-inch) greased and floured loaf pans. Bake 45–50 minutes. Allow bread to cool in pans for 10 minutes. Turn loaves out and allow to cool completely. Yields 2 loaves.

Cafe Oklahoma

Apricot Nibble Bread

2 (3-ounce) packages cream
  cheese, softened
⅓ cup sugar
1 tablespoon flour
1 egg
1 tablespoon grated orange
  rind
1 cup dried apricots
1½ cups warm water

2 cups flour
1 cup sugar
2 teaspoons baking powder
1 teaspoon salt
¼ teaspoon soda
¾ cup chopped pecans
1 egg
¼ cup vegetable shortening
½ cup orange juice

Cream together cream cheese, sugar, flour, egg, and grated orange rind and set aside. Mix dried apricots and warm water; let stand 5 minutes, drain well (reserve water), cut into small pieces and set aside.

Combine flour, sugar, baking powder, salt, soda, pecans, egg, and vegetable shortening. Mix together with orange juice and 1 cup water drained from apricots. Stir apricots into flour mixture. Turn ⅔ of batter into greased and floured 9x5-inch bread pan. Spoon cream cheese filling on top of batter, then add ⅓ of batter on top of cream cheese. Bake 65 minutes at 350°. May be baked in 8x10-inch pan.

Old and New

Cinnamon Bread

1 teaspoon baking soda
1 cup buttermilk
¼ cup margarine
1 cup sugar

1 egg
2 cups flour
½ cup sugar
1 tablespoon cinnamon

Mix the baking soda in the cup of buttermilk and let set 5 minutes. In another bowl, cream margarine, sugar, and egg. Add flour and buttermilk to mixture. Mix well. In still another bowl, combine ½ cup sugar and cinnamon. Grease 9x5x3-inch pan. Sprinkle liberally with sugar-cinnamon. Layer another ⅓ of batter and sprinkle with sugar-cinnamon. Layer remaining batter and sprinkle remaining sugar-cinnamon mixture on top. Bake at 350° for 50–60 minutes.

Centennial Cookbook

Oatmeal Bread

1 cup quick-cooking oats	2 cups boiling water
½ cup whole-wheat flour	1 package dry yeast
½ cup brown sugar, packed	½ cup warm water
1 tablespoon salt	5 cups all-purpose flour
2 tablespoons margarine	½ cup margarine

Combine oats, whole-wheat flour, brown sugar, salt, and margarine in bowl; mix well. Pour boiling water over all; mix well. Cool to room temperature. Dissolve yeast in warm water. Stir into oat mixture. Add all-purpose flour 1 cup at a time, stirring until dough is sticky but firm enough to handle. Knead on floured surface for 5–10 minutes or until smooth and elastic, adding enough flour to keep dough manageable. Place in greased bowl, turning to grease surface. Let rise, covered, until doubled in bulk. Punch dough down. Shape into 2 loaves. Place in greased 5x9-inch loaf pans.

Let rise, covered, until doubled in bulk. Bake at 350° for 30–40 minutes or until golden brown. Cool in pans for several minutes. Remove to wire rack to cool completely. Brush with margarine. May substitute half the all-purpose flour with whole-wheat flour and add 2 tablespoons dry milk solids and/or 2 tablespoons wheat germ or oat bran. Yields 24 servings.

Approx per serving: Cal 181; Prot 4g; Carbo 30g; Fiber 1g; T Fat 5g; 26% Cal from Fat; Chol 0mg; Sod 326mg.

Discover Oklahoma Cookin'

Cheese Popovers

Crisp and a lovely dark golden color, these popovers make a delightful change from the usual breads served with barbecue.

Light oil for coating pan
4 large eggs
1 cup milk
1 cup all-purpose flour

½ teaspoon salt
1 cup grated sharp Cheddar
cheese (do not pack cheese
into the cup)

Preheat oven to 450°. Brush popover cups with oil. Place the popover pan in the oven to get piping hot while mixing the batter. Combine all the ingredients in a blender. Blend on medium, stop and scrape down the sides of the blender jar. Blend again at high speed until the batter is well mixed. Remove the popover pan from the oven, close the oven door and pour batter into the cups, filling each about ⅔ full. Return to the oven and bake 20 minutes. Reduce heat to 350° and bake another 20 minutes. If the popovers seem to be browning too deeply, bake only 15 minutes. Makes 12.

Quick Breads, Soups & Stews

Bran Muffins

These muffins are just as enjoyable for a snack or breakfast, or served as part of a lunch or dinner.

½ cup egg replacer
2 cups skim milk
¼ cup oil
¼ cup maple syrup
1 tablespoon blackstrap
molasses

⅓ cup gluten flour
¾ cup wheat bran
1 cup oat bran
2 cups whole-wheat flour
1 tablespoon baking powder,
sifted

In a large plastic or glass bowl, whisk together the egg replacer, milk, oil, maple syrup, molasses, gluten, and brans. Heat for 1–2 minutes in the microwave, or until mixture is lukewarm. Let sit for 10 minutes.

Meanwhile, preheat oven to 375°. Grease muffin tins.

Stir in the flour and baking powder. Batter should be somewhat thick; add more flour if necessary. Fill muffin cups ¾ full. Bake for approximately 15 minutes; muffin middles should be peaked and firm. Yields 1½ dozen muffins.

Healthy America

Tumbleweeds

Delicious high fiber muffins

3 egg whites
½ cup water
½ cup vegetable oil
2 cups lowfat buttermilk
2½ cups flour
2½ teaspoons baking soda
½ teaspoon salt
2½ teaspoons cinnamon

2 cups bran cereal (not flakes)
1 cup quick-cooking oats
1 cup oat bran hot cereal, dry
1 cup Sugar Twin or sugar
  substitute
4 bananas, mashed (optional)
1 cup raisins (optional)

In a small bowl, combine egg whites, water, oil, and buttermilk. Set aside. In a large bowl, sift together flour, soda, salt, and cinnamon and then add remaining dry ingredients and stir to mix. Add buttermilk mixture to dry ingredients and stir, just until moistened. Stir in mashed bananas and raisins if desired. Spray muffin tins with nonstick cooking spray or line with paper cups. Fill ⅔ full and bake at 400° for 15–20 minutes or until golden brown. Yields 2 dozen.

Note: This recipe doubles nicely and batter stores well in refrigerator (before adding bananas and raisins).

Per muffin: Cal 171; Fat 6g; Chol 75mg.

Stir Ups

Orange Streusel Muffins

The true essence of orange was elusive, but after eight experiments, I finally caught it in a muffin. This lovely muffin and its variations are delicious with a cup of hot tea.

2 cups all-purpose flour
½ teaspoon salt
2 teaspoons baking powder
¼ cup sugar
Grated rind of 1 large orange
2 large eggs

½ cup orange juice
1 tablespoon lemon juice
½ cup milk
¼ cup butter or margarine,
  melted

Preheat oven to 425°. Brush 12 (2½-inch) muffin cups with melted butter or coat with vegetable spray. Combine the flour, salt, baking powder, sugar, and orange rind in a mixing bowl, blending thoroughly. In a separate bowl beat the eggs, orange

(continued)

(Orange Streusel Muffins continued)

juice, and lemon juice together. Add to the dry ingredients with the milk and melted butter, stirring rapidly with a rubber spatula until just moistened. Fill each muffin cup ¾ full. Top each muffin with about one tablespoon of streusel. Bake muffins 20 minutes until lightly golden.

STREUSEL:

½ cup cold butter
½ cup all-purpose flour

½ cup sugar
Grated rind of 1 large orange

Place all ingredients for the streusel in a food processor and whirl until the butter is thoroughly cut into the dry ingredients. The remainder of the streusel may be placed in a covered container and frozen for future use.

Quick Breads, Soups & Stews

The "Berry-Best" Muffins

1 cup butter, softened
2 cups sugar
4 eggs
2 teaspoons vanilla
4 cups flour
4 teaspoons baking powder

1 teaspoon salt
1 cup milk
4 to 5½ cups fresh or frozen
   blueberries, blackberries,
   raspberries or cranberries

Cream butter and sugar in large mixing bowl. Add eggs (one at a time) and vanilla. Blend thoroughly. Combine flour, baking powder and salt. Alternately add flour mixture and milk to first mixture (the batter will be very thick). Blend well. Fold in berries. Grease muffin tins. (Because batter will need to expand over the rim, it is best to grease or oil muffin tin beyond rims of cups. You may use paper liners, but top of tin should still be oiled to allow for overage.) So that muffins will take on a mushroom shape, heap batter above rim of muffin tins. This will produce a beautiful shape. Sprinkle generously with sugar and bake in preheated 425° oven for 10 minutes. After 10 minutes of baking, turn oven temperature down to 375° and bake an additional 15 minutes until muffins are done in center and a rich golden brown on top. Yields 16–18 muffins.

Stir Ups

Panhandle Casserole

Cookbook Committee's favorite brunch.

1 pound lean, hot sausage
1 pound Cheddar cheese, grated
1¼ pounds Monterey Jack cheese, grated

3 (4-ounce) cans green chiles, drained
9 eggs, beaten
1 cup milk
2 tablespoons flour

Brown sausage and drain between paper towels. Layer sausage with cheeses and whole chiles in a 9x13-inch glass baking dish. Combine eggs, milk, and flour until well blended. (Blender makes this step easier.) Pour liquid over layered mixture.

For a festive brunch, decorate top with strips of green chiles in a lattice design. Sprinkle with paprika and bake at 350° for 40–45 minutes. Slice and serve.

Stir Ups

Cheese Grits Casserole

1½ cups grits (quick cooking)
6 cups boiling water
1½ teaspoons salt
3 tablespoons Cheez Whiz
1 pound Velveeta cheese, grated
1 stick margarine

4 eggs, beaten
2 tablespoons chopped onion
Dash of celery salt
¼ teaspoon thyme
1 tablespoon Worcestershire
Dash of garlic salt
1 teaspoon paprika
1 tablespoon chopped parsley

Add grits to salted, boiling water and cook until done. (You may need to add more hot water if the grits get too thick before the grains are soft.) Then add cheese and margarine. When melted, add beaten eggs, one at a time, and beat well. Add onions, seasonings, and Worcestershire. Cook for 2 minutes. Pour into a greased 9x13-inch baking dish and bake, covered, for 40 minutes at 350° (longer if needed). Sprinkle paprika and parsley on top.

Dine with the Angels

Volunteer Egg and Sausage Casserole

1 pound sausage (cooked and cooled)
6 eggs
2 cups milk
1 teaspoon salt

1 teaspoon dry mustard
6 slices bread, broken into pieces
3 cups grated Cheddar or colby cheese

Beat eggs and milk. Add salt and mustard, then beat again. Fold in broken bread till moist. Add sausage and cheese. Pour into greased pan and sit overnight in refrigerator. Bake at 350° for 40 or so minutes till set.

Sequoyah's Cookin'

Butch's Rancher's Omelette

6 slices bacon, diced
2 tablespoons finely chopped onion
1 cup grated raw potato
6 eggs, slightly beaten

½ teaspoon salt
⅛ teaspoon white pepper
Dash of hot sauce
2 tablespoons minced fresh parsley

Fry bacon until crisp. Drain and set aside, reserving 2 tablespoons drippings in skillet. Sauté onion until soft in reserved drippings. Add potato and cook until light brown. Pour eggs into skillet. Add salt, pepper, and hot sauce. Cook over low heat, lifting up eggs with spatula to let uncooked egg mixture flow underneath. When firm, sprinkle with crumbled bacon and parsley. Fold omelette in half. Serve immediately. Serves 4–6.

Submitted by Butch McCain, Oklahoma City television personality.
The Oklahoma Celebrity Cookbook

Eggs À La Buckingham

Fit for a queen.

2 tablespoons butter or margarine
4 teaspoons all-purpose flour
Salt and pepper
¾ cup milk
1 (8-ounce) package smoked sliced beef, snipped
4 eggs
1 tablespoon milk
1 tablespoon butter or margarine
2 English muffins, split and toasted
½ cup (8 ounces) shredded sharp processed American cheese

Melt the 2 tablespoons butter or margarine; blend in flour and a dash each salt and pepper. Add ¾ cup milk. Cook and stir till bubbly; cook 1 minute more. Add beef; keep warm. Beat eggs with the 1 tablespoon milk and a dash each salt and pepper.

In skillet, melt 1 tablespoon butter. Add egg mixture. Cook over low heat just till set; lift and fold so uncooked part goes to bottom. Place muffins on baking sheet; spoon beef mixture over. Top with eggs. Bake in 350° oven 8 minutes. Sprinkle with cheese and bake 1 minute more. Makes 4 servings.

Shattuck Community Cookbook

Baked Eggs in Herbed Cheese Sauce

HERBED CHEESE SAUCE:

6 tablespoons butter	⅛ teaspoon cayenne pepper
6 tablespoons flour	Dash of Worcestershire
¼ teaspoon oregano	3 cups hot milk
½ teaspoon savory	3 cups grated Cheddar cheese

Melt butter in a saucepan and whisk in the flour, stirring rapidly. Add the oregano, savory, cayenne, and Worcestershire. Whisk thoroughly and let bubble 1 minute to give the herbs a chance to meld into the roux. Remove from the burner and add the hot milk all at once. Stir quickly with the whisk until smooth. Return to burner and continue cooking until thick and smooth. Add the cheese and blend until melted. For the baked eggs, this will be more sauce than needed, but the remainder can be used over broccoli or cauliflower or may be frozen for future use.

BAKED EGGS:

6 large eggs	1 tablespoon chopped parsley
½ cup bread crumbs	2 tablespoons butter
½ teaspoon dried basil	

Preheat oven to 350°. Brush a glass baking dish or a round attractive pottery plate with melted butter. Pour one-half the hot herbed cheese sauce in choice of dish. Break the 6 eggs, one at a time, into a saucer and slip each into the cheese sauce. Spoon a little sauce over each egg. Combine the bread crumbs, basil, parsley, and butter.

Sprinkle the crumb mixture over the eggs. Place the baking dish in shallow pan of hot water and cover loosely with aluminum foil. Bake the eggs about 25–30 minutes. If you are concerned about how done the eggs are, take a spatula and lift one of the eggs. If not done, bake a few more minutes. Serve each egg atop toast or a Holland Rusk.

Mary's Recipe Box

Almond Crusted Oven Pancakes

Oven pancakes make a spectacular breakfast and for all their puffed glory they are amazingly easy to prepare. Its concave center can be filled with fresh fruits or simply sprinkled with sugar and lemon juice. The pancake in its various forms will bring exclamations of admiration for your prowess in the kitchen.

3 large eggs
½ cup milk
½ cup all-purpose flour
½ teaspoon salt
1 teaspoon sugar

Pinch of nutmeg (optional)
2 tablespoons butter
½ cup blanched slivered
   almonds

Preheat oven to 425°. Select a round skillet or a quiche pan. Combine eggs, milk, flour, salt, and sugar and whirl in a blender or beat with a wire whip. If using a blender, scrape down its sides to be certain all the flour is in the batter, and whirl again until creamy. If you are baking the pancake in a skillet, place it over a burner, add butter and almonds and sauté the almonds for 2 minutes. If a quiche pan is used, place in the oven with the butter until melted, add the almonds and let cook about 2–3 minutes. Carefully pour in the batter and bake 20 minutes. The pancake will rise with the sides encrusted with almonds. Serve filled with fresh fruit if desired, or with cooked apples on the side. Serves 4 amply.

Quick Breads, Soups & Stews

Banana Oat Pancakes

½ cup egg replacer
1 cup skim milk
½ cup rolled oats soaked
  in ½ cup warm water
  for 10 minutes
1 teaspoon ground cinnamon

1 medium ripe banana,
  mashed
2 cups whole-grain pancake
  mix
Butter or soy margarine

Mix liquid ingredients, then stir in remaining ingredients. It is important for the batter to be of pancake consistency. If it is too thin, add more mix. Do not overstir. Cook 2 pancakes at a time in a large skillet using approximately 1 teaspoon margarine or butter. Cook over medium heat for approximately 5 minutes, then turn and cook approximately 3 more minutes. These will be thicker than traditional pancakes. Yields 10 pancakes.

Note: Any fresh, canned, or frozen (and thawed) fruit can be used in these pancakes. Store in sealable bags and simply reheat.

Healthy America

Everyday Waffle

1¾ cups sifted flour
½ teaspoon salt
3 teaspoons baking powder
2 beaten egg yolks

1¼ cups milk
½ cup Crisco oil
2 stiffly beaten egg whites

Sift dry ingredients; stir in combined egg yolks, milk, and Crisco oil. Fold in stiffly beaten egg whites. Do not overstir. Bake in hot waffle iron. Makes 8.

HOT MAPLE SYRUP:

1 cup white syrup
½ cup brown sugar
½ cup water

½ teaspoon maple flavoring
1 tablespoon margarine

Combine white syrup, brown sugar, and water; cook until sugar dissolves. Add maple flavoring and butter. Serve hot.

Spring Creek Club

Crisp Buttery Waffles

Heat your well-seasoned waffle iron.

2 cups sifted flour　　　　　　**½ teaspoon salt**
4 teaspoons baking powder　　**2 tablespoons sugar**

Sift these ingredients into a large mixing bowl, preferably one with a pouring spout.

2 eggs, separated　　　　　　**8 tablespoons butter, melted**
1¾ cups milk　　　　　　　　　**(or half butter and half**
　　　　　　　　　　　　　　　　shortening)

When you separate the eggs, place the yolks in one bowl and the whites in a clean non-plastic bowl. Beat the whites until they stand in stiff peaks. The volume will be greater if the eggs are room temperature when you beat them. Set this bowl aside. You can use the same beater to beat the yolks until they are thickened and lemon-colored. Add the milk and melted butter. Mix the liquid ingredients into the bowl of dry, sifted ingredients. Lightly fold the stiff egg whites through the batter. Do not overmix.

Bake the waffles in your heated waffle iron. Pour the batter into the center of the iron, but do not fill it too full. Close and do not open again until the steam stops pouring out of the sides of the iron. Serve the waffles on a heated plate, unstacked. When finished, let the waffle iron stand open to cool.

Have you tried sprinkling broken pecans over the batter after you pour it in the iron? Drained blueberries can be added the same way. Crumbled broiled bacon makes a delicious waffle to serve under creamed chicken. How about that for Sunday night suppers? Bake as usual. Serves 4–6.

Spiced with Wit

Oklahoma has some strange laws: Whale hunting is strictly forbidden; one could be fined or jailed for making "ugly faces" at dogs; it is illegal to wear your boots in bed; and in Tulsa, kisses lasting more than three minutes are forbidden.

Jell-O Flavored Syrups

½ small box cherry or
raspberry or strawberry or
your favorite flavor Jell-O

½ cup boiling water
1 pint white Karo

Dissolve Jell-O in boiling water. Stir into white Karo. Use over pancakes, waffles, fried mush or fritters.

Seems Like I Done It This A-Way II

Oklahoma Sandplum Jelly

Earliest kitchen memories of many an Oklahoman include the pickin' of sandplums for jelly makin'. Each family watched for a plum thicket to get the pickin's before everybody else discovered the plums were ripe (jelly the color of an Oklahoma sunrise being the coveted, reward for scratches gotten in the thicket). Sandplum Jelly is still a tradition on the Oklahoma Range...the tart red plums make the sampling just as pleasurable as the memories.

5½ cups prepared plum
juice

7½ cups sugar
1 box fruit pectin

To prepare plum juice: Wash plums, cover with cold water and boil until plums are soft and skins pop. Press through jelly bag, strain and measure. (At this point, juice may be frozen for later use.)

To prepare jelly: Mix plum juice with pectin and bring to a boil, stirring constantly. Add sugar, continue stirring, and boil hard for one minute. Pour in sterile jars. Let set for one minute and skim off top. Seal with new lids. Let jelly cool slowly as sudden temperature change can cause jar to explode. The foamy jelly skim makes a fun treat for little helpers as well as a tasty memory of jelly-making time!

Stir Ups

My Sister's Pear Preserves

4 quarts washed, peeled and   4 cups sugar
cut in eighths pears

In a 6–8 quart kettle, put 2 quarts of pears and 2 cups sugar, then another 2 quarts pears and 2 cups sugar. Let them stand overnight. Next morning put them on a low fire. Cook for about 4 hours or until they are dark red. They will cook down to about ½ of what you started with. But gee, they are really good. You can put a slice of lemon in if you like.

Seems Like I Done It This A-Way I

Ice Box Peach Jam

2½ cups peaches (2 pounds   5 cups sugar
or 7 large)   ¾ cup water
2 tablespoons lemon juice   1 box Sure-Jell fruit pectin

Peel peaches, chop or grind and mix with lemon juice. Add sugar. Mix well and let stand 10 minutes. In small pan, mix water and Sure Jell. Boil 1 minute stirring constantly. Add this to the fruit mixture and continue stirring for 3 minutes. Ladle into screw-top jars or plastic containers with snap lids. Makes 5 cups. Cover and let stand at room temperature for 24 hours to set. Refrigerate. Surplus can be frozen.

Seems Like I Done It This A-Way III

Heavenly Jam

5 cups finely cut rhubarb   1 (20-ounce) can crushed
5 cups sugar   pineapple
Juice of 1 lemon   2 boxes strawberry Jell-O

Boil rhubarb, sugar, lemon juice, and crushed pineapple. Remove from heat and add to regular boxes of strawberry Jell-O. Stir until dissolved. Pour into jars and seal with paraffin wax or freeze.

Home Cookin' Is a Family Affair

Better Meal Sandwich

1 loaf French bread
1 long stick Polish sausage
2 or 3 tablespoons mustard
⅔ cup French Onion Dip
½ cup chopped onion

Dill pickle chips
Crumbled fried bacon or
  bacon bits
¾ cup grated Cheddar
  cheese

Split French bread (leave connected on the bottom). Spread the sides with mustard. Place pre-baked Polish sausage in bread. Spread Polish sausage with French onion dip. Push pickle chips and onions down into French onion dip. Sprinkle with bacon bits. Top with grated cheese. Wrap in foil and bake at 450° for 10 minutes or until cheese melts. Cut in serving-size pieces.

What's Cooking in Okarche?

Hot Ham Sandwich

¼ cup mayonnaise
2 tablespoons horseradish
  mustard
1 tablespoon poppy seed

2 tablespoons grated onion
Rye bread or buns
Slivered ham
Swiss cheese

Mix first four ingredients. On bread or bun, layer the sauce, slivered ham and Swiss cheese. Wrap in foil and heat at 350° for 30 minutes.

Company Fare II

Stromboli

2 loaves white frozen
  unbaked bread
1 can mushrooms, drained
1 green pepper, chopped

1 tablespoon butter
1 package pepperoni
1 package Canadian bacon
1 package Provolone cheese

Let bread thaw and rise for 4 hours. Punch bread down flat. Sauté mushrooms and pepper in 1 tablespoon butter. Layer all ingredients in center of bread loaves. Cut sides into strips and fold strips over the top. Bake at 350° for 30 minutes or until done.

Seasoned with Love

Ready-To-Eat Breakfast Cereal

8 cups rolled oats
2 cups bran
3 cups wheat germ
3 cups flaked coconut
2 cups packed brown sugar
½ teaspoon salt
1 cup water

½ cup oil
1 tablespoon vanilla extract
1 cup chopped dates
1 cup chopped pecans
1 cup raisins
1 cup chopped dried apricots

Combine oats, bran, wheat germ, coconut, brown sugar, and salt in bowl; mix well. Stir in mixture of water, oil, and vanilla. Spread in a thin layer on nonstick baking sheet. Bake at 275° for 45 minutes, stirring frequently. Add dates, pecans, raisins, and apricots to cooled baked mixture; mix well. Store in cool place. Yields 20 servings.

Approx per serving: Cal 510; Prot 12g; Carbo 87g; Fiber 11g; T Fat 17g; 28% Calories from Fat; Chol 0mg; Sod 73mg.

Discover Oklahoma Cookin'

Soups

Chickasha's Muscle Car Ranch represents nostalgic Americana featuring thousands of antique automotive signs, muscle cars, vintage motorcycles, a 1900s Dairy Farm, and a fully restored 1940s diner collected by owner Curtis Hart. The ranch hosts the Annual Muscle Car Ranch Swap Meet twice a year on the 70-acre farm.

Chicken Chowder

1 cup chopped onion
1 cup chopped celery
1 cup chopped carrots
4 tablespoons butter
2 tablespoons flour
1 cup milk
2 cups chicken broth

1 (10-ounce) package mixed
   vegetables
1 tablespoon chicken soup
   base
2 cups chicken
8 ounces Velveeta cheese
Salt and pepper

Sauté onion, celery, and carrots in butter until crisp. Add flour and stir. Add milk, then broth and vegetables. Add soup base to taste. When hot, add cut-up chicken and cheese. Add salt and pepper to taste. Heat and serve.

Here's What's Cookin' at Zion

Chicken Vegetable Gumbo

A lowfat recipe.

1 cup coarsely chopped onion
1 cup sliced fresh mushrooms
½ cup sliced celery
½ cup chopped green pepper
2 cloves minced garlic
2 (14½-ounce) cans
   chopped tomatoes,
   undrained
1 (10½-ounce) can chicken
   broth
½ cup dry sherry

1 teaspoon chicken flavored
   bouillon granules
1 teaspoon dried Italian
   seasoning
¼ teaspoon pepper
2 cups cubed cooked chicken
   breasts
⅔ pound fresh okra (tipped,
   stemmed and sliced) or 1
   (10-ounce) package frozen
   sliced okra

Coat large Dutch oven with cooking spray. Over medium heat cook onion, mushrooms, celery, green pepper, and garlic 5 minutes. Add tomatoes, chicken broth, sherry, bouillon granules, Italian seasoning, and pepper. Bring to a boil, cover and simmer 1 hour or until vegetables are tender. About ½ hour before done, add cubed chicken and okra. Finish cooking. Preparation time: 1½ hours. Makes 2 quarts.

Cooking A+ Recipes

Spicy Chicken Tomato Pasta Soup

Those who love pungent full-meal soups with cornbread sticks or muffins will be warmed to their cockles when served this soup before a roaring fire in the mid-winter.

6 cups canned or homemade chicken broth
1 cup chopped onion
1 cup diced zucchini
½ cup diced carrot
1 cup diced celery
1 bay leaf
¼ teaspoon thyme
1 large garlic clove, peeled and minced
¼ cup finely chopped parsley
Grindings of black pepper

3 sprigs fresh basil or 1 teaspoon dried basil
1 (1-pound 12-ounce) can crushed tomatoes with purée
Approximately ½ cup Ro-Tel brand tomatoes and green chiles (½ of one 10-ounce can)
1 cup elbow macaroni or tiny pasta
2 cups cooked chicken, chopped
Salt to taste

Measure the chicken broth into a soup kettle, bring to a boil and add the onion, zucchini, carrots, celery, bay leaf, thyme, garlic, parsley, pepper, and basil. Bring to a simmer and cook 15 minutes uncovered until vegetables are tender. Add the crushed tomatoes, Ro-Tel tomatoes and green chiles and pasta. (If a spicier soup is desired, add the remaining half can of Ro-Tel tomatoes and green chiles.) Bring to a boil, lower to simmer and cook gently 20 minutes until the pasta is tender. Add the chicken and simmer until thoroughly heated. If the soup becomes too thick after the pasta is added, add 1–2 cups additional chicken broth to suit your own taste. Adjust for salt. Serves 10–12.

Quick Breads, Soups & Stews

Russian Borscht

1–2 pounds beef-stew-type
   meat, cut up
1–2 quarts water
2 fresh tomatoes, diced
1 cup chopped onion
3 sprigs parsley
Pepper to taste
3 cups coarsely shredded
   cabbage (about 1 pound)

4 medium carrots, sliced
2 tablespoons sugar
1 (1-pound) can beets,
   undrained (tastes better
   with 2 fresh beets, peeled
   and cut into pieces)
Sour cream

In a skillet, brown the meat with a little oil. Transfer to large stew pot; add water and cook for 30–60 minutes. Add all other ingredients, except sour cream. Bring to a boil, then turn down to low and cook for 2–3 hours. May also be cooked using a slow cooker.

To serve, put hot mixture in bowl, add 1 tablespoon sour cream and stir.

Sequoyah's Cookin'

Santa Fe Taco Soup

3 chicken breast halves
½ medium onion, chopped
1 clove garlic, minced
2 tablespoons oil
1 package taco seasoning mix
1 (15-ounce) can diced
   tomatoes
1 (8-ounce) jar green chili
   salsa

1 (4-ounce) can green chiles
1 can corn with peppers
1 (15-ounce) can Ranch-Style
   beans
1 (15-ounce) can black beans
2 cups chicken broth
1 cup shredded Cheddar
   cheese

Cook chicken breasts in water to cover; save broth. Cool and shred. Set aside. Sauté onion and garlic in oil. Set aside. In large saucepan, combine taco seasoning mix, tomatoes with juice, salsa, green chiles, corn, ranch beans, black beans, chicken broth, chicken breasts, and sautéed onions and garlic. Simmer 45 minutes. Top with shredded Cheddar. Serve with warm buttered tortillas. Serves 6.

Gourmet Our Way

Taco Soup

2 pounds hamburger
1 large onion, finely chopped
2–3 cloves garlic, minced
1 small can chopped green
  chiles
3 cans diced tomatoes
1 can corn
1 can red kidney beans

1 can pinto beans
1 can black-eyed peas
1 package Old El Paso Taco
  Seasoning
1 package Hidden Valley
  Original Ranch Dressing Mix
2 cups water

Brown hamburger with onion and garlic; drain. Add remaining ingredients and bring to boil; simmer at least 2 hours.

100 Years of Cooking

Terry's White Chili

Terry Davis is a full blood Cherokee Indian, an expert on chili, and the fine chef of Mary's Bread Basket in Tulsa. Terry's avocation is following chili contests in Arkansas, Texas, New Mexico, Colorado and Kansas. His cooking apparel is a handsome apron with Seminole patchwork in red and green and a big bright red pepper below the patchwork—and he wins those chili cookoffs!

6 cups chicken broth	1 cup chopped onion
3 cups navy beans (small white beans)	½ teaspoon white pepper
	½ teaspoon ground cloves
2 teaspoons cumin	1 pound cooked chicken, cut
1 teaspoon oregano	in pieces
8 ounces canned green chiles, chopped	Salt to taste
1 clove garlic, peeled and minced	

Combine in a soup kettle the chicken broth, beans, cumin, oregano, chiles, garlic, onion, white pepper, and cloves. Place over medium heat and bring to a boil, then lower heat and simmer until the beans are tender, 1½–2 hours. When the beans are tender, add the chicken, bring to a simmer, and salt to taste. Simmer 10–15 minutes to allow ingredients to meld. Serves 10.

Quick Breads, Soups & Stews

Black Beans and Rice Soup

16 ounces smoked turkey sausage	15 ounces canned black beans
2 (4.3-ounce) boxes Rice-A-Roni long grain and wild rice	1 tablespoon Mrs. Dash extra spicy seasoning
	5 cups water
16–24 ounces chopped canned tomatoes	

Cut sausage into slices. Place all ingredients in a large kettle and simmer until rice is tender.

Shattuck Community Cookbook

Chuck Wagon Bean Hot Pot

1 pound Western dry beans	1 teaspoon salt
½ cup butter	1 can tomato sauce
1 large onion	1 can tomatoes
1 teaspoon chili powder	1 teaspoon garlic
1 teaspoon paprika	1 cup water
1 tablespoon red pepper	1 pound ground beef

Cook Western dry beans for 2½ hours after soaking in hot water for 1 hour. Cook butter, onion, chili powder, paprika, red pepper, salt, tomato sauce, tomatoes, garlic and water in saucepan. Cook beef alone and then drain off grease. Mix beans, tomato mixture and beef together. Let cook for 1 hour.

Oklahoma Cookin'

8 Bean Soup

½ cup pinto beans	½ cup red kidney beans
½ cup split peas	½ cup Great Northern beans
½ cup small red beans	½ cup lentils
½ cup black turtle beans	½ cup black-eyed peas

HERBS:

¾ tablespoon basil	½ tablespoon tarragon
¾ tablespoon chili powder	½ tablespoon rosemary
¾ tablespoon thyme	¼ tablespoon black pepper
¾ tablespoon dried onions	

Pour dry beans in a large bowl and mix thoroughly. Soak the beans overnight in water. Pour off this water and rinse beans. Place the beans in a slow cooker and cover with water. Add herbs and cook on low heat until tender.

The Homeplace Cookbook

Creamy Carrot Soup

Children love this soup because of the natural sweetness of the carrots.

1 small onion, coarsely
   chopped
6 carrots, scrubbed, coarsely
   chopped
1 white potato, coarsely
   chopped; or 1 (16-ounce) can
   white beans, drained

1½ cups vegetable or
   nonfat chicken broth
½ cup skim milk or
   evaporated skim milk

Place the onion, carrots, potato, and broth in a saucepan and bring to a boil. Simmer, covered, until vegetables are tender. Place in a blender and purée until smooth, adding milk until the desired consistency.

Note: This recipe will work for most all favorite vegetables. It's a quick and easy way to have a delicious, healthy soup.

Healthy America

Creamy Potato Soup

6 medium potatoes, cubed
1 large onion, chopped
2 carrots, diced small
2 ribs celery, chopped
6 cups water or 3 cups water
   and 3 cups chicken broth

1 tablespoon salt
1 teaspoon pepper or to taste
1 (12-ounce) can evaporated
   milk
2 cups cubed Velveeta cheese

In large pot, boil first 7 ingredients until vegetables are tender, about 30 minutes. Add milk and cheese. If you prefer this soup thick, mix 4 tablespoons flour in ⅓ cup cold water. Add ½ cup hot soup gradually; return to entire pot, stirring gently. Serves 8.

Country Cooking

What's in a name? Some say the town of Enid was named for a restaurant that had the sign turned upside down. The sign said "DINE."

Potato Bacon Chowder

8 slices bacon, cut up
1 cup chopped onion
4 cups cubed potatoes
1 cup water
1 can cream of chicken soup

1 cup sour cream
1¾ cups milk
½ teaspoon salt
Dash of pepper

Fry bacon until crisp. Remove bacon and sauté onion in drippings. Remove onion and drain on paper towel. Cook potatoes in the 1 cup water; add soup, onion, and bacon (save some to crumble on top), sour cream, and milk, plus seasonings. Simmer, but do not boil. Serves 6.

Stir Ups

Crab and Corn Chowder

3 tablespoons butter
1½ cups finely chopped onion
1½ cups finely chopped celery
6 medium potatoes, peeled and cubed
2 cups clam juice or chicken stock

1 cup whipping cream
Salt and pepper to taste
½ teaspoon red pepper flakes (or more if you like spicy)
2 cups frozen corn
2 cups crab
½ cup fresh coriander or parsley

Heat butter in large saucepan. Sauté onion and celery. Add potatoes and stock. Cook until potatoes are done. Add cream, salt, pepper, red pepper flakes, corn, and crab. Simmer 6–8 minutes. To serve, garnish with coriander or parsley. Serves 4 as a main course, 6 as appetizer.

Note: This soup can be put together in 45 minutes. A fast winter meal with bread and salad, or a wonderful way to start a dinner party.

Gourmet Our Way

Low-Fat Clam Chowder

8 medium potatoes, diced
1 large onion, diced
2 stalks celery, diced
Water
2 cups 1% milk

¼ cup flour
2 cans undrained clams
1½ tablespoons chicken
    bouillon
Coarse ground pepper

Place potatoes, onions, and celery in 4-quart saucepan. Add water to top of potatoes. Cook until potatoes are tender. Do not drain. Add milk to flour to make a smooth paste. Add milk-flour mixture to potatoes and add clams. Stir in bouillon and ground pepper. Heat until thickened and flour is cooked. Stir to prevent scorching. Serves 8.

(Per serving: 1g Fat)

Come Grow with Us

Salads

Talimena Skyline Drive winds through the Ouachita National Forest providing 54 miles of amazing vistas and excellent photo opportunities. It is the only scenic byway located in Mid-America, stretching from Talihina, Oklahoma, to Mena, Arkansas. Its name comes from the combination of both towns.

Chicken Salad
with Cranberry Dressing

4 cups cooked and cubed
  chicken
1 cup chopped celery
2 cups seedless green or red
  grapes
½ teaspoon salt

½ teaspoon pepper
½ cup mayonnaise
½ cup sour cream
½ cup sliced almonds,
  toasted

CRANBERRY DRESSING:

½ cup jellied cranberry
  sauce
¾ cup vegetable oil
¼ cup wine vinegar
1 teaspoon salt

1 teaspoon sugar
½ teaspoon paprika
¼ teaspoon dry mustard
Dash pepper

Combine salad ingredients. Whip cranberry sauce and other dressing ingredients. Pour over salad. Serves 4.

Gourmet Our Way

Cotillion Chicken Salad

4 cups cooked, cubed chicken
1 cup thinly sliced celery
1 tablespoon chopped green
  onions
¼ cup coarsely chopped
  pecans

¼ teaspoon salt
⅓ cup reduced-calorie
  mayonnaise
1 teaspoon fresh lemon juice
½ teaspoon Dijon mustard
1 cup peeled, cubed kiwi fruit

In large bowl, combine chicken, celery, green onions, pecans, and salt. Set aside. Combine mayonnaise, lemon juice, and mustard in small bowl; pour over chicken mixture and toss gently. Cover and chill to meld flavors. Just before serving, stir in kiwi. Yields 4–6 servings.

Nutritional information per ¾ cup serving: 141 calories.

Sounds Delicious!

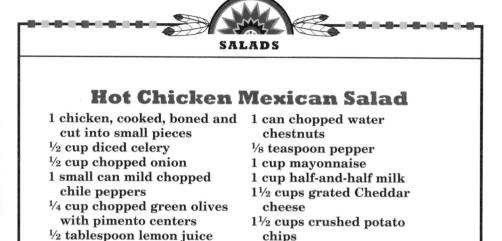
Hot Chicken Mexican Salad

1 chicken, cooked, boned and
  cut into small pieces
½ cup diced celery
½ cup chopped onion
1 small can mild chopped
  chile peppers
¼ cup chopped green olives
  with pimento centers
½ tablespoon lemon juice

1 can chopped water
  chestnuts
⅛ teaspoon pepper
1 cup mayonnaise
1 cup half-and-half milk
1½ cups grated Cheddar
  cheese
1½ cups crushed potato
  chips

Combine chicken, celery, onion, chili pepper, olives, lemon juice, water chestnuts, and pepper in mixing bowl; mix well. Mix together mayonnaise and half-and-half and add to chicken. Stir in ½ of cheese and potato chips. Pour into a large Pyrex baking dish. Bake at 375° for 20 minutes. Add remaining cheese and chips and bake an additional 10 minutes.

Kitchen Klatter Keepsakes

Chicken and Pasta-Stuffed Tomatoes

1 cup uncooked 4-color rotini
1 (7-ounce) can chicken white
  meat, drained
½ cup plain lowfat yogurt
½ cup shredded cucumber
¼ cup shredded carrot

2 tablespoons reduced-calorie
  mayonnaise
¼ teaspoon dillweed
¼ teaspoon salt
⅛ teaspoon pepper
4 medium tomatoes

Cook pasta using package directions; drain. Combine chicken, yogurt, cucumber, carrot, mayonnaise, dillweed, salt and pepper in medium bowl. Add pasta; toss to mix well. Remove a ½-inch section of core from each tomato with sharp knife; invert tomatoes on work surface. Cut each tomato into 6 wedges, cutting to, but not through bottom. Place on serving plates; spread wedges gently. Fill with chicken mixture. Yields 4 servings.

Approx Per Serving: Cal 178; T Fat 4g; Cal from Fat 18%; Prot 16g; Carbo 21g; Fiber 3g; Chol 4mg; Sod 379mg.

The Pioneer Chef

Shanghai Shrimp and Pasta Salad

½ pound linguini
¼ cup sesame oil, divided
¼ cup peanut oil, divided
1 pound fresh mushrooms, sliced
2 tablespoons grated fresh ginger
2 cloves garlic, minced

1½ pounds shrimp, cooked and peeled
1 pound snow peas, steamed one minute (until just crisp and bright green)
⅓ cup soy sauce
¼ cup sesame seed, toasted

Cook linguini in boiling salted water until al dente. Drain and rinse under cold water; transfer to a large bowl. Toss linguini with ½ teaspoon of the sesame oil and ½ teaspoon of the peanut oil. Sauté mushrooms, ginger, and garlic in remaining sesame and peanut oils. Let cool and add to linguini. Add shrimp, snow peas, soy sauce, and toasted sesame seeds. Toss to mix well. Cover and chill. Serves 6–8.

Note: If you plan to chill longer than 2 hours, store the snow peas separately and add shortly before serving to retain their bright green color and crispness.

Gourmet Our Way

Pasta Salad

1 (16-ounce) bag of your favorite pasta (elbow macaroni, curly pasta, or any fun shape variety pasta)
2 cucumbers, peeled and chopped
1 green bell pepper, chopped
1 red bell pepper, chopped
1 (2¼-ounce) can black olives, chopped and drained

1 onion, chopped
1 (16-ounce) can tuna (packed in water), drained
¼ teaspoon basil, crushed
¼ teaspoon tarragon, crushed
¼ teaspoon thyme, crushed
¼ teaspoon dill, crushed
1 large bottle zesty Italian salad dressing

Boil pasta, then drain water. Let cool; does not need to be cold. Prepare other ingredients while pasta is boiling. When pasta is cooled, add all other ingredients and serve.

The Homeplace Cookbook

Ham-Pecan-Blue Cheese Pasta Salad

Grab a glass of white wine and pleasurize your palate with this tasty salad.

1 (12-ounce) package bow tie pasta
4 ounces cooked ham, cut into strips
1 cup coarsely chopped pecans
1 (4-ounce) package blue cheese
⅓ cup chopped fresh parsley
2 tablespoons fresh rosemary or 2 teaspoons dried rosemary
1 clove garlic, minced
½ teaspoon coarsely ground pepper
¼ cup olive oil
⅓ cup grated Parmesan cheese

Cook pasta according to directions. Drain. Rinse with cold water and drain. Combine pasta and remaining ingredients, except Parmesan cheese, tossing well. Sprinkle with Parmesan cheese. Serve immediately or chill if desired. Serves 6.

Cooking A+ Recipes

Zucchini and Basil Pasta Salad

4 medium zucchini
1 teaspoon salt
1½ cups chopped fresh basil
½ cup olive oil
4 garlic cloves
¼ teaspoon dried oregano
6 cups chicken broth

¾ pound orzo*
¼ cup lemon juice
¼ cup grated Parmesan
  cheese
3 tablespoons chopped parsley
Salt and pepper

Grate zucchini coarsely and place in a colander. Sprinkle with salt and toss. Let stand 30 minutes, stirring once or twice. Squeeze zucchini dry and transfer to a large bowl. Blend basil, oil, garlic, and oregano together in food processor or blender. Add to zucchini.

Bring chicken broth to a boil in a large pot. Add orzo and reduce heat, cooking until orzo is just tender, 9–12 minutes. Drain well. Stir pasta into zucchini. Add the lemon juice, grated cheese, and parsley. Season to taste with salt and pepper. Serve warm, at room temperature, or chilled. Makes 8 servings. May be served as a main dish or side dish with barbecued meats.

*Orzo is a rice-shaped pasta. Any small pasta may be used.

Applause!

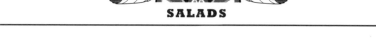
Lebanese Tabouleh Salad

In the 1930s tabouleh was brought to Oklahoma by Lebanese and Syrian immigrants, a number of whom opened restaurants or delicatessens where the salad was sold as a specialty item. Fifty years later it is a standard item in restaurant salad bars, and bulghur, the sun-parched wheat used to make tabouleh, is widely available in supermarkets.

1 cup bulghur wheat (medium grind)
½ cup water
1½ cups chopped green onions (green part, too)
1½ cups chopped parsley
1 cup chopped mint leaves
2 large tomatoes, cut in ½-inch wedges

DRESSING:
⅔ cup lemon juice
⅔ cup olive oil
2 teaspoons salt, or to taste

Wash bulghur 3 times. Soak wheat in ½ cup water for 2 hours or until water is absorbed and wheat is tender. Add onions, parsley, mint, and tomatoes. Mix dressing ingredients and stir into salad. Refrigerate after 2 hours.

Cleora's Kitchens

Creamy Corn Bread Salad

1 (6-ounce) package corn bread mix
½ cup chopped green onions
½ cup chopped green bell pepper
½ cup chopped tomatoes
4 ounces ham slices, chopped
4 ounces cream cheese, softened
¼ cup salad dressing
¼ cup creamy cucumber ranch salad dressing
½ teaspoon salt
2 tablespoons dry mustard

Prepare and bake cornbread using package directions. Cool; crumble into large bowl. Add green onions, green pepper, tomatoes and ham; toss well. Blend cream cheese, salad dressing, cucumber salad dressing, salt, and mustard in small bowl. Pour over cornbread mixture; mix well.

Watonga Cheese Festival Cookbook 17th Edition

Hot Chili Mexican Salad
(Microwave)

1 pound ground beef
1 medium onion, chopped
1 (15½-ounce) can kidney
   beans, drained
⅓ cup ketchup
¼ cup mayonnaise or salad
   dressing
½ teaspoon salt

1 teaspoon chili powder
1 cup shredded Monterey
   Jack cheese
2 tomatoes, coarsely chopped
1 small avocado, peeled and
   sliced
1 head lettuce, shredded

Combine ground beef and onion in 2-quart glass casserole. Cover with glass lid or Saran Wrap. Microwave on HIGH for 5 minutes; drain. Stir in beans, ketchup, mayonnaise, salt, and chili powder. Mix well; recover. Microwave on MEDIUM (or ROAST) for 5–6 minutes or until hot. Let stand, covered, 3 minutes before serving.

Toss cooked ingredients with cheese, tomatoes, and avocado. Serve on a bed of lettuce. Serves 4–6.

Thunderbird Cookers of AT&T

Ramen Noodle Salad

1 package Low Fat Oriental
  Flavor Ramen Noodle Soup
  Mix
1 (3-ounce) package slivered
  almonds (optional)
½ head Napa cabbage

4 green onions, chopped
1 (11-ounce) can mandarin
  oranges
4 boneless, skinless chicken
  breasts, cooked and diced
  (optional)

Crumble Ramen Noodles into 9x13-inch baking pan and spread evenly over bottom of pan. Mix the almonds in with the noodles and bake for 10 minutes at 350°. Allow to cool. In the meantime, tear the tender outer edges of the cabbage into bite-sized pieces and place in a large salad bowl. Add the green onions, mandarin oranges, chicken, and toasted Ramen Noodle/almond mixture. Pour dressing over and toss.

DRESSING:

¼ cup canola or corn oil
2 tablespoons sugar
3 tablespoons vinegar
Oriental spice mix from
  Ramen Noodle Soup Mix

½ teaspoon salt
Dash of black pepper

Place all ingredients in a jar and shake. Keeps well in the refrigerator for several days.

Note: With the chicken, this makes a spectacular main course salad. Serves 8.

Per serving with chicken: Cal 251; Fat 9g; Chol 3mg.

Stir Ups

Once known as Indian Territory, Oklahoma is still home to more American Indians than any other state in the Union. Thirty-nine tribal headquarters and members of at least sixty-five tribes make their home here. Native American art galleries, museums, historic sites, powwows, dances, and festivals are part of life in Oklahoma.

Herman's Slaw

This is the original slaw served at Herman's Fish Market—a favorite of many in the 1930s and '40s.

1 (4-pound) head cabbage	1 teaspoon dry mustard
2 medium onions	2 teaspoons salt
½ cup plus 2 tablespoons	1 teaspoon celery seed
sugar	1 clove garlic, minced
1 cup cider vinegar	½–¾ cup salad oil

Shred cabbage and onions. Cover with the ½ cup sugar. Set aside. Boil vinegar, 2 tablespoons sugar, mustard, salt, and celery seed; pour over cabbage while hot. (Add grated carrots or diced pimientos for color.) Add garlic and salad oil. Let set 24 hours; serve cold. It's quite tart, so add sugar "to taste." Will keep in refrigerator for weeks.

Four Generations of Johnson Family Favorites

Caesar Salad

2 large cloves garlic, peeled and crushed	Pinch of sugar
½ teaspoon salt	8 cups loosely packed romaine lettuce leaves, torn into bite-size pieces
¼ teaspoon black pepper	
⅓ cup fresh squeezed lemon juice (or more to taste)	⅓ cup grated Parmesan cheese
⅔ cup olive oil	1–2 cups croutons (depending on how many you like in your salad)
2 teaspoons Worcestershire or 1 anchovy, mashed, or ¼ teaspoon anchovy paste	

In a small bowl, blend together garlic, salt, and pepper. Whisk in lemon juice. Slowly add oil. Add Worcestershire or anchovy and a pinch of sugar. Whisk until blended well. In a large bowl, gently toss together lettuce and dressing, adding Parmesan cheese and croutons. Serves 4.

Gourmet: The Quick and Easy Way

Spinach Salad

One of my favorites! A secret is in the onions. Mild, meaty Texas 1015, or sweet purple onions make a difference.

1 bunch (about a pound)
stemmed spinach
Few sprigs of cilantro,
chopped (optional)
1 (8-ounce) can mandarin
oranges, drained

½ onion, chopped or sliced
thin
½ cup sliced almonds or
chopped pecans, toasted
(275°–15 minutes)
½ cup sliced mushrooms

Wash and drain spinach thoroughly. Add chopped onions, cilantro, toasted nuts, mandarin oranges, mushrooms, crumbled bacon (from dressing below). Toss thoroughly. Warm dressing almost to boiling and pour over salad mix. Serves 2–4.

DRESSING:

2 slices bacon
3 tablespoons vegetable oil
½ onion, chopped
½ teaspoon cornstarch
½ cup cider or wine vinegar
2 tablespoons raspberry
vinegar (or other vinegar)

¼ teaspoon salt
¼–½ cup sugar, depending
on your taste (a sugar free
sweetener can be substituted
if added just after cooking)

Fry bacon until crisp; remove and drain on paper towel. Retain the grease. Over low heat, add oil, and sauté onion until translucent. Add cornstarch. Stir until cornstarch is absorbed. Add vinegars, stir, and heat until boiling. Add salt and sugar. Remove from heat. Stir until sugar dissolves.

When a Man's Fancy Turns to Cooking

Sour Cream Spinach Salad

2 heads bibb lettuce
2 large heads iceberg lettuce
2 pounds fresh spinach
2 bunches green onions,
　sliced thin
2 pounds bacon, cooked until
　crisp and crumbled
½ cup sour cream

1 pint cottage cheese
¼ cup sugar
3 tablespoons vinegar
2 teaspoons horseradish
½ teaspoon dry mustard
¼ teaspoon salt
1 cup pecan pieces (optional)

Wash and dry lettuce and spinach. Tear into bite-size pieces. Add green onions, ½ of bacon, and nuts, if used. Blend sour cream, cottage cheese, sugar, vinegar, horseradish, mustard, and salt. Blend well and toss carefully with greens. Sprinkle balance of bacon over salad. Serves 6–8.

Cleora's Kitchens

Summer Tomato Salad with Brie

5 medium garden fresh
　tomatoes, cut into chunks,
　save juice
½ pound Brie cheese, rind
　removed, torn into pieces
½ cup fresh basil, snipped
　into strips with scissors

3 large garlic cloves, minced
⅓ cup olive oil
½ teaspoon salt
½ pound fresh pasta,
　linguini, shells, etc.
½ cup freshly grated
　Parmesan cheese

Combine tomatoes and juice, Brie, basil, garlic, olive oil, and salt. Leave at room temperature at least 2 hours. Cook pasta as directed on package. Drain and immediately toss with tomato mixture. Brie should melt. Mix. Sprinkle with Parmesan. Add more salt to taste. Serve at room temperature. Serves 6–8.

Note: Freeze Brie for 20 minutes to remove the rind easily.

Gourmet Our Way

Zucchini-Artichoke Salad

1 (8-ounce) bottle Italian
salad dressing
2 (4-ounce) envelopes Ranch
Style dressing mix
4 small zucchini, sliced
2 (14-ounce) cans artichoke
hearts, drained and cut in
thirds

1 (8-ounce) can whole
mushrooms, drained
1 (6-ounce) can pitted ripe
olives, drained
1 (8-ounce) can bamboo
shoots, drained
1 (2-ounce) jar diced pimento,
drained

Combine Italian salad dressing and Ranch dressing. Mix. Stir in remaining ingredients. Cover and chill overnight. Serves 12–14.

United Methodist Cookbook 1993

Shoe Peg Salad

1 can shoe peg corn
1 can Le Sueur peas
1 can green beans
1 (4-ounce) jar diced pimentos
1 bunch chopped green
onions
1 small green pepper,
chopped

1 teaspoon salt
1½ teaspoons pepper
½ cup vinegar
½ cup salad oil
½ cup sugar

Drain corn, peas, green beans, and pimentos. Place drained vegetables in large bowl and add chopped green onions, chopped green pepper, salt and pepper. Mix together well.

In small pan place vinegar, salad oil, and sugar. Boil together and pour over vegetables. Mix well. Let set in refrigerator for 24 hours.

Thank Heaven for Home Made Cooks

Just a few inches more and Cavanal Hill would be a mountain; at 1,999 feet, it has been designated the World's Highest Hill. From the top it offers an unparalleled panoramic view of the broad fertile Poteau Valley and the spectacular mountain ranges of southeastern Oklahoma.

Cauliflower Salad

1 small head cauliflower, cut
  into bite-size pieces
1 small can chopped ripe
  olives
1 small green pepper,
  chopped

¼ cup chopped green onions
1 small jar pimientos, chopped
Salt to taste
Bottled vinegar and oil
  dressing

Mix all ingredients. Moisten with dressing. Cover; refrigerate.
Chill several hours, stirring occasionally.

What's Cooking in Okarche?

Mushroom Salad

1 large package fresh
  mushrooms, sliced
2 bunches green onions (tops
  too), chopped

1 package mild Cheddar
  cheese, cubed

DRESSING:
½ cup salad oil
¼ cup wine vinegar
1 tablespoon sugar

3 heaping teaspoons
  Cavender's Greek Seasoning

Place mushrooms, onions, and cheese in bowl. Mix all dressing
ingredients together. Pour over salad just before serving.

Shattuck Community Cookbook

Summer Potato Salad

1 pound small-curd cottage
  cheese
1½ cups mayonnaise
2 tablespoons frozen chives

Salt to taste
2 cups chopped fresh spinach
5 large potatoes, cooked,
  peeled and diced

Mix first 5 ingredients. Combine with potatoes and chill. Makes
10 large portions

Pow Wow Chow

Sweet Potato Apple Salad

4 cups cubed cooked sweet
potatoes
1 (20-ounce) can pineapple
chunks, drained
1 (10-ounce) package
miniature marshmallows
4 red Delicious apples,
chopped

½ cup flaked coconut
½ cup chopped walnuts
¾ cup mayonnaise
1 (12-ounce) carton frozen
whipped topping

In a large bowl gently toss first 6 ingredients. Combine mayonnaise and whipped topping; fold into fruit mixture. Cover and chill at least 1 hour. Yields 32 servings.

Old and New

Fruit Salad with Cardamom

2 tablespoons sugar
½ cup water
½ cup orange juice
½ teaspoon ground
cardamom
Segments of 2 oranges
1 apple, diced

1 pear, diced
2 bananas, sliced
2 plums, diced
Assorted soft fruit for garnish
such as: grapes, cherries,
blueberries, and raspberries
Fresh mint (use for garnish)

In a small saucepan, combine the sugar and water over medium heat. Simmer until the sugar is dissolved. Leave to cool. Add the orange juice and cardamom. Combine the oranges, apple, pear, bananas, and plums in a glass bowl and pour the cardamom mixture over the fruit. Chill 30 minutes and add the soft fruits; garnish with mint.

The Homeplace Cookbook

Waldorf Salad

DRESSING:

¼ cup Miracle Whip Salad
    Dressing
Sugar or sweetener to taste
¼ teaspoon salt

1 tablespoon lemon juice
1–2 cups small marshmallows
    (kids like 2 cups or more)

Prepare the dressing by mixing ingredients together.

3 medium tart apples such as:
    Granny Smith, Winesap, Fuji
2 stalks celery, coarsely
    chopped

½ cup chopped pecans
    toasted 15 minutes at 300°

Pare apples or leave peelings on if you prefer. Cube the apples into bite-sized pieces. Place them in the dressing, and stir thoroughly so that the apples won't turn brown. Add chopped celery and nuts. Stir in marshmallows just before serving. Makes about 6 servings.

When a Man's Fancy Turns to Cooking

Cucumber Salad

1 (3-ounce) package lemon
    Jell-O
1 cup boiling water
2 small cucumbers, peeled,
    finely chopped
2 tablespoons onion, finely
    chopped

1 cup sour cream
½ cup mayonnaise
¼ teaspoon salt
⅛ teaspoon pepper
1 tablespoon vinegar

Dissolve Jell-O in water, refrigerate until slightly thickened. Stir in the finely chopped cucumbers and onion. Add the sour cream, mayonnaise, salt, pepper, and vinegar. Stir well. Refrigerate.

Come Grow with Us

Frosted Salad

2 packages lemon Jell-O
2 cups boiling water
2 cups 7-Up
2 large bananas

1 cup small marshmallows
1 (20-ounce) can crushed
  pineapple, drained (save
  juice)

Dissolve Jell-O in water, then add 7-Up and stir. Add rest of ingredients and pour into a 9x13-inch pan. Refrigerate until set and top with the following:

½ cup sugar
2 tablespoons flour
2 tablespoons butter

1 cup pineapple juice
1 egg, beaten
2 cups Cool Whip

Combine all except Cool Whip and cook until it boils. Cool and add Cool Whip.

Come Grow with Us

Mom's Blueberry Salad

2 packages grape Jell-O
2 cups boiling water

1 can crushed pineapple
1 can blueberry pie filling

TOPPING:

1 (8-ounce) package cream
  cheese, softened
½ cup sugar
½ pint sour cream

Few drops lemon juice
½ cup chopped nuts
1 teaspoon vanilla

Add grape Jell-O to boiling water and dissolve. Add crushed pineapple (do not drain) and blueberry pie filling. Mix well and let congeal in a 9x13-inch dish. Blend first 4 ingredients of topping and add nuts and vanilla. Spread over gelatin and return to the refrigerator, covered.

Note: This makes a big salad, and is so rich it could be served as a dessert.

Sisters Two and Family Too

Cranberry Orange Salad

2 (3-ounce) packages
  raspberry gelatin
2 cups boiling water
½ cup undiluted frozen
  orange juice
½ cup apple juice and 1 cup
  cold water

1 cup mini marshmallows
1 can cranberry-orange relish
1 cup chopped celery
1 cup chopped nuts
1 apple, grated

Stir boiling water into gelatin until dissolved. Thaw orange juice and add with apple juice and cold water. Stir well. Refrigerate until slightly set. Add marshmallows, relish, celery, nuts, and grated apple. Pour into large 11x9x2-inch Pyrex dish. Refrigerate.

Centennial Cookbook

Ribbon Salad

2 (3-ounce) boxes lime Jell-O
1 (3-ounce) box lemon Jell-O
1 (8-ounce) package cream
  cheese
¼ pound little marshmallows

1 can crushed pineapple
1 cup whipped cream
2 (3-ounce) boxes cherry
  Jell-O

Mix lime Jell-O with 2 cups hot then 2 cups cold water; pour in large cake pan and let harden. Mix lemon Jell-O with 1 cup hot water; dissolve cream cheese and marshmallows in hot Jell-O; let set partially. Add pineapple and whipped cream. Pour on set lime Jell-O and let set. Mix cherry Jell-O with 2 cups hot then 2 cups cold water. When it starts to cool and jell, pour on top of second layer. Let set; cut when cool.

Here's What's Cookin' at Zion

7-Up Salad

2 small packages lemon Jell-O
2 cups hot water
2 cups 7-Up
2 (8-ounce) cans crushed
   pineapple, well drained
1 cup miniature marshmallows
2 bananas, sliced

Mix Jell-O and water. Let cool slightly. Add 7-Up and let set until ropey. Stir sliced bananas into pineapple and let set 10 minutes so that bananas will not darken. Add marshmallows and combine all with 7-Up mixture. Pour into pan and chill.

TOPPING:

2 tablespoons flour
½ cup sugar
1 egg, well beaten
1 cup pineapple juice
2 tablespoons butter
2 cups (1 package) prepared
   Dream Whip

Mix flour, sugar, egg, and juice. Cook until thick, stirring constantly. Add butter and cool. Fold in Dream Whip. When salad is set, spread on topping. Sprinkle with grated cheese, nuts, cherries, etc.

Feeding Our Flock

Quick Salad

1 (8-ounce) package cream
   cheese, softened
1 can Eagle Brand Milk
1 can lemon pie filling
1 (8-ounce) carton Cool Whip
1 (15½-ounce) can crushed
   pineapple, drained
Nuts (if desired)

Mix the cream cheese and Eagle Brand Milk together. Add the rest of the ingredients together and stir. Spread in a long dish and chill.

Centennial Cookbook

Visitors may be surprised to see ostriches roaming the plains around Sayre. This little town is home to some of the country's biggest ostrich farms.

French Dressing

This has been used for 36 years or more and is one of the best of its kind.

1 can tomato soup	½ cup vinegar
1 cup salad oil	Dash of garlic salt
¼ cup sugar	Dash of paprika

In a quart fruit jar combine all ingredients. Cover jar and shake thoroughly. Makes 3 cups.

Seems Like I Done It This A-Way I

Ranch Dressing

Cowboys were never known for their love of fresh greens. Some clever cookie invented this sensational dressing made with those cowboy favorites, buttermilk and mayonnaise (both used with a heavy hand in modern ranch cooking), and cowboys have been asking for seconds of salad ever since.

¾ cup mayonnaise	1 clove garlic, crushed
¼ cup buttermilk	through a press
⅓ cup minced celery with	¼ teaspoon dried thyme
leaves	¼ teaspoon celery seed
2 tablespoons chopped fresh	¼ teaspoon salt
parsley	⅛ teaspoon freshly ground
1 tablespoon grated onion	pepper
(1 small onion)	

In a medium bowl, combine all the ingredients. Cover and refrigerate until ready to use, up to 5 days. Makes about 1½ cups.

Variation: Cucumber Ranch Dressing: Peel a medium cucumber. Cut in half lengthwise and scoop out the seeds with the tip of a spoon. Grate on the large holes of a cheese grater. A handful at a time, squeeze out the excess liquid from the grated cucumber. Stir the grated cucumber into the prepared ranch dressing.

National Cowboy Hall of Fame Chuck Wagon Cookbook

Pasta, Pizza, Rice, Etc.

COURTESY OF OKLAHOMA TOURISM

Oklahoma's 50 state parks reflect the beauty and diversity of the state. From the pine forests of southeastern Oklahoma to the spectacular mesas of the Panhandle, and from the northeastern lakes and forests to the rugged mountains of the Southwest, you are surrounded by Oklahoma's natural wonders. Many parks feature cabins like these at Hugo Lake State Park.

Indian Tacos

INDIAN FRY BREAD:

2½ pounds self-rising flour　　1 quart vegetable oil
Whole milk

Mix flour and whole milk slowly together until you have a wet dough. Pinch off a handful of the dough; pat out using flour or vegetable oil on hands. Place the prepared pieces in hot vegetable oil and deep fry until golden brown on each side. Drain on paper towels.

TOPPING:

2 pounds ground beef
6 rounds Indian Fry Bread
½ pound sharp Cheddar
　cheese, grated
1 head iceberg lettuce,
　shredded

3 ripe medium tomatoes
1 can diced green chiles
1 cup chopped green onion
Salsa (optional)

Brown ground beef. Divide among the six fry breads. Sprinkle with cheese, lettuce, tomatoes, chiles, and green onions. Serve with salsa, if desired. The ground beef may be substituted with 2 cans of beef chili.

Oklahoma Cookin'

Cavattini

½ onion, chopped
1 pound hamburger
1 stick smoked sausage,
　diced
½ pound regular sausage
1 pound package rotini
　macaroni

1 large jar Prego spaghetti
　sauce
1 large can sliced mushrooms
Pepperoni
3 cups grated Mozzarella
　cheese
2 cups grated Cheddar cheese

Cook onion, hamburger, and sausage until done. Boil macaroni. Drain and add Prego, mushrooms, and meat. Layer (in 9x13-inch greased pan) with pepperoni and both cheeses. Bake at 350° for 20 minutes.

100 Years of Cooking

Terrific Tortilla Torte

2 cups pinto beans, cooked
Vegetable cooking spray
½ cup chopped onion
1 clove garlic, minced
¼ teaspoon cumin, ground
¼ cup Picante Sauce
1 cup chopped green chiles

4 (8-inch) flour tortillas
¾ cup shredded Jack cheese
2 tablespoons sliced ripe
  olives
2 cups shredded lettuce
1 medium tomato, chopped
2 jalapeños, sliced thin

Place beans in strainer and drain. Coat a large skillet with cooking spray over medium heat. Add onion and garlic; sauté until tender. Turn heat to low and add beans and cumin. Cook uncovered 25 minutes, stir occasionally. Mash beans with masher, set aside but keep warm.

Combine Picante Sauce and green chiles; set aside. Heat tortillas in oven until warm; wrap with foil to keep from drying out. Cook 8 minutes. Lightly coat a baking sheet with cooking spray. Place a tortilla on it; top with ⅓ of bean mixture, ¼ cup cheese, 2 teaspoon olives. Repeat layers twice. Top with remaining tortillas. Cover with foil and bake at 350° for 15 minutes.

Transfer to serving platter, arrange lettuce around torte, top with lettuce, tomatoes, garnish with jalapeño slices.

PICANTE SAUCE:

9 tomatoes, peeled and diced
1½ large onions, diced
6 hot chiles, chopped fine
1½ cups tomato sauce
1 small clove garlic, minced
1½ large green peppers,
  diced

½ cup vinegar
1½ tablespoons sugar
½ tablespoon black pepper
Salt to taste

Combine tomatoes, onions, and chiles in a large pot over medium heat. Add all other ingredients and cook about 1½ hours. This can be canned in hot jars to be used later. Make sure jars seal. Or can be frozen for future use.

Note: This makes about 5 pints, so if smaller quantities are desired, cut recipe accordingly.

Helen's Southwest Specialties

Chicken Lasagna

SAUCE:

3 tablespoons butter
½ cup chopped onion
½ cup chopped green bell
  pepper
¼ pound fresh mushrooms,
  sliced (or 3 ounces canned,
  drained mushrooms)

1 (10½-ounce) can cream of
  chicken soup
⅓ cup milk
¼ cup diced pimiento,
  drained
½ teaspoon crumbled dried
  basil

Heat butter in large skillet over medium heat. Sauté onion, bell pepper, and mushrooms until soft. Add soup, milk, pimiento, and basil. Heat until blended.

NOODLES:

8 ounces lasagna noodles,
  cooked and drained
1½ cups cottage cheese,
  drained
3 cups cooked, diced chicken

2 cups shredded American or
  Cheddar cheese
½ cup grated Parmesan
  cheese

In buttered 9x13-inch casserole, place half of noodles; cover with half of sauce. Top with half of cottage cheese, half of chicken and half of cheeses. Repeat layering second time. Preheat oven to 375°. Bake 30 minutes or until lightly browned and bubbly. Yields 8 servings.

Sounds Delicious!

Confetti Turketti

1¼ cups cooked elbow
  macaroni
2 cups cooked, diced turkey
¼ cup pimento
¼ cup chopped green pepper
½ cup chopped onion
1 can cream of mushroom
  soup
1 tablespoon sage
1½ cups turkey broth
1 teaspoon pepper
½ cup shredded yellow
  cheese (no-fat)

Preheat oven to 350°. Combine all ingredients in casserole dish. Sprinkle cheese on top. Bake for 45 minutes.

The Homeplace Cookbook

Mexican Lasagna

1 pound lean ground beef
1 (16-ounce) can refried beans
2 teaspoons oregano
1 teaspoon cumin
¾ teaspoon garlic powder
12 lasagna noodles
2½ cups water
2½ cups picante sauce
2 cups sour cream
¾ cup finely sliced green
  onions
1 (2-ounce) can sliced black
  olives, drained
1 cup shredded Monterey
  Jack cheese

Combine ground beef, beans, oregano, cumin, and garlic powder in bowl; mix well. Layer ⅓ of the uncooked lasagna noodles and ½ of the ground beef mixture in nonstick 9x13-inch baking pan. Repeat layers, ending with noodles. Pour mixture of water and picante sauce over top. Bake, covered, at 350° for 1½ hours or until noodles are tender. Spoon mixture of sour cream, green onions, and olives over top. Sprinkle with cheese. Bake for 5 minutes or until cheese melts. Yields 12 servings.

Approx per serving: Cal 372; Prot 18g; Carbo 35g; Fiber 4g; T Fat 19g; 45% Cal from Fat; Chol 51mg; Sod 557mg.

Discover Oklahoma Cookin'

Calzones

FILLING:

1 pound ground turkey breast
    or chicken breast
½ cup chopped onion
½ teaspoon oregano
½ teaspoon caraway seeds

⅓ cup fat-free Italian salad
    dressing
¼ teaspoon salt
1 cup 1% cottage cheese

Brown meat and onion in large skillet sprayed with nonstick cooking spray. Add oregano, caraway seeds, fat-free Italian dressing and salt. Stir and cook until meat is done. Remove from heat and add cottage cheese.

CRUST:

6 egg roll wrappers
2 egg whites, slightly beaten

½ cup shredded fat-free
    cheese

Dip one side of the egg roll wrapper in egg white. The egg white side should be the outside. Place ½ cup filling in the center of the wrapper and add about 1 tablespoon fat-free cheese. Fold each corner of the wrapper to the center and form a sort of package. Place on baking sheet sprayed with nonstick cooking spray and bake at 375° for 20–25 minutes or until golden brown. Makes 6 servings.

Grams of Fat Per Serving 2. Calories Per Serving 227.

Fat Free & Ultra Lowfat Recipes

Wood Chuck

2 cups medium white sauce
1 medium can mushrooms
½ pound grated American or
    Cheddar cheese
1 can mushroom soup
1 small jar pimentos, chopped

½ green pepper, chopped
    (optional)
1½ cups cubed, cooked ham
6 hard-boiled eggs, chopped
2 cans Chinese noodles

Blend together all ingredients except eggs and Chinese noodles. Simmer over low heat and stir eggs in just before serving. Serve over 2 cans Chinese noodles. Serves 10.

Four Generations of Johnson Family Favorites

Spaghetti Sauce with Meat Balls

SAUCE:

2 medium-large onions,
   chopped
½ teaspoon garlic salt
2 bay leaves
1 tablespoon Worcestershire
1 teaspoon salt
1 tablespoon sugar
½ teaspoon pepper
½ teaspoon chili powder
   (optional)

2 teaspoons oregano
2 teaspoons Italian seasoning
3 tablespoons dried parsley
2 (16-ounce) cans tomatoes
2 (8-ounce) cans tomato sauce
1 (1.5-ounce) package
   spaghetti sauce with
   mushrooms

In a large kettle, combine onions, garlic salt, bay leaves, Worcestershire, salt, sugar, pepper, chili powder, oregano, Italian seasoning and parsley. Chop or break up tomatoes; add to pan. Add tomato sauce, spaghetti sauce mix and 3 cups water. Bring to a boil; reduce heat and simmer 2 hours. Stir occasionally across the bottom of the pan to prevent sticking.

MEATBALLS:

1½ pounds ground beef
1 cup soft fine bread crumbs
2 eggs
½ cup milk

½ cup Parmesan cheese
½ teaspoon salt
¼ teaspoon pepper
1 teaspoon Italian seasoning

In a medium bowl, combine ground beef, crumbs, eggs, milk, cheese, salt, pepper and Italian seasoning. Mix well with hands. Shape into small balls. In a large skillet, heat a small amount of oil. Fill skillet with meat balls. Brown lightly on both sides, turning as necessary to brown evenly. Drain meat balls in a colander. Add to sauce; simmer an additional hour. Discard bay leaves. Serve sauce over hot, cooked spaghetti. Serves 8.

Note: I usually double the recipe and freeze the sauce and meat balls in amounts for 1 meal.

Something Special Cookbook

Chicken Quiche
in Lemon Pastry Shell

PASTRY:

1½ cups flour
½ teaspoon salt
9 tablespoons butter
1 teaspoon (heaping)
    shortening

Grated rind and juice of ½
    lemon
¼ cup (scant) ice water

Sift flour and salt. Cut in butter and shortening until crumbly. Add lemon rind, juice, and ice water. Mix lightly. Form ball and roll out on lightly floured board. Roll 1½ inches larger than 10-inch pie plate. Place in plate and trim to 1 inch beyond plate. Roll edge under, form into rim and flute. Bake at 425° until partially done (10 minutes).

FILLING:

2 whole chicken breasts,
    skinned, boned and cut into
    1-inch cubes
½ teaspoon salt
⅛ teaspoon white pepper
¼ cup corn oil
1 large onion, thinly sliced
    and separated into rings
1 large firm tomato, peeled,
    seeded, cubed and drained
3 large eggs

¾ cup milk
¾ cup light cream
4½–5 ounces Gruyère
    cheese (or Swiss), cubed or
    grated
¼ cup freshly grated
    Parmesan cheese
Pinch of nutmeg
1 teaspoon salt
1 teaspoon butter, cut into
    small pieces

Add salt and pepper to chicken. Heat corn oil. Sauté chicken slowly, 5–6 minutes. Remove. Add onion rings to oil and cook until nearly tender. Add tomato. Cover and cook 7 minutes or until moisture evaporates. Beat eggs. Add milk, cream, cheeses, nutmeg, and salt. Arrange onion, tomato, and chicken in bottom of pastry shell. Pour egg mixture over and dot with butter. Bake in oven preheated to 375° for 35–40 minutes. Check for doneness by inserting knife 3 inches from edge. Quiche is done when knife comes out clean. Serve with Sauce. Makes 6 servings.

(continued)

(Chicken Quiche in Lemon Pastry Shell continued)

SAUCE:

10 small mushrooms, chopped
3 tablespoons butter
Salt and pepper to taste
2 tablespoons flour
½ cup light cream

2 tablespoons chutney, chopped
½ pint sour cream
¼ cup dry sherry

Sauté mushrooms in butter. Add salt and pepper to taste. Add flour and blend. Add cream and cook, stirring constantly, until sauce is thickened. Add chutney, sour cream and sherry. Cook until heated through. Serve over Quiche.

Come Grow with Us

Fast Fettuccine

SAUCE:

⅔ cup water or dry white wine
¼ cup butter, softened
2 tablespoons dried parsley
1 teaspoon dried basil, crumbled

½ teaspoon oregano
1 (8-ounce) package cream cheese, softened
1 teaspoon Italian herbs
Salt and pepper to taste

Combine the water (or dry white wine), butter, parsley, basil, and oregano. Cook over low heat. Blend in the cream cheese, stirring constantly. Season this mixture with the Italian herbs. Salt and pepper to taste. Keep warm, but do not burn.

FETTUCCINE:

1 (10-ounce) package fettuccine, cooked and drained
¼ cup butter

1 garlic clove, smashed
¾ cup grated Romano cheese

Cook the pasta according to package directions and drain. Set it aside. Melt ¼ cup butter in small skillet over low heat. Add the garlic and cook about 1–2 minutes. Do not burn. Pour this garlic butter over the warm pasta and toss gently. Sprinkle with ½ of the Romano cheese and toss again. Transfer this mixture to a serving platter and spoon the cream sauce over the top and sprinkle with the remaining cheese. Serve immediately.

Gourmet: The Quick and Easy Way

Cleo's Pizza

1 pound sausage or ground
  beef
1 can tomato sauce
1 medium onion, diced

1 can mushroom sauce
1 unbaked pie crust
Grated cheese

Cook sausage or ground beef. Drain off fat. Mix tomato sauce, onion, and mushroom sauce. Add this to the cooked drained meat. Pour over an unbaked crust and cover with grated cheese.

CRUST:
1 envelope dry yeast
Warm water

½ teaspoon sugar
Flour

Dissolve yeast in small amount of warm water with ½ teaspoon sugar added. Add flour to make dough. Roll out ⅛-inch thick and spread over cookie sheet. Bake at 375° until cheese is melted and crust is brown. This is fit for a king!

Seems Like I Done It This A-Way II

Crock Pot Pizza

1 (12-ounce) package mini-
  lasagna noodles or other
1½–2 pounds hamburger
  and/or sausage
1 onion, chopped
1 green pepper, chopped
1 package pepperoni (may
  use more, if desired)

1 can mushrooms, drained
2 (14-ounce) jars or 1 large
  jar spaghetti sauce
1 (14-ounce) jar pizza sauce
1 (8-ounce) package shredded
  Cheddar cheese
1 (8-ounce) package shredded
  Mozzarella cheese

Cook noodles as package instructs. Brown meat and drain grease. Add chopped onion, pepper, pepperoni, mushrooms, and spaghetti and pizza sauce. Simmer 30 minutes. Layer in crock pot or 9x12-inch casserole dish, the meat sauce mixture, noodles, and cheeses; repeat. Top with extra pepperoni slices to decorate top, if desired.

Cook on low in crock pot for 2 hours, or if baking in casserole dish, bake at 350° for 30 minutes, loosely covered with foil. Makes about 10–12 servings.

Spring Creek Club

Onion Cheese Pie

Ultra lowfat. One of my favorites.

2 large fat-free flour tortillas
Buttermist nonstick cooking
 spray
1 teaspoon Molly McButter
1 (16-ounce) carton fat-free
 cottage cheese
⅓ cup fat-free liquid egg
 product
2 teaspoons dry onion flakes
1 medium onion, thinly sliced

⅓ cup fat-free Parmesan
 cheese
5 slices fat-free Swiss cheese
⅓ cup grated fat-free
 Cheddar cheese
1 large ripe tomato, thinly
 sliced
Garlic salt
Black pepper to taste

Preheat oven to 325°. Place 1 tortilla in large pie plate sprayed with nonstick cooking spray. Spray tortilla lightly with Buttermist and sprinkle with ½ teaspoon Molly McButter. Repeat process with second tortilla on top of the other.

In large bowl, combine cottage cheese, egg product, and onion flakes and mix with spoon. Pour half over tortillas and gently smooth and spread with spoon.

Add layers in this order: half of the sliced onion, all the Parmesan and Swiss cheese, remaining cottage cheese mixture, all the Cheddar cheese, remaining sliced onion, and all the sliced tomato. Sprinkle top with garlic salt and black pepper. Bake at 325° for 1 hour and 20 minutes. Cool slightly before slicing. Makes 8 servings.

Grams of Fat Per Serving 1. Calories Per Serving 128.

Fat Free 2

Wild Rice Baron

2 cups raw wild rice
4 cups water
2 teaspoons salt
2 pounds lean ground beef
1 pound fresh mushrooms
1 cup chopped onion
½ cup chopped celery

½ cup butter
¼ cup soy sauce
2 cups sour cream
2 teaspoons salt
¼ teaspoon pepper
½ cup slivered almonds

Gently cook wild rice in water and 2 teaspoons salt (uncovered) for 45 minutes or until rice is done. Drain if necessary. Brown ground beef. Rinse mushrooms; slice and sauté with onion and celery in butter for 5–10 minutes.

Combine soy sauce, sour cream or soup (see Note), and remaining salt and pepper. Add cooked wild rice, beef and onions, mushrooms, celery mixture, and almonds. Toss lightly and place in 3-quart buttered casserole. Bake at 350° about 1 hour, uncovered. Add a little water during baking if necessary and stir several times during baking.

Note: May use 2 cans cream of mushroom soup, undiluted, instead of sour cream and fresh mushrooms, or use both.

United Methodist Cookbook 1993

Orange Rice

3 tablespoons butter
⅔ cup sliced celery
2 tablespoons chopped onion
1½ cups water
2 tablespoons grated orange
  peel

1 cup orange juice
1¼ teaspoons salt
1 cup raw rice

Melt butter in heavy saucepan with a cover; add celery and onion and cook, stirring occasionally until tender. Stir in water, orange peel, juice, and salt; then bring to a boil. Add rice, cover and steam over low heat for 20–25 minutes or until rice is tender. Serves 6.

Pow Wow Chow

Wild Rice Bake

1 cup uncooked wild rice
2 (14-ounce) cans chicken
 broth
6 slices bacon, cut into 1-inch
 pieces
1 cup chopped onion

2 cups sliced mushrooms
¼ teaspoon each thyme and
 marjoram
⅛ teaspoon pepper
¾ cup chopped carrots

Rinse uncooked rice. Bring to a boil in chicken broth in 2-quart saucepan; reduce heat. Simmer, covered, for 40–50 minutes or just until tender; do not drain. Cook bacon in skillet until crisp; remove with slotted spoon and drain, reserving 2 tablespoons drippings in skillet. Sauté onion in reserved drippings for 3–4 minutes or until tender. Stir in mushrooms, thyme, marjoram, and pepper. Sauté for 2 minutes longer. Add mushroom mixture, bacon, and carrots to rice; mix well. Spoon into buttered 2-quart baking dish. Bake at 350° for 35–40 minutes or until bubbly. Let stand for 5 minutes before serving. Yields 6 servings.

Approx per serving: Cal 170; Prot 10g; Carbo 25g; Fiber 1g; T Fat 4g; 22% Cal from Fat; Chol 6mg; Sod 528mg.

Discover Oklahoma Cookin'

Rice Almondine

2 cups raw rice
3 envelopes Lipton Chicken
 Noodle Soup
8½ cups boiling water
2 pounds pork sausage

1 bunch celery, chopped
2 medium onions, chopped
1 green pepper, chopped
2 medium cans pimientos
1 can chopped almonds

Combine rice, soup mix and water. Cook for 30 minutes. Fry sausage. Reserve some of the fat to cook celery, onions, and pepper. Cook until soft, then add pimientos and almonds. Combine with rice mixture and bake uncovered at 350° for 30 minutes.

What's Cooking in Okarche?

Simply Southwest

This recipe takes less than 15 minutes to get to the table and tastes fantastic!

1 (14½-ounce) can chicken broth
2¼ cup quick-cooking brown rice
2 teaspoons sunflower oil
1 medium onion, chopped
2 garlic cloves, minced
2 cups diced cooked turkey breast

2 cups (2 small) thinly sliced zucchini
1 medium red bell pepper, chopped (use the seeds)
1 teaspoon ground cumin
½ cup picante sauce

Bring broth to boil; add rice. Cover and simmer on lowest heat 8–10 minutes. While it simmers, sauté onion and garlic in the oil. Add remaining ingredients to the onion/garlic mixture, and cook for just a very few minutes—just till the vegetables are tender-crisp. Serve the turkey mixture on top of the rice. Makes 4 large servings.

Note: This dish can be made extra hot and spicy by the kind of picante sauce you use. Green bell pepper can be substituted for red, but the red pepper makes this a beautiful dish, plus it ups the beta carotene a tremendous amount. Also, you can use leftover cooked chicken or turkey. I like to bake a small turkey just to have meat available for dishes like this. You can also use Louis Rich Oven Roasted Turkey Breast.

Variation: Try thin carrot slices and bite-size pieces of cauliflower. Be creative. Enjoy!

Per serving: Cal 345; Fat 7g; Sod 545mg; Fiber 4.5g.

15 Minute, Lowfat Meals

Delicious Rice

2 cups uncooked long grain
  rice
4 tomatillos (green Spanish
  tomatoes), rinsed and
  chopped
½ cup chopped cilantro
2 jalapeño peppers, diced
1 large clove garlic, minced
2 teaspoons salt
1½ ounces butter
1 can chicken broth and 1 can
  water
6 green onions, diced

Prepare rice according to directions on package/box. Add remaining ingredients and simmer 12–15 minutes.

Court Clerk's Bar and Grill

Salmon Patties

1 (16-ounce) can salmon,
  drained, flaked
¾ cup crushed saltine
  crackers (16–18)
½ cup chopped celery
½ cup milk
2 eggs, beaten
2 tablespoons chopped onion
1 tablespoon lemon juice
½ teaspoon salt
Dash of pepper
Slices of process cheese
  spread

Heat oven to 350°. Combine salmon, crackers, celery, milk, eggs, onion, lemon juice, and seasonings; mix well. Form into 6 patties. Bake at 350° for 25 minutes. Top each patty with a slice of cheese; return to oven until cheese melts. Makes 4 servings.

Cookbook of Treasured Recipes

Tartar Sauce

1 small onion, chopped fine
1 or 2 dill or sour pickles
  (chopped)
10–12 stuffed olives (chopped)
Mayonnaise
Lemon juice

Take first 3 ingredients and mix with just enough mayonnaise to mix. A drop of lemon juice may be added.

Seems Like I Done It This A-Way III

Ham Delicacy

1 (5-ounce) package noodles, cooked and drained
1 pound Cheddar cheese grated
1 can cream of chicken soup undiluted
1 can whole grain corn, drained
1 green pepper, diced
1 can pimiento, diced
1 pound cooked ham, diced

Combine all ingredients. Bake uncovered at 350° for 30 minutes. Serves 12.

Company Fare I

Crystalline Pickles

1 quart hamburger sliced dill pickles
2½ cups sugar
1 teaspoon celery seed
1 teaspoon mustard seed
1 tablespoon dried minced onion
1 tablespoon dried crushed red pepper

Drain pickles, reserving the liquid. Place pickles and other ingredients in large bowl, stirring to mix well. Cover and let sit in refrigerator overnight. (Sugar will make liquid to almost cover pickles.) Stir and place in jar, adding liquid from original pickles, if needed, to cover pickles. A few days curing makes them even better.

Come Grow with Us

J.J.'s Pepper Relish

24 sweet peppers, part red
5 hot peppers
7 medium onions
3 cups vinegar
3 cups sugar
2 tablespoons salt
2 tablespoons mustard seed

Grind peppers; chop onions and combine with vinegar and sugar; add salt and mustard seed. Boil 30 minutes. Very good.

Seems Like I Done It This A-Way II

Vegetables

Although the Santa Fe Depot stopped receiving rail passengers long ago, it still welcomes visitors to Shawnee who come to see its unusual castle-like architecture and local history exhibits. Built in 1904—before statehood (1907)—the depot is the last of its kind on the old route to the West. Shawnee is just 30 minutes east of downtown Oklahoma City.

Honey-Dijon Carrots

3 tablespoons butter
1 tablespoon honey or maple
  syrup

1 tablespoon Dijon mustard
2 cups steamed sliced carrots

Combine butter, honey, and mustard in saucepan. Heat for several minutes until flavors are blended, stirring constantly. Pour over hot steamed carrots. Yields 4 servings.

Approx Per Serving: Cal 130; T Fat 9g; Cal from Fat 59%; Prot 1g; Carbo 13g; Fiber 3g; Chol 23mg; Sod 174mg.

The Pioneer Chef

Company Carrots

1 pound carrots, thinly sliced
¼ cup golden raisins
¼ cup butter
3 tablespoons honey

1 tablespoon lemon juice
¼ teaspoon ground ginger
¼ cup sliced, unpeeled
  almonds

Preheat oven to 300°. Cook carrots, covered, in ½-inch boiling water for 8 minutes; drain. Place carrots in a 1-quart baking dish. Stir in raisins, butter, honey, lemon juice, and ginger. Bake, covered, for 30 minutes, stirring occasionally. Watch. Don't let burn. Sprinkle with almonds before serving. Serves 4.

Gourmet: The Quick and Easy Way

Copper Pennies

2 pounds carrots
1 small green pepper
1 medium onion
1 can tomato soup
½ cup salad oil

1 cup sugar
¾ cup apple cider vinegar
1 teaspoon prepared mustard
1 teaspoon Worcestershire

Slice and boil carrots in salted water until fork tender. Cool. Alternate in layers with carrots, pepper rings, and onion slices. Beat remaining ingredients well with beater until completely blended. Pour over vegetables. May be served hot or cold. May be prepared several days before serving.

Company Fare II

Sensational Spinach and Zucchini Pie

PASTRY:

2⅔ cups flour
1 teaspoon salt

1 cup vegetable shortening
7–8 tablespoons ice water

Combine flour and salt in bowl. With pastry blender, cut in shortening until mixture resembles coarse crumbs. Sprinkle on water 1 tablespoon at a time, tossing with fork until mixture holds together. Shape into 2 balls, one slightly larger than the other; flatten. Wrap and refrigerate until ready to use.

FILLING:

1 pound bulk sweet Italian sausage
2 tablespoons butter or margarine
3 cups coarsely chopped zucchini
2 teaspoons Knorr Aromat Seasoning or 1 teaspoon seasoned salt
1 (10-ounce) package frozen chopped spinach, thawed and squeezed dry

1 (15-ounce) container ricotta cheese
1 (8-ounce) container soft cream cheese with herb and garlic
1 cup shredded Mozzarella cheese
2 large eggs, lightly beaten
1 tablespoon hot pepper sauce
1 large egg, beaten with 1 tablespoon water

Preheat oven to 425°. Brown sausage in skillet over medium heat. Drain. Meanwhile, melt butter in another skillet over high heat. Add zucchini, sprinkle with seasoning and cook just until tender. Combine sausage, spinach, ricotta cheese, cream cheese, Mozzarella, eggs, and pepper sauce in large bowl. Stir in zucchini.

On lightly floured surface, roll larger pastry to a 12-inch circle. Fit into 10-inch pie plate. Spoon in filling. Roll remaining pastry to 11-inch circle; make decorative cutouts for vents. Brush rim of pie with egg glaze and place pastry circle on top. Flute edges. Brush top with egg glaze. Bake 15 minutes. Reduce oven temperature to 375° and bake 35–45 minutes more, until golden. Cool on wire rack 30 minutes. Serve warm or at room temperature. Makes 10 servings.

Watonga Cheese Festival Cookbook 17th Edition

Spinach Cups

½ cup butter, melted
12 slices white bread, crusts removed
1 (10-ounce) package frozen chopped spinach, thawed
2 eggs, beaten lightly
½ cup cream-style cottage cheese
2 tablespoons Parmesan cheese, grated
½ cup cream
½ teaspoon Worcestershire
Garlic salt to taste
Pinch of sugar
Paprika for garnish

Melt the butter in a skillet. Cool. Coat both sides of bread slices with cooled butter. Press each slice into a muffin cup (or use a muffin tin).

Squeeze as much water as possible out of spinach, using your hands. In a mixing bowl combine spinach and the remaining filling ingredients except paprika. Spoon about 2 tablespoons of filling into each bread cup. Sprinkle with paprika. Bake at 325° for 25–30 minutes. Let cool a minute. Use a fork to lift out the baked spinach cups. Makes 8 servings.

Applause!

Broccoli Balls

2 pounds fresh broccoli or 3 (10-ounce) packages frozen broccoli
1 (12-ounce) carton small curd cottage cheese
⅓ cup plus ½ cup grated Parmesan cheese, divided
⅓ cup fine bread crumbs
½ teaspoon salt
2 eggs, beaten
⅓ cup flour
¼ cup margarine

Cook broccoli in a small amount of water just until tender; drain and chop. Combine broccoli, cottage cheese, ⅓ cup Parmesan cheese, bread crumbs, salt, and eggs. Mix well. Shape into 8 balls; refrigerate overnight.

Roll balls in flour and place in a buttered 9x13-inch baking dish. Dot with margarine. Bake at 400° for 10 minutes. Sprinkle with ½ cup Parmesan cheese and bake 5 minutes longer. Makes 8 generous servings.

United Methodist Cookbook 1993

Cheesy Broccoli Casserole

1½ pounds fresh broccoli
2 slightly beaten eggs
¾ cup cottage cheese
½ cup shredded Cheddar
  cheese (2 ounces)
2 tablespoons finely chopped
  onion

1 teaspoon Worcestershire
½ teaspoon salt
⅛ teaspoon pepper
¼ cup fine dry bread crumbs
1 tablespoon butter or
  margarine, melted

Wash and trim broccoli; cut stalks into spears. Cook broccoli, covered in a small amount of boiling unsalted water about 10 minutes or until crisp-tender; drain. Meanwhile in a bowl, combine eggs, cheeses, onion, Worcestershire, salt and pepper. Arrange broccoli spears in a shallow 1½-quart baking dish; spoon cheese mixture on top. Stir together bread crumbs and melted butter or margarine; sprinkle over cheese mixture. Bake uncovered in a 350° oven for 15–20 minutes or until heated through and egg mixture is set. Serve immediately. Makes 4–6 servings.

Old and New

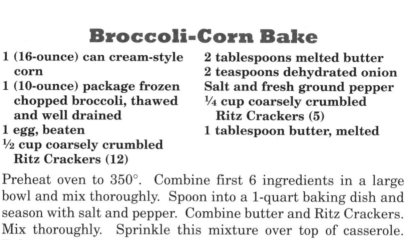

Broccoli-Corn Bake

1 (16-ounce) can cream-style corn
1 (10-ounce) package frozen chopped broccoli, thawed and well drained
1 egg, beaten
½ cup coarsely crumbled Ritz Crackers (12)

2 tablespoons melted butter
2 teaspoons dehydrated onion
Salt and fresh ground pepper
¼ cup coarsely crumbled Ritz Crackers (5)
1 tablespoon butter, melted

Preheat oven to 350°. Combine first 6 ingredients in a large bowl and mix thoroughly. Spoon into a 1-quart baking dish and season with salt and pepper. Combine butter and Ritz Crackers. Mix thoroughly. Sprinkle this mixture over top of casserole. Bake uncovered until golden brown, about 30 minutes.

Gourmet: The Quick and Easy Way

Cheese Corn Bake

2 tablespoons butter or margarine
4 teaspoons all-purpose flour
⅛ teaspoon garlic powder
¼ cup milk
6 ounces sharp American cheese, shredded (1½ cups)

1 (3-ounce) package cream cheese, cut up
3 (10-ounce) packages frozen, whole kernel corn, thawed
3 ounces diced ham

In large saucepan, melt margarine or butter. Stir in flour and garlic powder. Add milk all at once. Cook and stir over medium heat until thickened and bubbly. Stir in cheeses and cook over low heat until melted.

Add corn and ham. Transfer mixture to a 2-quart casserole dish. Bake in a 350° oven for 45 minutes or until heated through. Makes 10–12 servings.

Sequoyah's Cookin'

The final resting place of the great Apache warrior, Geronimo, is in Lawton. Quanah Parker, Santatanta, and Santank are also buried there.

Jalapeño Corn Pudding

Some corn puddings are wimpy, tenderfoot food, but not this one. If you can find them, Kent suggests adding 1 cup drained canned cactus (nopales) pieces.

2 (16-ounce) cans cream-style corn
2 cups (8 ounces) shredded sharp Cheddar cheese
½ cup yellow cornmeal
½ cup vegetable oil

2 large eggs, beaten
2 tablespoons canned chopped green chiles, drained
2 cloves garlic, minced
½ teaspoon salt

Preheat the oven to 350°. Lightly butter a 12x7-inch baking dish. In a medium bowl, whisk the corn, 1 cup of the cheese, the cornmeal, oil, eggs, chiles, garlic, and salt. Spread the batter in the baking dish, then sprinkle with the remaining 1 cup cheese. Bake until the center feels set when pressed gently with a finger, about 1 hour. Let stand 5 minutes before serving. Makes 4–6 servings.

National Cowboy Hall of Fame Chuck Wagon Cookbook

Fried Corn

Select 12 ears of corn at the perfect stage. Husk the corn and remove silk by brushing back and forth with a soft brush or cloth. Cut from the cob with a very sharp knife. Cut only half the depth of the kernel. Use the back of the knife to scrape out the remaining pulp and juice. Should yield 5 cups of corn. Heat ½ cup of butter, sizzling hot in heavy skillet. Add corn and enough water to give consistency of thin gravy. Season with salt and pepper, stirring constantly. Cook 5 minutes. Reduce heat to simmering. Cover tightly and cook about 20 minutes longer. The corn will be thick. Serve hot. Very good with fried chicken.

Oklahoma Cookin'

Chile Corn Casserole

An easy dish to prepare for pot luck suppers, etc.

1 can whole kernel corn,
  drained
1 can cream corn
1 (8-ounce) package cream
  cheese

1 small can green chiles, do
  not drain
Bread crumbs, buttered

Butter 1½-quart casserole. Combine both cans of corn and cream cheese (cut in small pieces) in small pan. Heat over low flame, stirring constantly until cheese melts. Add chiles; stir well. Pour into buttered casserole dish and top or edge with buttered bread crumbs. Bake at 300° for 15 minutes or until lightly browned. Serves 8.

Note: Chilies may be mild to hot depending on choice of cook.

Cooking A+ Recipes

Hominy Casserole

1 medium onion, chopped
1 stalk celery
Butter
2 cans yellow hominy (drain
  ½ juice off)

1 (8-ounce) carton sour cream
¼ cup pimento
1 cup grated cheese
  (American)

Sauté onion and celery in butter. Combine all ingredients and pour in buttered casserole dish. Bake in slow oven until bubbling (20–30 minutes).

Seems Like I Done It This A-Way III

Route 66, the fabled "Main Street of America," crosses Oklahoma for 392-plus miles. The "Mother Road" was in fact born in Oklahoma, as the road's architect, Cyrus Avery, lived in Tulsa. Travelers find neon-lit diners, drive-in theatres, mom-and-pop gas stations, and rustic trading posts along the route. You can still "get your kicks on Route 66."

Fried Green Tomatoes

Green tomatoes
Salt and pepper
1 egg, beaten
3 tablespoons milk

Flour
½ cup bread crumbs
½ cup cornmeal
4 tablespoons oil

Slice tomatoes in ¼-inch slices. Salt and pepper tomatoes. Mix egg and milk together. Dip tomatoes in flour, then in egg mixture and into bread crumbs and cornmeal mixture. Then fry in oil in cast iron skillet until brown on both sides.

Oklahoma Cookin'

Grilled Green Tomatoes

4 large green tomatoes
2 tablespoons Dijon mustard
2 tablespoons balsamic
   vinegar

2 tablespoons olive oil
1 tablespoon fresh oregano

Slice off sides to flatten tomatoes. Make ½-inch vertical slices. Make marinade of next 4 ingredients. Combine, then whip with a small wire whip. Spread on both sides of tomatoes and let marinate about one hour at room temperature. Grill 5 minutes, turn, grill 3 or 4 minutes. Serve with grilled chicken breasts. Delicious!

Court Clerk's Bar and Grill

Basil Tomato Tart

Great to serve when your garden is bountiful with fresh tomatoes and basil.

1 unbaked 9-inch pie crust
1½ cups shredded
  Mozzarella cheese
6 Roma or 4 medium
  tomatoes
1 cup loosely packed fresh
  basil leaves

4 cloves garlic, minced
½ cup mayonnaise
¼ cup freshly grated
  Parmesan cheese
⅓ teaspoon ground white
  pepper
Fresh basil leaves

Place pie crust in quiche dish or glass pie plate. Flute edges and prick bottom and sides. Bake in preheated 475° oven 8–10 minutes until light brown. Sprinkle with ½ cup of the Mozzarella cheese. Cool on a wire rack.

Cut tomatoes into wedges; drain on paper towels. Arrange tomato wedges atop melted cheese in the baked pie shell. In a food processor combine basil and garlic and chop coarsely. Sprinkle over tomatoes.

In medium mixing bowl combine remaining Mozzarella cheese, mayonnaise, Parmesan, and pepper. Spoon cheese mixture over basil mixture spreading evenly cover the top. Bake in 375° oven 35–40 minutes or until golden and bubbly. Serve warm. If desired, sprinkle with basil leaves. Serves 6.

Gourmet Our Way

Baked Herbed Tomatoes

3 large tomatoes
¾ cup bread crumbs
2 tablespoons chopped fresh
  basil or 1½ teaspoons dried

3 tablespoons chopped
  parsley
2–3 tablespoons melted butter

Preheat oven to 350°. Rub a baking sheet, 10x17, lightly with oil. Core tomatoes and slice each in half. The slices should be about ¾-inch thick. Combine the bread crumbs, basil, and parsley. With a fork stir in the melted butter until well mixed. Sprinkle the crumb mixture on top of the tomatoes. Bake, uncovered in preheated oven for 20–25 minutes. Makes 6 servings.

Mary's Recipe Box

Garden Goulash

This is an original recipe which my family loved, and since we raised a large vegetable garden, I had all the vegetables on hand. I often add other vegetables as well, such as eggplant and summer squash.

5 cups sliced okra
Meal, flour and salt
1 small chopped onion
1 cup whole kernel corn

⅛ cup chopped green pepper
1 small chopped jalapeño
  pepper (seeded)
2–3 fresh tomatoes

Toss the okra in a mixture of cornmeal, flour and salt. Brown slightly in oil. Don't overbrown. Then add remaining ingredients except tomatoes. Simmer slowly until done. Do not stir frequently. When done, peel and cut fresh tomatoes into chunks; place atop mixture. Simmer until tomatoes are slightly soft.

Recipes and Remembrances

Ataloa Lodge in Muskogee houses one of the best collections of privately owned traditional and contemporary Native American art in the United States. One of the unique attractions at Ataloa Lodge is the fireplace made of rocks from around the world, including a fossilized dinosaur egg.

Okra Creole Style

¼ cup margarine	1½ cups canned tomatoes
½ cup chopped onion	1½ cups sliced okra
1 green pepper, chopped	Salt and pepper to taste

Melt margarine; add onion and pepper. Cook until transparent. Add other ingredients and cook covered until okra is tender. Serves 6.

Home Cookin' Is a Family Affair

Squash with Eggs

1 large onion, chopped	½ teaspoon allspice
2 tablespoons butter	(optional)
1 pound squash, minced	1 teaspoon salt
2 eggs	½ teaspoon pepper

Sauté chopped onion in butter for 5 minutes. Wash and cut squash in very fine pieces. Add minced squash to sautéed onion; cover and cook slowly until squash is tender.

Make 2 wells in squash and add an egg in each well; add spices. As eggs begin to set, fold into squash gently. Stir gently until eggs are done. Serves 3.

Cookbook of Treasured Recipes

Elegante Squash

2 (8-ounce) packages squash, cooked and drained	1 cup water chestnuts, sliced
	½ cup shredded cheese
½ cup chopped onion	1 egg
½ cup chopped green pepper	1 tablespoon sugar
½ cup margarine	½ cup bread crumbs
½ cup mayonnaise	

Cook squash; drain and set aside. Sauté onion and green pepper in margarine until clear. Add squash, mayonnaise, chestnuts, and cheese. Beat egg with sugar; spread over vegetables in casserole. Cover with bread crumbs and bake at 350° until bubbly, about 30 minutes. Good!

Country Cooking

Red Cabbage with Wine

2 pounds red cabbage,
  shredded (7 cups)
4 slices bacon, diced
1 onion, chopped
2 tablespoons sugar
1 teaspoon salt

1½ cups water
6 tablespoons tarragon
  vinegar
1 tart apple, peeled and
  chopped
4 tablespoons sherry wine

Shred cabbage coarsely. Place diced bacon and chopped onion in kettle; cook until onion is glazed. Add sugar, salt, water, and vinegar; bring to a boil. Add cabbage and apple; mix thoroughly. Cover and simmer until cabbage is tender, about 25 minutes. Add wine. Increase sugar or vinegar as desired. Wine vinegar may be used instead of tarragon.

Thunderbird Cookers of AT&T

Escalloped Asparagus

1 can asparagus
4 hard-boiled eggs, sliced
White Sauce

Butter
Grated cheese

Layer ½ asparagus, sliced eggs and remaining asparagus. Cover with White Sauce then dots of butter and grated cheese. Bake 1–2 hours at 325°.

WHITE SAUCE:

3 tablespoons butter
⅓ cup flour

Milk
Salt and pepper, to taste

Brown butter, add flour, stir. Add milk to make a medium thickened sauce. Add salt and pepper to taste.

Here's What's Cookin' at Zion

There are dinosaur footprints in the Panhandle. Millions of years ago, these prehistoric giants left their footprints now preserved in a sandstone creek bed about six miles north of Kenton near Boise City. Dinosaur signs on SH-325 guide you there.

Molly's Landing Marinated Mushrooms

At the west edge of the twin bridges in Verdigris is Molly's Landing, an upscale restaurant with an unexpected twist.

1½ cups vegetable oil	3 tablespoons sugar
½ teaspoon dry mustard	2 teaspoons Worcestershire
1½ cups vinegar	1 tablespoon salt
1½ tablespoons fresh garlic, minced	1 pound fresh mushrooms, cleaned

Combine all ingredients except mushrooms. Pour mixture over mushrooms and marinate for 24 hours in the refrigerator. Makes 5–6 servings.

The Route 66 Cookbook

Stuffed Baked Onions
(Ultra Lowfat)

4 large sweet onions
2 stalks celery, chopped fine
3½ cups boxed stuffing mix
(should contain only 1 gram
fat per serving for mix only)
Salt to taste

Black pepper to taste
1 egg white, slightly beaten
4 tablespoons lite sour cream
2 cups chicken broth (use
canned and remove fat from
top)

Preheat oven to 350°. Remove centers of onion, leaving outside shell to stand alone after center is removed. To remove centers, cut top and bottom from onion and carefully remove several inside layers from the onion, starting with the center and working out. Save enough of the onion centers to provide ½ cup chopped onion to mix with stuffing.

Brown chopped onion and celery in skillet sprayed with nonstick cooking spray Set aside to cool slightly. In large bowl combine stuffing mix, browned onion and celery, salt, pepper, and egg white. Fill each onion with stuffing mix.

In small bowl stir lite sour cream until creamy. Gradually add chicken broth and stir until all chicken broth is added. Place stuffed onions in baking dish sprayed with nonstick cooking spray. Pour a small amount of cream sauce over each stuffed onion and pour the rest of the sauce in the bottom of the baking dish. Bake uncovered at 350° for 35–40 minutes or until onions are tender. Serve as a side dish with meat if desired. Makes 4 servings.

Grams of Fat Per Serving: 3. Calories Per Serving: 264.

Fat Free & Ultra Lowfat Recipes

Started in 1871 by George Miller and his sons Joe, Zack and George, the 101 Ranch, south of Ponca City, stretched across 101,000 acres and into four counties, Noble, Pawnee, Osage, and Kay. The self-contained ranch had its own tannery, dairy, and a store for goods. Many of the first western movies were made here. The 101 Ranch Room, full of memorabilia, is open to the public.

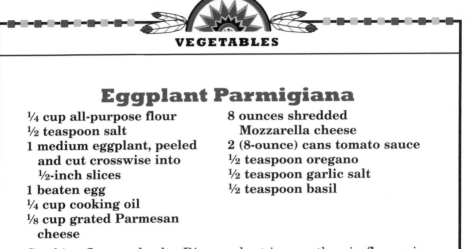

Eggplant Parmigiana

¼ cup all-purpose flour
½ teaspoon salt
1 medium eggplant, peeled
  and cut crosswise into
  ½-inch slices
1 beaten egg
¼ cup cooking oil
⅛ cup grated Parmesan
  cheese

8 ounces shredded
  Mozzarella cheese
2 (8-ounce) cans tomato sauce
½ teaspoon oregano
½ teaspoon garlic salt
½ teaspoon basil

Combine flour and salt. Dip eggplant in egg, then in flour mixture. Brown eggplant, half at a time, in hot oil about 3 minutes per side. Drain well. Using ½ of the eggplant, place a single layer in a 10x6x2-inch baking dish. Sprinkle with half the Parmesan. Mix tomato sauce, oregano, garlic salt, and basil. Top eggplant with half the sauce and half the Mozzarella. Repeat layers. Bake uncovered in a 400° oven for 15–20 minutes or until hot. Serves 6.

Kitchen Klatter Keepsakes

Eggplant—Chick Pea Dinner

2 medium eggplants
2 medium onions, slivered
1 clove garlic, chopped
¼ cup olive oil

1 can chick peas, drained
1 (14½-ounce) can tomatoes
Salt, pepper, cinnamon (to
  taste)

Wash eggplants, peel and cut into 3-inch cubes. Sauté onions and garlic in oil until limp. Add chick peas and stir-fry for a few minutes. Add eggplant, tomatoes, and spices. Cover and simmer for 15 minutes. You may also add squash and potatoes for a complete vegetable dinner.

Cookbook of Treasured Recipes

In territory days, outlaws like Frank and Jesse James and Belle Starr used the caves and tunnels in the San Bois Mountains as hideouts between sprees in Kansas and Texas. More civilized today, but no less secluded, Robbers Cave State Park offers visitors a chance to see it for themselves.

Bart Conner's Eggplant Parmigiana

1 egg, slightly beaten
1 cup milk
1 tablespoon vegetable oil
1 cup flour
2 medium eggplant, peeled and cut into ½-inch slices
Hot vegetable oil
1 (20-ounce) can tomato sauce
1 (12-ounce) can tomato paste
1 (16-ounce) can tomatoes, drained
¼ cup Burgundy wine
1 teaspoon dried whole oregano
½ teaspoon dried whole basil
¼ teaspoon dried whole thyme
¼ teaspoon garlic salt
10–16 ounces sliced Mozzarella cheese
Grated Parmesan cheese

Combine egg, milk, 1 tablespoon vegetable oil; gradually add to flour, beating until smooth. Dip eggplant in flour mixture; fry in hot oil until golden. Drain well on paper towels; set aside. Combine next 8 ingredients in medium saucepan, mixing well. Simmer sauce 10 minutes.

Arrange half of eggplant slices in a lightly greased 13x9x2-inch baking dish. Top with half of Mozzarella slices. Spoon half of tomato mixture over cheese. Repeat layers. Top with Parmesan cheese. Bake at 350° for 30–40 minutes or until sauce is bubbly. Serves 6–8.

Sooner Sampler

Potato Pancakes

A great side dish—or serve with a salad for a delicious meal!

½ cup egg replacer
1¼ cups skim milk
2 medium red potatoes,
   scrubbed, grated
3 green onions, sliced

1–2 tablespoons parsley,
   chopped
1 cup whole-wheat flour
Oil, butter, or soy margarine

In a large bowl combine the egg replacer and milk. Stir in the potatoes, green onions, and parsley. Stir in the flour until just combined.

In a large skillet, heat 2 teaspoons of your choice of fat over medium heat. Spoon the batter into the skillet, making 2 or 3 pancakes. Spread them out with a spoon if necessary (batter will be thick). Turn the heat down to medium-low and cook for approximately 3 minutes on each side. Yields 8 pancakes.

Healthy America

Kugulas

This famous Lithuanian recipe has been handed down from generation to generation. Now it is your turn to follow Grandma Michus' version. Patience will lead you to a successful dish. The potatoes need to be grated, preferably by hand. It is difficult, time-consuming, and usually results in a few skinned knuckles. It is definitely worth the effort, however.

1 large onion	1 small can evaporated milk
4 eggs	2 tablespoons sugar
5 slices bacon	Salt to taste
¼ pound margarine	5 pounds potatoes

Grate onion, have eggs ready to mix into the potatoes, fry bacon until crisp. Combine the bacon grease with margarine. Have a small can of evaporated milk available; 2 tablespoons of sugar and salt (to taste) will be added. Keep the peeled potatoes under water prior to grating—this will keep them from turning brown. Grate potatoes. Do this all at once. Also, squeeze some of the water out of the grated potatoes before you combine them with the other ingredients. If you have everything ready to go before you grate the potatoes and then combine the grated potatoes immediately with the other ingredients, the Kugulas will be lighter and a beautiful yellow in color.

Grease a large roasting pan (3 inches deep); have the oven preheated to 400°. In a large bowl combine the potatoes, onion, eggs, crumbled bacon, evaporated milk, sugar, bacon grease/margarine mixture. Add salt to taste. Pour the mixture into the roasting pan. There should be enough to fill the pan so that the Kugulas is about 3 inches deep. Bake for 15 minutes at 400° and then turn the temperature down to 350° and bake for 1½ hours. Remove from the oven and let the Kugulas set for a few minutes before cutting it into slices for serving. Enjoy!

Cooking A+ Recipes

Laredo Potato

So many people love this dish! It's quick to fix, it's very tasty, very low in fat, and it's filled with energy.

1 medium potato	½ ounce (⅓ cup) shredded
¼ cup chili hot beans	low moisture, part skim,
½ tomato, chopped	Mozzarella cheese
2 tablespoons chopped green	Salsa
onion	

Bake potato in microwave 4 minutes, or till done; split and mash a bit. Top with the beans. Heat in microwave. Top with tomato, onion, and cheese. Now add salsa for great Mexican flavor. Makes 1 serving.

Per serving: Cal 320; Fat 3g; Sod 560mg; Fiber 9.5g.

15 Minute, Lowfat Meals

Prairie Schooners

4 large baked potatoes	Salt and pepper to taste
1 (15-ounce) can Ranch-Style	1 green pepper, chopped
beans	1 onion, chopped
1 cup sour cream	1 cup grated mild Cheddar
1 stick butter, room	cheese
temperature	

Slice off top ⅓ of baked potato lengthwise. Scoop out potato with a teaspoon leaving ¼-inch around potato skin. Mash scooped-out potato until free of lumps. Drain beans thoroughly, reserving sauce. Mash beans. Whip sour cream, butter, mashed beans, salt and pepper. Add to mashed potatoes, adding enough bean juice to moisten. Spoon mixture lightly into potato shells. Top with grated cheese, onion, and green pepper. Bake at 425° until browned. Serves 4.

Sooner Sampler

The "prairie schooner," typical of the covered wagon traveled in by most of the homesteaders, became the spirit symbol for the University of Oklahoma Sooners.

My Favorite Potatoes

6 potatoes	Rosemary leaves
1 stick butter, melted	1 package onion soup mix

Do not peel potatoes. Wash thoroughly. Slice in ¼-inch to ½-inch thickness. Combine melted butter and onion soup mix. Layer potatoes in pan and cover with butter, onion soup mix. Sprinkle with rosemary leaves. Cover. Bake 1 hour at 375°.

United Methodist Cookbook 1993

Gourmet Potatoes

6 medium potatoes	⅓ cup finely chopped green onions
2 cups shredded Cheddar cheese	1 teaspoon salt
¼ cup butter	¼ teaspoon pepper
1½ cups sour cream	2 tablespoons butter
Paprika	

Cook potatoes in skins and cool. Peel and shred coarsely. In a saucepan over low heat, combine cheese and the ¼ cup butter; stir occasionally until almost melted. Remove from heat and blend in sour cream, onion, and seasonings. Fold in potatoes. Turn into a greased 2-quart casserole. Dot with 2 table-spoons butter and sprinkle with paprika. Bake uncovered in 350° oven for 30 minutes or until heated through. Serves 8.

Thank Heaven for Home Made Cooks

Company Scalloped Potatoes

2 pounds frozen hash browns
½ cup margarine, melted
1 teaspoon salt
¼ teaspoon pepper
½ cup chopped onion
1 can cream of chicken soup

1 pint sour cream
2 cups grated Cheddar cheese
2 cups crushed cornflakes
 mixed with ¼ cup melted
 butter

Defrost potatoes; combine everything except cornflakes. Pour into a 3-quart greased casserole. Top with cornflakes and butter mixture. Bake at 350° for 45 minutes. Serves 16.

What's Cooking in Okarche?

Cowboy Potato and Vegetable Bake

The best way to get cowboys to eat their vegetables is to mix them with plenty of potatoes. No one at the dinner table will turn up their noses at this casserole.

½ cup (1 stick) unsalted
 butter, melted
4 medium baking potatoes
 (about 2½ pounds), peeled
 and sliced ⅛-inch thick
3 medium carrots, sliced ¼
 inch thick
2 medium zucchini, scrubbed
 and sliced ½ inch thick
4 ounces fresh mushrooms,
 sliced ¼ inch thick

1 medium onion, chopped
1 medium green bell pepper,
 seeded and chopped into
 ½-inch pieces
1 teaspoon salt
¼ teaspoon freshly ground
 pepper
½ cup (4 ounces) shredded
 sharp Cheddar cheese

Preheat the oven to 400°. Brush the inside of a 13x9-inch baking dish with some of the melted butter.

Add the vegetables, drizzle with the remaining melted butter, sprinkle with the salt and pepper, and toss well.

Bake, stirring occasionally, until the potatoes are tender, about 1 hour. During the last 15 minutes, sprinkle with the cheese. Makes 6–8 servings.

National Cowboy Hall of Fame Chuck Wagon Cookbook

Linda's Sweet Potato Casserole

3 cups sweet potatoes (4 or 5)
½ cup sugar
½ cup butter

2 eggs, beaten
1 teaspoon vanilla
⅓ cup milk

Boil and mash potatoes. Mix in sugar, butter, eggs, vanilla and milk. Put in 13x9-inch dish.

TOPPING:

⅓ cup melted butter
1 cup brown sugar

½ cup flour
1 cup chopped nuts

Mix the topping ingredients together and sprinkle on top of potato mixture. Bake at 350° for 25 minutes. Serves 10–12.

Sisters Two and Family Too

Summer Vegetable Casserole

6 slices bacon, diced
1 cup slivered almonds
1 large onion, chopped
1 pound sliced zucchini
1 pound diced eggplant
1 tablespoon flour
2 cups diced fresh or 1
  (16-ounce) can undrained
  tomatoes

1 teaspoon minced or ¼
  teaspoon powdered garlic
1½ teaspoons salt
¼ teaspoon pepper
1 teaspoon basil
1 (6-ounce) package sliced
  Swiss cheese

In large skillet, sauté bacon and nuts till brown. Remove and set aside. Add the next 3 ingredients to drippings and cook, covered, for 15 minutes. Stir or shake often to keep from sticking. Stir in flour, then tomatoes. Add garlic and seasonings. In 2-quart casserole, layer vegetables, bacon, nuts, and cheese slices. Reserve some bacon and nuts for top. Bake at 400° for 15–20 minutes or till bubbly.

Can be served later if covered and refrigerated. Bake at the same temperature but allow at least 15 minutes longer baking time.

Thunderbird Cookers of AT&T

Vegetable Patties

These make a wonderful entrée, or a great substitute for a burger on a whole-wheat bun!

1 small onion, quartered	1 (15-ounce) can white beans,
2 stems broccoli or 1 large	well drained
zucchini	½ cup whole-wheat flour
¼ cup skim or evaporated	½ cup whole-wheat bread
skim milk	crumbs
1 (16-ounce) can green beans,	Olive or safflower oil
drained	

Steam onion and broccoli together for 5–6 minutes, or until broccoli is tender. Place in a food processor bowl. Add milk and both beans. Process until smooth. Place mixture in a large bowl. Stir in flour and bread crumbs. "Dough" should be soft but not runny. Add more bread crumbs if necessary.

Heat 1 teaspoon of oil over medium heat in a large skillet. Form a patty the size of a burger and place it in the skillet. Reduce heat to medium-low. Cook approximately 4 minutes on each side; cook longer over higher heat if a crisper patty is preferred. Patties should be golden brown. Serves 4–6.

Note: To make whole-wheat bread crumbs, simply dry out whole-wheat bread heels overnight, or bake in a 200° oven. Crumble using a food processor. Store in the refrigerator.

Healthy America

Vegetable Medley

Are you in the mood for a cool meal, one that requires no cooking, is very lowfat, takes just a few minutes to prepare and tastes fantastic? Then write down these ingredients now and pick them up at your store today! You're familiar with A Hole In One? Well, this is A Meal In One.

2 cups frozen peas	2 ribs celery, sliced
2 cups frozen corn	½ cup chopped onion
2 cups chopped tomatoes	Shredded low moisture, part
1 cup broccoli florets	skim Mozzarella cheese,
1 cup sliced, fresh mushrooms	optional

FAT-FREE ITALIAN DRESSING:

1¼ cups water	1 packet Italian Good Seasons
2 tablespoons vinegar	Fat-Free Dressing Mix
1 clove garlic, minced	

To thaw the corn and peas, put them in a large microwaveable dish and microwave on high for 4 minutes. Prepare the remaining vegetables and add to the corn and peas.

Put all the dressing ingredients in a container with a tight lid, and shake vigorously till mixed. Add to vegetable mixture and stir. That's it! Enjoy! Serves 5.

Per serving: Cal 130; Fat .7g; Sod 64mg; Fiber 4.5.

Note: This is a complete meal in itself—the peas and corn make a complete protein—but if you want to add a small sprinkling of shredded Mozzarella, go ahead. This will give the meal some vitamin B12, and a small amount of fat.

Variations: Try red or green bell pepper, zucchini and/or yellow squash, cucumbers, green onion, cauliflower, etc. (I always use tomatoes as they just MAKE this dish.)

15 Minute, Lowfat Meals

The Mason-Dixon Line goes through the rural community of Aline, located in the valley of the Eagle Chief. It is the home of four Centennial Award Farms—farms owned and operated by the same families for more than 100 years.

Vegetable Casserole
(Green Beans and Corn)

1 quart drained green beans
1 quart corn
½ cup sour cream
1 can cream of chicken soup

½ cup cheese, shredded
Salt and pepper to taste
½ cup chopped onion
 (optional)

TOPPING:

1 package (or 1 stack) Ritz
 crackers, rolled fine

1 stick margarine

Mix together first 6 (or 7) ingredients. Place crackers and margarine in fry pan and stir until margarine is melted. Do not brown. Spread on top of vegetables and bake at 350° for 45 minutes.

Here's What's Cookin' at Zion

Vegetable Casserole
(Lima Beans and Broccoli)

1 (10-ounce) box frozen lima
 beans
1 box frozen broccoli (partially
 cooked)
1 small package dry Lipton's
 Onion Soup

1 can mushroom soup
1 cup sour cream
1 can sliced water chestnuts,
 drained
1 cup Rice Krispies
½ cup butter, melted

Mix first six ingredients together and pour into a buttered casserole. Top with Rice Krispies which have been mixed with melted butter or margarine. Bake at 325° for 30 minutes. (For a large Pyrex, 9x13 inches, double the recipe.)

Cookbook of Treasured Recipes

The Gloss Mountains, just west of Orienta, were named by early explorers intrigued by the reflections of shiny mineral deposits scattered across the surface of these red mesas.

Green Beans Supreme

2 (16-ounce) cans French-cut
  green beans, drained
1 (4-ounce) can water
  chestnuts, diced or sliced
1 can cream of mushroom
  soup
1 (3½-ounce) can French
  fried onions
¼ cup water

Layer beans in small casserole with water chestnuts until all are used. Spoon mushroom soup that has been thinned with water over top. Bake at 350° for 25–30 minutes. Top with onions and brown at 400° for 10 minutes. Serves 6.

Company Fare I

Italian Green Beans

2 slices bacon
2 (16-ounce) cans green
  beans
1 (16-ounce) can stewed
  tomatoes
1 medium onion, chopped
1 tablespoon margarine

Fry bacon until crisp. Dry with paper towel and crumble. Place green beans and tomatoes in large pot. Add onion, margarine, and crumbled bacon. Bring to boil and cook until juice is reduced to half.

Shattuck Community Cookbook

Southwestern Pinto Beans

1 (16-ounce) package pinto
  beans
½ pound bacon, cut up
2 cups chopped onions
3 garlic cloves, minced
2 (8-ounce) cans tomato sauce

2–3 tablespoons chili powder
½ teaspoon oregano leaves
½ teaspoon salt
½ teaspoon pepper
⅛ teaspoon cumin

Rinse beans well. Soak overnight in 6 cups water; do not drain. Cover; simmer beans for 3–3½ hours until tender. In larger skillet, cook bacon, onions, and garlic over medium heat until bacon is crisp. Do not drain. Add bacon mixture, tomato sauce, chili powder, oregano, salt, pepper, and cumin to beans; stir well. Simmer, uncovered an additional 20–30 minutes. These are good as a main dish. They can also be used as a burrito filling, or can be served over cooked white rice and topped with your favorite shredded cheese.

Oklahoma Cookin'

Crazy Beans

8 slices bacon
1 cup chopped onion
½–1 cup brown sugar,
  firmly packed
½ teaspoon salt
1 teaspoon dry mustard
½ cup vinegar

2 (15-ounce) cans butter
  beans
1 (15-ounce) can lima beans
1 (15-ounce) can kidney
  beans
2 (15-ounce) cans pork and
  beans, undrained

Fry bacon; remove, drain and crumble. Add onion, sugar, salt, mustard, and vinegar to bacon drippings. Stir; cover and simmer 20 minutes. Drain butter, lima, and kidney beans; place in 2½-quart casserole. Add pork and beans, bacon and onion mixture; combine well. Preheat oven to 350°. Cover and bake one hour. Yields 8–10 servings.

Sounds Delicious!

Cotton Eyed Joe's Baked Beans

On the south edge of Claremore, just across the railroad track from Route 66, is Cotton Eyed Joe's, a serious barbecue stop.

2 (16-ounce) cans pork and
  beans
⅛ teaspoon salt
3½ tablespoons brown sugar
2 tablespoons Worcestershire

¼ cup barbecue sauce
1 teaspoon powdered mustard
3 drops liquid smoke
1 teaspoon powdered onion

Combine all ingredients in a large container and bake at 300° for one hour. Makes 10 servings.

The Route 66 Cookbook

Sweet and Tangy Beans

Not every good bean recipe starts with dried beans. In this one, canned pintos get dressed up with barbecue sauce, apples, and raisins. They make a perfect pairing with baked ham.

3 strips bacon
1 medium apple, peeled,
  cored, and cut into ½-inch
  pieces
1 medium onion, finely
  chopped
1 cup golden raisins

1 cup prepared barbecue
  sauce
¾ cup packed light brown
  sugar
3 (16-ounce) cans pinto
  beans, drained

Preheat the oven to 350°. Rub the inside of a 2-quart round flameproof casserole with one of the bacon strips to lightly grease, and place the bacon strip in the bottom of the casserole. Cut the remaining 2 bacon strips into 1-inch pieces.

In a large bowl, stir the apple, onion, raisins, barbecue sauce, and sugar until well combined. Stir in the beans. Transfer to the prepared casserole. Top with the bacon pieces.

Cover and bake for 30 minutes. Uncover and continue baking until bubbling throughout and the bacon is browned, about 30 more minutes. Serve the beans hot. Makes 4–6 servings.

National Cowboy Hall of Fame Chuck Wagon Cookbook

Calico Beans

1 can butter beans
1 can kidney beans
1 large can pork and beans
2 tablespoons liquid smoke
  (optional)
4–6 slices bacon, fried and
  chopped
1 pound hamburger, fried and
  drained

1 large onion, chopped
½ cup ketchup
2 teaspoons mustard
½ cup brown sugar
2 teaspoons vinegar
2 tablespoons Worcestershire

Do not drain the liquid from the beans. Combine all ingredients.
Bake until bubbly.

Centennial Cookbook

Poultry

Roman Nose State Park near Watonga was once a winter campground of the Cheyenne tribe. The park is named for Chief Roman Nose, who lived in this rugged canyon from 1887 until his death in 1917. He is remembered as a peacemaker who helped his people make the transition from a nomadic lifestyle to a settled existence.

Honey Dijon Oven Chicken

Ultra low fat. Wonderful flavor.

½ cup honey
¼ cup Dijon mustard
1 clove garlic, pressed
1 small onion, finely chopped

4 boneless, skinless chicken
breasts
2 cups crushed cornflakes
Salt and black pepper to taste

Preheat oven to 350°. In small bowl, combine honey, mustard, garlic, and onion. Dip chicken breasts in mixture and roll in cornflakes. Place on baking sheet sprayed with non-stick cooking spray and sprinkle with salt and pepper. Discard any remaining honey mustard mixture when finished. Bake at 350° for 30–35 minutes. Recipe makes 4 servings.

Grams of Fat Per Serving 4. Calories Per Serving 397.

Fat Free 2

Marinated Chicken Breasts

3 cups pineapple juice
⅔ cup sugar
¾ cup soy sauce
1½ teaspoons garlic
powder

1 cup sherry (dry)
1½ teaspoons powdered
ginger
½ cup red wine vinegar
10–12 boned chicken breasts

Mix all ingredients and pour over chicken breasts. Marinate at least 12 hours or overnight. Cook over charcoal grill. Submitted by Rhonda Walters, wife of former Governor of Oklahoma.

The Oklahoma Celebrity Cookbook

"Big Mac" is the nickname for the Oklahoma State Penitentiary in McAlester. The Oklahoma Prison Rodeo, one of the state's biggest events, is the world's largest rodeo held entirely behind prison walls.

Colby's Cheesy Chicken

8 chicken breast filets
¾ cup Head Country
  Barbecue Sauce
3 ounces green chiles,
  peeled, chopped

½ cup chopped green bell
  pepper
½ cup shredded Monterey
  Jack cheese
½ cup shredded colby cheese

Rinse chicken and pat dry. Place in ungreased 9x13-inch baking dish. Brush generously with barbecue sauce. Bake at 325° for 25 minutes. Top with mixture of green chiles and green pepper. Bake for 15 minutes longer. Place on serving plate; sprinkle with cheese while hot. Yields 8 servings.

Approx per serving: Cal 216; Prot 31g; Carbo 4g; Fiber <1g; T Fat 8g; 35% Cal from Fat; Chol 86mg; Sod 337mg.

Discover Oklahoma Cookin'

Peachy Chicken Casserole

This is great for family and entertaining friends.

6 chicken breasts (skinless)
2 teaspoons salt
Pepper to taste
1½ teaspoons paprika
¾ cup flour
½ cup butter
½ cup slivered almonds
1 cup water

2 cans beef consommé
2 tablespoons ketchup
2 cups sour cream
1 large can sliced peaches,
  drained
¼ cup grated Parmesan
  cheese

Preheat oven to 350°. Dredge chicken with mixture of salt, pepper, paprika, and flour. Reserve remaining flour mixture. Brown chicken on all sides in hot butter. Place in 3-quart casserole. Lightly brown almonds in drippings in skillet. Stir in remaining flour. Gradually stir in water and consomme. Add ketchup; cook and stir until thickened. Remove from heat and stir in sour cream. Pour over chicken and bake, uncovered, for about 1 hour. Arrange sliced peaches on top of chicken. Sprinkle with cheese and return to oven for 10 minutes. Serves 8–12.

Four Generations of Johnson Family Favorites

Ro-Tel Chicken Casserole

1 frying chicken or 8 chicken
  breasts (boiled)
2 onions
2 large green peppers
1 stick margarine
1 (17-ounce) package
  spaghetti

1 package onion soup mix
1 can Ro-Tel tomatoes
2 tablespoons Worcestershire
1 can green peas
1 large can mushrooms
1 pound American cheese
Salt and pepper to taste

Boil chicken in enough water to get 1½ quarts broth; chop and sauté peppers and onions in margarine. Cook spaghetti in chicken broth, onion soup, tomatoes (mashed) and Worcestershire. Cook till thick. Add peas and mushrooms (drained). Add onions, peppers, and cheese. Stir till cheese is melted. Season with salt and pepper (or Lawry's Seasoned Salt). Add chicken. Bake at 350° for 30–40 minutes.

Court Clerk's Bar and Grill

Mexican Chicken

2 pounds chicken breast or 1
  (3-pound) whole chicken,
  cooked and boned
1 cup chicken broth
½ cup onion
1 can Ro-Tel tomatoes
½ pound American cheese,
  grated

1 can cream of mushroom
  soup
1 can cream of chicken soup
1 (7-ounce) bag tostados
  chips (broken in small bits,
  but not crushed)

Mix everything but chips. Stir good. Butter casserole dish. Pour some of the mixture in the bottom of the pan. Layer with chips (repeat with about 3 layers). Bake uncovered 350° for 30 minutes or less. Check oven occasionally.

Note: Leftover turkey may be substituted for chicken.

Seems Like I Done It This A-Way III

Chicken Asparagus Casserole

3 whole chicken breasts
1½ teaspoons Accent
½ cup canola oil
2 packages frozen asparagus
1 can cream of chicken soup
¼ teaspoon pepper
½ teaspoon curry powder
½ cup mayonnaise
1 teaspoon lemon juice
1 cup shredded sharp Cheddar
   cheese

Sprinkle Accent over chicken. Sauté chicken in oil. Remove. Cook asparagus slightly. (Heat water. Drop asparagus in; turn heat off. Let set 6 minutes, then drain.) Place asparagus on bottom of dish, chicken on top. Mix soup, pepper, curry powder, mayonnaise, and lemon juice. Pour over chicken. Sprinkle cheese on top. Cover with foil. Bake 30 minutes at 375°.

Court Clerk's Bar and Grill

Aztec Casserole

1 (10¾-ounce) can cream of
   mushroom soup
1 (10¾-ounce) can cream of
   chicken soup
1 (7-ounce) can green salsa
   sauce or (7-ounce) can
   chopped green chiles
   (undrained)
¾ cup milk
12 corn tortillas, cut into
   1-inch squares
4 boneless, skinless chicken
   breasts, cooked and cubed
1 small onion, minced
½ pound Monterey Jack
   cheese, grated
½ pound Cheddar cheese,
   grated

In a medium bowl, combine soups, salsa, and milk for sauce and set aside. Spray 9x13-inch baking dish with nonstick vegetable spray. Alternate layers in dish beginning with a small amount of sauce, tortillas, chicken chunks, onion, sauce, and cheeses. Repeat layers, cover and refrigerate overnight to soak and set mixture. Bake in oven preheated to 325° for 1–1½ hours or until bubbly. Yields 8 servings.

Cafe Oklahoma

Chicken Cannelloni
(Low Calorie)

SAUCE:

1 tablespoon oil
¾ cup thinly sliced celery
½ cup thinly sliced carrot
½ cup sliced fresh
  mushrooms
1 small onion, sliced

1 clove garlic, minced
1 (8-ounce) can tomato sauce
1 (7½-ounce) can tomatoes,
  undrained and cut up
1 teaspoon Italian seasoning
¾ teaspoon sugar

Heat oil in large saucepan. Cook next 5 ingredients until onion is tender. Stir in tomato sauce, tomatoes, Italian seasoning, and sugar. Bring to boiling; reduce heat. Cook, uncovered, over low heat for 20 minutes.

3 medium chicken breasts
½ cup ricotta cheese
3 tablespoons grated
  Parmesan cheese
1 tablespoon chopped green
  onion

½ teaspoon Italian seasoning
Dash of pepper
2 ounces Mozzarella cheese

Pound chicken breasts between 2 pieces of plastic wrap to ¼-inch thickness. Combine ricotta cheese, grated Parmesan cheese, chopped green onion, Italian seasoning, and pepper. Place about 1½ tablespoons of the cheese mixture on each chicken piece. Roll up; place, seam-side-down, in 8x8x2-inch baking dish. Pour sauce over chicken rolls. Bake, covered, in a 375° oven for 25–30 minutes or until tender. Place 2 ounces of Mozzarella cheese, cut into thin strips, in a lattice design on top. Bake 2–3 minutes more. Makes 6 servings.

Thunderbird Cookers of AT&T

Homemade Shake & Bake

2 cups flour
2 cups cracker meal
2 tablespoons sugar
1 teaspoon garlic salt

1 teaspoon onion salt
1 tablespoon paprika
¼ cup vegetable oil

Blend ingredients with a fork and store in airtight container (marked). When using, preheat oven to 325°–350°. Place ½ cup in bag, add more as needed. Moisten meat evenly with water or milk. Shake meat to cover and mix (1 piece at a time). Place meat in a greased pan. Bake about 1 hour or until tender. Use on chicken, fish, chops, or tenderized steak, etc.

Come Grow with Us

Miss Bonnie's Fried Chicken with Her Original Chicken Fried Biscuits

Mama has made these biscuits for years, and finally she shared her secret. They are wonderful when accompanied with your favorite fried chicken. This is a favorite summer meal with fresh corn on the cob and a good salad. With fresh strawberries and your favorite homemade ice cream—big city guests will be in for a fantastic country dinner!

1 whole fryer, cut into pieces	Salt
Buttermilk	Pepper
Flour	Crisco oil

Wash and dry chicken parts. Marinate in buttermilk 1 hour. Preheat oil in electric skillet, 375°, while preparing chicken. (Tip—heat skillet slightly before pouring in oil.) Put 2 cups flour into large brown bag. Place chicken parts which have been coated in buttermilk into bag and shake well. Place in heated oil and sprinkle with salt and pepper. Cover and cook 20 minutes per side. For crispy chicken, do not cover. Larger pieces can finish cooking in a 325° oven. Cover with foil if you don't wish to have a crisp crust.

Note: Removing skin from chicken does get rid of extra fatty layers and some extra calories as well. This buttermilk method allows for a good crisp crust. If you desire a few extra crunchies, add ¼ cup grits or cracker crumbs to the flour. Salt and pepper the chicken as you begin frying. The salt will help the chicken to bleed and give up some of its own juices—thus making more flavorful biscuits as well as gravy.

BISCUITS:

2 cups flour	½ teaspoon salt
1 tablespoon baking powder	1¼ cups milk
1 tablespoon sugar	

Remove chicken from frying pan (hold in oven to keep warm). Sift dry ingredients together. Stir in milk. Mixture will be gooey. Drop by teaspoonful into 375° or 400° oil in skillet in which you have just prepared chicken. All the little crunchies will adhere to these biscuits. Turn once. Each side should be golden brown. Make sure oil is correct temperature. These biscuits are light and crisp and they do not absorb oil. Drain on paper towels.

Stir Ups

Chicken Fricassee with Dumplings

1 (2½- to 3-pound) fryer, cut up
1 cup Bisquick Baking Mix
2 teaspoons salt
1 teaspoon paprika
⅛ teaspoon pepper
2 tablespoons shortening
1 tablespoon butter
1 can cream of chicken soup
1½ cups milk

Wash chicken pieces and pat dry. Mix baking mix, salt, paprika, and pepper in paper or plastic bag. Shake 2 or 3 pieces of chicken at a time in bag to coat thoroughly. Melt shortening and butter in large skillet; brown chicken on all sides. Remove chicken. Drain fat from skillet; stir in soup and milk; add chicken. Cover and simmer about 1 hour or until thickest pieces are tender. Twenty minutes before end of cooking time, prepare Dumplings.

DUMPLINGS:

2 cups Bisquick Baking Mix
¼ teaspoon poultry seasoning
½ teaspoon parsley flakes
⅔ cup milk

Mix 2 cups Bisquick, poultry seasoning and parsley flakes. Add milk until soft dough forms. Drop dough by spoonfuls onto hot chicken. Cook, uncovered, 10 minutes; cover and cook 10 minutes longer. Makes 4 servings.

Feast in Fellowship

Mother's Chunky Chicken and Strip Dumplings

1 (4½- to 5-pound) chicken
cut into serving pieces
3 tablespoons butter
3 tablespoons oil
1 carrot, halved
1 onion
2 cloves

Bouquet garni composed of 2
ribs celery, chopped, 3 sprigs
parsley, 1 small bay leaf
7 cups chicken stock or
chicken broth, enough to
cover chicken

In a large heavy skillet, sauté chicken in butter and oil until it is lightly colored; add carrot, onion stuck with cloves, and bouquet garni. Add stock or broth and bring to a boil, skimming off the froth that rises to the surface. Simmer chicken, covered, for 1 hour and 30 minutes until just tender. Transfer chicken with tongs to a plate and keep it warm. Skim fat from stock. Strain stock and return it to the kettle.

DUMPLINGS:

1½ cups flour
½ teaspoon baking powder
½ teaspoon salt

1 tablespoon shortening
1 small egg, lightly beaten
⅓ cup cold water

In a large bowl, sift together flour, baking powder and salt. Cut in shortening until mixture resembles meal. Make a well in the center. Add egg and water. Stir liquid into flour mixture to form a dough.

Turn the dough out on a floured surface and knead for 10 minutes or until elastic. Chill dough, covered, for 30 minutes. Roll out half the dough very thin on a floured surface. Cut the dough into 1½-inch strips and let the dumpling noodles dry for 10 minutes. Bring stock to a boil over high heat and stir mixture with a wooden spoon. Reduce heat to low and cook dumplings for 5–7 minutes. Skin and bone chicken and cut into 2-inch pieces. Add chicken to kettle and simmer until it is just heated through. Garnish the dish with minced parsley and shredded carrot. Serves 4–6.

Cleora's Kitchens

Crispy Herb Chicken

⅔ cup mashed potato flakes
¼ cup grated Parmesan
  cheese
2 teaspoons parsley flakes
½ teaspoon onion powder
¼ teaspoon garlic salt

⅛ teaspoon paprika
Dash of pepper
⅓ cup margarine or butter,
  melted
1 whole chicken, quartered
  skinned, rinsed, patted dry

Heat oven to 375°. Grease or line with foil a 15x10-inch jelly roll pan or a 13x9-inch pan. In medium bowl, combine potato flakes, Parmesan cheese, parsley flakes, onion powder, garlic salt, paprika, and pepper; stir until well mixed. Dip chicken pieces into margarine; roll in potato flake mixture to coat. Place in greased pan. Bake for 60–75 minutes or until chicken is tender and golden brown. Makes 4–5 servings.

The Oklahoma Celebrity Cookbook

Route 66 Diner Philly Chicken

One of the specials at the Route 66 Diner in Tulsa is the Philly Chicken.

½ cup chopped celery
½ cup chopped onion
¼ medium green pepper,
  chopped
3 tablespoons vegetable oil
½ teaspoon tarragon
¼ teaspoon lemon pepper
2 cloves garlic, minced
1 pint heavy cream

1 (8-ounce) package cream
  cheese, softened
¾ cup milk
1 chicken, cooked, skinned
  and deboned (approximately
  3 cups diced)
¼ cup grated Parmesan
  cheese
Wild rice or pasta

In a large saucepan, sauté the celery, onion, and pepper in vegetable oil. Add the tarragon, lemon pepper, and garlic. Cook until vegetables are tender. Add cream, cream cheese, milk, and chicken and heat to simmer but do not boil. Sprinkle with Parmesan cheese and serve over wild rice or pasta. Makes 6–8 servings.

The Route 66 Cookbook

Chicken Enchiladas
with Sour Cream

18 corn tortillas
6 cups Green Chile Sauce
4½ cups cooked chicken,
  minced
1½ pounds Jack cheese,
  grated

⅓ cup minced onion
½ teaspoon salt
1 pint sour cream

Heat tortillas on a hot griddle. Keep warm. Mix 1 cup of Green Chile Sauce with the chicken. Put ¼ cup of chicken sauce mixture on each tortilla and roll up. Place in baking dish. Cover the enchiladas with the cheese. Add the onion and salt to the remaining chile sauce and pour over the enchiladas. Bake at 350° for about 25 minutes. Add sour cream on top of enchiladas and cook an additional 10 minutes. Serves 8.

GREEN CHILE SAUCE:

2 cloves garlic, minced
¾ cup finely chopped onion
3 tablespoons salad oil
1½ tablespoons flour

1½ cups chopped green chiles,
  (fresh or canned)
6 cups chopped tomatoes
  (fresh or canned)

Sauté garlic and onion in oil over low heat. Add flour and stir. Add chiles and tomatoes. Mix well, bring to boil and simmer 8–12 minutes.

Helen's Southwest Specialties

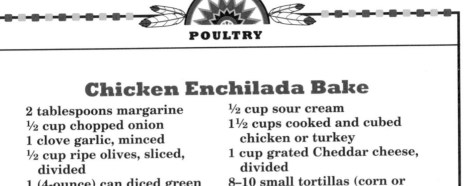
Chicken Enchilada Bake

2 tablespoons margarine
½ cup chopped onion
1 clove garlic, minced
½ cup ripe olives, sliced, divided
1 (4-ounce) can diced green chiles, drained
1 (10¾-ounce) can cream of chicken soup
½ cup sour cream
1½ cups cooked and cubed chicken or turkey
1 cup grated Cheddar cheese, divided
8–10 small tortillas (corn or flour)
¾–1 cup milk

Heat oven to 350°. In medium saucepan, melt margarine; sauté onion and garlic in margarine until tender. Stir in ¼ cup of ripe olives, green chiles, soup, and sour cream; mix well. Reserve ¾ cup sauce; set aside. Fold in chicken or turkey and ½ cup of the cheese to remaining sauce.

Warm tortillas as directed on package. Fill tortillas with chicken or turkey mixture; roll up. Place, seam-side-down, in ungreased 12x8-inch baking dish. In small bowl, combine reserved ¾ cup sauce and enough milk to make a thick, smooth sauce; spoon over tortillas. Bake at 350° for 30–35 minutes or until bubbly. To serve, sprinkle with remaining cheese and olives.

United Methodist Cookbook 1993

Chicken Tetrazzini

1 (4- to 5-pound) hen
4 cups chicken broth
1 large green pepper, chopped
1 large onion, chopped
8 ounces long spaghetti
1 medium-sized can mushrooms
½ pound butter
⅔ cup flour
1 quart milk
½ pound Old English Cheese
½ pound American cheese
Salt and pepper to taste

Cook hen until tender. Remove from bone. Dice. Add green pepper, onion, and spaghetti to 4 cups of chicken broth. Cook until spaghetti is barely tender. Add mushrooms and diced chicken. Melt butter in heavy skillet; add flour, milk, and cheeses. Cook until thickened. Add to spaghetti and chicken mixture. Salt and pepper to taste. Bake for 30 minutes at 350°.

Seems Like I Done It This A-Way I

Chicken Tetrazzini

Delicious served with a tossed green salad and sliced French bread or bread sticks.

8 chicken breasts
4 cups water
1 (12-ounce) package spaghetti
2 teaspoons Worcestershire
2 teaspoons paprika
1 can cream of chicken soup
1 can cream of mushroom soup
1 (8-ounce) carton sour cream
1 (4-ounce) can chopped ripe olives

1 (4-ounce) can sliced mushrooms, drained
1 onion, chopped, ½ green pepper, chopped, and ½ cup celery, chopped and sautéed in 2 tablespoons butter (optional)
1 pound Cheddar cheese, grated and divided in half

Simmer the chicken breasts in water for 1 hour. Remove the chicken breasts from the broth (reserve broth); let them cool. Cut breasts into bite-size pieces. Boil the spaghetti in reserved chicken broth for 10 minutes. Drain spaghetti in a colander. Mix the chicken bites, cooked spaghetti, Worcestershire, paprika, soups, sour cream, olives, and mushrooms together. Optional sautéed vegetables may be added at this time. Add half the Cheddar cheese to this mixture and stir.

Spoon into a greased 3-quart baking dish. Cover the chicken mixture with the remaining grated Cheddar cheese. Bake covered with foil at 350° for 30 minutes until the cheese melts and the casserole is hot. Serves 8.

Gourmet: The Quick and Easy Way

MANGUMRATTLESNAKEDERBY.COM

Rattlesnake roundups lure danger-seekers who compete to catch the deadly poisonous snakes. In April, such events as the Rattlesnake Hunt and Carnival in Waurika, the Rattlesnake Derby in Mangum, and the Waynoka Rattlesnake Hunt—which features the den of Death snake pit—attract participants and visitors from all over the world.

Chicken Waikiki Beach

2 whole chicken legs and
breasts or cut-up chicken
for big meal
½ cup flour
⅓ cup salad oil or shortening

1 teaspoon salt
¼ teaspoon pepper
1 large green pepper, cut in
¼-inch circles or small cubes

Coat chicken with flour and heat oil in large skillet. Brown all sides. Remove and put in roasting pan, skin-side-up; salt and pepper. Preheat oven to 350°.

SAUCE:

1 (1-pound, 4-ounce) can
sliced pineapple
1 cup sugar
2 tablespoons cornstarch

¾ cup cider vinegar
1 tablespoon soy sauce
¼ teaspoon ginger
1 chicken bouillon cube

Drain pineapple, pouring into 2-cup measure. Add water to have 1¼ cups of liquid. In medium saucepan, combine sugar, cornstarch, pineapple syrup, vinegar, soy sauce, ginger, and bouillon cube. Bring to boiling, stirring constantly. Boil 2 minutes. Pour over chicken. Bake, uncovered, 30 minutes. Add pineapple slices or cubes and green pepper. Bake 30 minutes longer or until chicken is tender.

Centennial Cookbook

Chicken Spaghetti

Chicken
1 medium onion, chopped
1 package fresh mushrooms, sliced
3 celery stalks, finely sliced
2 cans cream of chicken soup or cream of mushroom soup
½–1 cup sour cream
Black olives, sliced, optional
Spaghetti

Precook, microwave, or bake chicken. The amount depends on how much chicken you desire. Cube chicken. Sauté onion and mushrooms until almost tender. Add finely sliced celery and cover for about 3 minutes. Drain liquid. Mix soup and sour cream and add to first mixture. Add olives if desired. Bring to a boil. Add cubed chicken. If sauce is too thick, thin with chicken broth. Either mix with or serve on top of thin spaghetti.

Dine with the Angels

White Chili

1 pound large white beans, soaked overnight in water and drained
6 cups chicken broth
2 cloves garlic, minced
1 medium onion, chopped and divided
1 tablespoon oil
2 (4-ounce) cans chopped green chiles
2 teaspoons ground cumin
1½ teaspoons dried oregano
¼ teaspoon ground cloves
¼ teaspoon cayenne pepper
4 cups diced cooked chicken breasts
3 cups grated Jack cheese

Combine beans, chicken broth, garlic, and half the onions in large soup pot; boil. Reduce heat and simmer 3 hours or more (until beans are very soft). Add more chicken broth if necessary. Sauté remaining onions until tender in oil. Add chiles and seasonings and thoroughly mix. Add to beans. Add chicken and simmer one hour. Serve topped with grated cheese. Suggested condiments: tomatoes, parsley, olives, guacamole, sour cream, tortilla chips, salsa and/or cornbread.

Court Clerk's Bar and Grill

Turkey Vegetable Pot Pie

PASTRY SHELL:

1 cup whole-wheat pastry
  flour (or unbleached
  all-purpose flour)

½ teaspoon salt
¼ cup vegetable oil
2 tablespoons ice water

In medium bowl combine flour and salt. Blend in oil with fork. Sprinkle water over mixture; mix well. Shape into ball; chill 1 hour.

FILLING:

3 carrots, cut into 1-inch
  pieces
2 large onions, chopped
3 tablespoons light margarine
¼ cup all-purpose flour
½ teaspoon salt
¼ teaspoon dried thyme,
  crumbled

¼ teaspoon freshly ground
  pepper
2 cups chicken bouillon
½ cup frozen peas
2 cups chopped, cooked
  turkey or chicken

Cook carrots and onions in water in medium pan until tender-crisp, about 10 minutes. Drain; set aside. In same pan, melt margarine over low heat. Blend in flour, salt, thyme, and pepper; cook 1 minute, stirring. Gradually add bouillon, stirring constantly, until sauce is thick. Set aside.

In 2-quart casserole, combine carrot mixture, sauce, peas, and turkey; mix well.

Roll dough out between 2 pieces of wax paper. Remove top layer of paper; invert pastry over top of casserole. Remove paper; seal pastry around dish. Cut slits in top for steam to escape. Bake 30 minutes at 400° or until pastry is golden brown. Yields 6 servings.

Hint: If prebaked pie shell is needed for another use, bake in preheated 450° oven 10–12 minutes.

Per serving: 485 calories.

Sounds Delicious!

Turkey Croquettes

2 cups shredded turkey (use
 food processor with metal
 blade)
1 tablespoon finely chopped
 onion
1 recipe Thick White Sauce
¼ teaspoon each: paprika,
 salt, pepper

Dash of nutmeg
2 teaspoons lemon juice
1 tablespoon chopped cilantro
 or parsley
1 egg plus 2 tablespoons
 water, slightly beaten
Bread crumbs

Mix first 7 ingredients thoroughly. Wet your hands, then form
the mixture into balls about an inch in diameter. Dip the balls
into the egg mixture, then cover with bread crumbs. Roll
between your hands to form cones, or leave in the original ball
shape. Fry in deep oil for about 3 minutes. Serves 4 or 5.

THICK WHITE SAUCE:

¼ cup margarine
¼ cup flour
¼ teaspoon salt

¼ teaspoon pepper
1 cup milk

Melt butter. Over low heat, add flour, salt, and pepper to make
a bubbling paste. Stir in milk gradually. Stir constantly to
avoid sticking. (White sauce loves to scorch on the bottom of the
pan.) Continue until mixture thickens and starts to bubble.

When a Man's Fancy Turns to Cooking

Cranberry Sauce

1 quart cranberries
1 orange, rind included
2 cups water
2½ cups sugar

2 small packages lemon Jell-O
1 cup chopped celery
1 cup chopped pecans

Grind together cranberries and orange. Boil water and sugar
until dissolved. Remove from heat. Add Jell-O and stir. Add
other ingredients and pour into a 9x12-inch pan and refrigerate.

Cookbook of Treasured Recipes

Meats

Capture Old West adventure at one of the many working ranches across Oklahoma. Western-style cowboy vacations can include hiking, horseback riding, hunting, fishing, barn dances, and chuck wagon dining (shown here at Coyote Hills Ranch near Cheyenne).

Steve's Favorite Mexican Casserole

2 pounds hamburger
1 large onion, chopped
Salt and pepper
Tabasco
1 package dry taco seasoning

1 can cream of chicken soup
1 large can evaporated milk
1 large can green chiles
10 corn tortillas
2 cups grated cheese

Brown hamburger with onion. Drain. Add salt and pepper to taste and a small amount of Tabasco sauce. Add taco seasoning, chicken soup, evaporated milk, and green chiles. In a large oblong dish, place a layer of corn tortillas; cover with some of above mixture, then repeat until used up. Bake at 350° for 20 minutes, uncovered. Remove from oven. Cover completely with grated cheese; return to oven until cheese has melted.

Watonga Cheese Festival Cookbook 17th Edition

Ground Beef Casserole

1 pound hamburger
1 medium onion, chopped
1 (16-ounce) package corn chips
1 can Ranch-Style beans

1 can enchilada sauce
2 cups grated cheese
1 can cream of mushroom soup
½ cup picante sauce

Brown ground beef and onion, stirring until crumbly; drain. Line 9x13-inch baking dish with half the corn chips. Stir beans and enchilada sauce into ground beef mixture. Pour half the mixture over corn chips. Top with half the cheese. Mix soup and picante sauce in bowl. Pour over cheese. Layer remaining corn chips, ground beef mixture and cheese over soup mixture. Bake at 300° until cheese is melted. Yields 8 big servings.

Centennial Cookbook

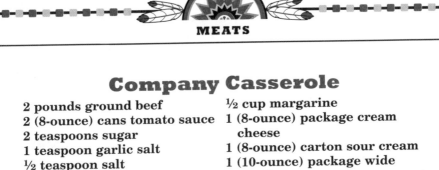
Company Casserole

2 pounds ground beef
2 (8-ounce) cans tomato sauce
2 teaspoons sugar
1 teaspoon garlic salt
½ teaspoon salt
½ teaspoon black pepper
1 cup chopped onion
½ cup margarine
1 (8-ounce) package cream cheese
1 (8-ounce) carton sour cream
1 (10-ounce) package wide noodles
1 cup grated Cheddar cheese

In large skillet, brown ground beef. Drain fat. Add tomato sauce, sugar, garlic salt, salt and pepper. Simmer 20 minutes. Set aside.

In saucepan, sauté onion in margarine. Add cream cheese and sour cream; stir until melted. Cook noodles according to directions on package. Drain.

Pour noodles in buttered baking dish. Cover with onion mixture. Pour meat mixture over top. Bake at 350° for 30 minutes. Add cheese last 5 minutes. Freezes well.

Feeding Our Flock

Beef and Potato Casserole

1 pound ground beef
1 medium onion, chopped
1 can mushrooms, chopped
1 can cream of mushroom soup
1 can Ranch-Style beans
1 package grated Cheddar cheese
1 package frozen O'Brien potatoes (hash browns)

Brown meat; drain and add onion; cook until done. Add mushrooms, soup, and beans. Pour mixture into a greased 9x13-inch pan over the O'Brien potatoes. Top with grated cheese and bake 25–30 minutes in 375° oven until heated through or cheese is melted. Very good!

Seasoned with Love

Taco Salad Casserole

Here's a one-dish meal with its tomato, lettuce, cheese, and olive garnish that looks great on a supper or buffet table, and it will round up compliments for taste, too.

1 tablespoon olive oil
2 pounds ground round
1 medium onion, chopped
2 cloves garlic, minced
2 tablespoons chili powder
1 tablespoon sweet Hungarian paprika
1 teaspoon salt
1 teaspoon dried oregano
½ teaspoon ground cumin
⅛ teaspoon ground hot (cayenne) pepper
2 (16-ounce) cans stewed tomatoes, undrained
1 (4-ounce) can chopped green chiles, drained

2 cups small-curd cottage cheese
1 cup (4 ounces) shredded Monterey Jack cheese
1 large egg
12 corn tortillas
2 cups shredded iceberg lettuce
4 ripe plum tomatoes, seeded and chopped
1 cup (4 ounces) shredded sharp Cheddar cheese
½ cup sliced ripe black olives
2 scallions, chopped

In a large skillet, heat the oil over medium-high heat. Add the ground round, onion, and garlic. Cook, stirring to break up the meat with a wooden spoon, until the meat loses its pink color, about 6 minutes. Tilt the pan to drain off the excess fat. Add the chili powder, paprika, salt, oregano, cumin, and hot pepper. Stir for 1 minute.

Stir in the stewed tomatoes with their juices and the chiles. Bring to a simmer and reduce the heat to low. Simmer, uncovered, until the excess liquid is evaporated, about 30 minutes. Preheat the oven to 350°. Lightly oil a 9x13-inch baking dish. In a medium bowl, combine the cottage cheese, Monterey Jack, and egg.

Place an overlapping layer of half the tortillas in the baking dish. Spread with the meat mixture. Top with the remaining tortillas, then spread with the cheese mixture.

Bake until the topping is firm in the center, about 30 minutes. Let the casserole stand for 5 minutes.

Top the casserole with a layer of lettuce, then sprinkle with the tomatoes, Cheddar cheese, olives, and scallions. Cut into rectangles and serve immediately. Makes 8–10 servings.

National Cowboy Hall of Fame Chuck Wagon Cookbook

Sloppy Joes

1 pound ground beef
1 onion, chopped
2 tablespoons chili powder
3 tablespoons barbecue sauce
Dash Worcestershire
½ cup ketchup

1 tablespoon sugar
½ cup milk
2 tablespoons vinegar
1 tablespoon flour
Salt and pepper to taste

Brown beef and onion. Stir in other ingredients. Simmer for 5 minutes. Serve on toasted buns.

Kitchen Klatter Keepsakes

Bierocks
(Mama Burgers)

DOUGH:

½ cup warm water	2 teaspoons salt
2 packages yeast	1 stick margarine
1½ cups lukewarm milk	7–7½ cups flour
½ cup sugar	2 eggs

Dissolve yeast in water. Combine milk, sugar, salt, margarine, and 2 cups flour. Add eggs and yeast. Combine well and add more flour until kneadable. Knead until smooth, but a little sticky. Let rise until double. Prepare filling while dough is rising.

FILLING:

2 pounds hamburger	3 cups shredded cabbage
1 medium onion, chopped	Garlic powder to taste
1 envelope beefy onion soup mix	Salt and pepper
3 cups grated cheese (12 ounces)	

Brown meat and onions. Drain. Add soup mix, cheese, cabbage, and salt and pepper to taste. Divide dough in half. Roll dough thin (⅛ inch) and cut in 4-inch squares (or larger if desired). Place approximately ¼ cup filling in center. Pinch together opposite corners to seal. Place seam-side-down on lightly greased cookie sheet and let rise for ½ hour. Bake at 375° for 15–20 minutes on middle rack. Makes 24.

Sisters Two and Family Too

The Meers Store is all that remains of Meers, a boom town in the turn-of-the-century gold rush in the Wichita Mountains. The store was once a drugstore, doctor's office, newspaper office, and later a general store. Meers population has dwindled from the gold rush peak of 500 to one family of six people, eight cats and a dog. "It's our fault" they boast of the Meers Fault—a 15-mile crack in the earth's crust that scientists believe could produce a major earthquake. Today the prosperous family restaurant is famous for "Meersburgers"—7-inch diameter burgers made exclusively from the Texas Longhorn beef raised on the family's ranch. The beef is free from antibiotics, pesticides and growth hormones and is lower in cholesterol than chicken.

Rock Cafe Old Fashioned Hamburger

In Stroud, the Rock Cafe has been a part of Route 66 history since it opened on July 4, 1939.

¼ pound coarsely ground
  beef
½ teaspoon salt, or to taste

¼ teaspoon pepper
1 teaspoon finely chopped
  onion

Mix all ingredients; lightly pat into a burger about ½ inch thick. If you want a juicy burger, don't pack the meat. If the meat is too lean, mix a little ground suet with the patty. Fry patty on grill or in iron skillet for a few minutes, turn and cook a few minutes longer. Overcooking dries out the meat.

Lightly butter the top and bottom of a bun, place on grill until golden brown. Spread mustard on bottom half, pile with chopped onions, pickles, and meat patty. Spread mayonnaise or mustard on top half of bun. Pat the top of the bun with a spatula loaded with hamburger grease. Provide lettuce, tomato, and ketchup to be used as desired.

The Route 66 Cookbook

Barbecued Meatballs

3 pounds hamburger
1 (13-ounce) can evaporated
  milk
2 cups quick oatmeal
2 eggs

½ teaspoon garlic powder
½ teaspoon pepper
2 teaspoons chili powder
1 chopped onion
2 teaspoons salt

SAUCE:
2 cups ketchup
2 tablespoons liquid smoke
½ teaspoon garlic powder

½ chopped onion
1½ cups brown sugar

Form into desired size balls. Place in shallow pan. Mix sauce. Bring to a boil. Pour over meatballs. Bake 1 hour at 350°.

Sisters Two and Family Too

Poor Man Steak

2 pounds hamburger
1 cup cracker crumbs
1 cup milk
1 teaspoon salt
¼ teaspoon pepper

Chopped onion
Flour
1 can mushroom soup
1 soup can water

Mix first 6 ingredients and shape into a loaf. Chill overnight.
Cut into slices and dip in flour; brown on both sides. Place in
roaster; cover with soup/water mixture. Bake at 350° for 1½
hours.

Here's What's Cookin' at Zion

Spoon Meat Loaf

1 pound hamburger meat
1 large onion, diced
2 tablespoons diced green
pepper
4 cups cooked elbow
macaroni

1 can tomato sauce or
tomatoes
1 cup grated American cheese

Place hamburger in skillet. Add chopped onion and pepper.
Brown slowly until partially done. Drain off fat. Place a thin
layer of cooked macaroni, well drained, in the bottom of a baking dish or pan; put a layer of meat mixture over macaroni, then
a layer of tomatoes or sauce. Sprinkle a layer of grated cheese
over this. Repeat layers. Bake at 350° for about 35–45 minutes.
Serves 8.

Seems Like I Done It This A-Way I

Mexicali Meat Loaves

1 pound ground beef	1 tablespoon minced onion
½ cup oats	1 teaspoon chili powder
1 egg	Salt to taste
1 (8-ounce) can tomato sauce	½ teaspoon garlic powder
1 (4-ounce) can chopped	½ cup shredded Cheddar
green chiles	cheese

Combine meat, oats, egg, ¼ cup tomato sauce, 3 tablespoons green chiles, 1 tablespoon onion, chili powder, and salt; mix well. Shape to form 4 loaves; place in an 8-inch square dish. Cook in microwave oven on HIGH 6–7 minutes, rotating after each 2 minutes. Combine remaining tomato sauce, chiles, onion, and garlic powder in glass measuring cup. Cook on HIGH 1 minute. To serve, spoon sauce over meat; sprinkle with cheese.

United Methodist Cookbook 1993

Opal's Meat Loaf

2 pounds ground beef	½ cup shredded Cheddar
1 large onion, finely chopped	cheese
1 egg, beaten	2 teaspoons garlic salt
½ cup cracker crumbs	1 teaspoon salt
½ cup milk	1 (10-ounce) can tomato soup

Combine ground beef, onion, egg, cracker crumbs, milk, cheese, garlic salt, and salt in bowl; mix well. Shape into loaf; place in greased pan. Bake at 350° for 30 minutes. Spoon soup over top. Bake for 30 minutes longer. Garnish with parsley. Yields 8 servings.

Approx Per Serving: Cal 332; T Fat 21g; Cal from Fat 56%; Prot 25g; Carbo 11g; Fiber 1g; Chol 112mg; Sod 1217mg.

The Pioneer Chef

Route 66, dubbed the "Will Rogers Memorial Highway," rolls within a few blocks of the Will Rogers Memorial in Claremore. The Will Rogers birthplace is in near by Oologah.

Russian Sauerkraut

1 pound hamburger	1 (16-ounce) can tomatoes
1 pound sausage	(mashed)
2 tablespoons oil	3 cups sauerkraut
1 medium onion, chopped	1 small carton sour cream
1 green pepper, chopped	Salt and pepper to taste

Brown hamburger and sausage. Add oil, onion, and green pepper, and cook about 5 minutes. Add tomatoes, sauerkraut and sour cream, and let simmer for one hour.

Court Clerk's Bar and Grill

Concession Chili

4 pounds hamburger meat	4 (1.62-ounce) packages
1 large onion, chopped	Lawry's chili seasoning mix
4 (28-ounce) cans Gardenside	¾ tablespoon garlic salt
tomatoes	2 tablespoons brown sugar
1 (12-ounce) can tomato paste	Salt and pepper to taste

Brown hamburger meat and drain completely. Add onion and tomatoes which have been put through a food processor. Add tomato paste and chili seasoning which has been liquefied in water. Add garlic salt and brown sugar.

Put ingredients in a large, round roaster and fill with water; let chili boil slowly for 3 hours. Add water if it boils down before that time. Stir often and cook slowly so that it does not stick to bottom of pan. You can add salt and pepper to taste. Freezes well.

Dine with the Angels

Herbal Chili

This recipe freezes well. I usually make a big batch and freeze several servings for future use. Use zipper plastic bags or foil containers. I find it best to freeze without the beans.

2 pounds ground beef and/or prepared beef chuck*
1 medium onion (about ¾ cup), chopped
2–3 cloves garlic, minced
1 stalk celery, minced finely
2 tablespoons green chile, chopped
1 (16-ounce) can tomatoes or 3 cups peeled fresh tomatoes

2 cups chicken stock or broth
2 cups water
2 chicken bouillon cubes
2 tablespoons raspberry vinegar, or red wine vinegar
½ cup red wine
5 tablespoons Rice's Red Herbal Chile Blend

Using a large pot, brown the ground beef. Add prepared chuck. Sauté onion, garlic, and celery in the grease left after browning the meat. Cook until onion turns translucent. Stir in all the remaining ingredients. Simmer over heat for at least 2 hours. Serves about 4–6 people.

*To prepare beef chuck: Brown cubes of chuck or other beef. Cool and shred beef cubes with the metal blade of a food processor.

Variations: (1) Liquefy water, onion, celery, garlic, and green chile in a blender. Add directly to the beef without sautéing. (2) Substitute ground and shredded turkey for beef. (3) Substitute apple juice for the water. (4) Add 1–2 cups cooked pinto or other beans.

RICE'S RED HERBAL CHILI BLEND:

1 cup chili powder
½ teaspoon sage
6 tablespoons cumin
5 teaspoons sugar
3 tablespoons paprika
1 teaspoon black pepper
3 teaspoons oregano

2 teaspoons dried cilantro
3 teaspoons garlic powder
½ teaspoon coriander
2 teaspoons salt
½ teaspoon marjoram
½ teaspoon thyme

Makes enough for 10 pounds of meat; 2 pounds of meat requires 5 tablespoons mix.

When a Man's Fancy Turns to Cooking

Hot 'N' Spicy Chunky Beef Chili

2¼ pounds lean boneless
  beef chuck, cut into ¾-inch
  pieces
1 cup coarsely chopped onion
2 cloves garlic, minced
2 tablespoons vegetable oil
1 teaspoon salt
1 (28-ounce) can plum
  tomatoes, broken up
1 cup water
1 (6-ounce) can tomato paste

3 tablespoons chili powder
1 teaspoon dried oregano
  leaves
1 teaspoon crushed red
  pepper pods
1 cup chopped green bell
  pepper
6 tablespoons each: shredded
  Cheddar cheese and sliced
  green onion

Brown beef (half at a time) with onion and garlic in oil in large frying pan or Dutch oven. Pour off drippings. Sprinkle salt over beef. Add tomatoes, water, tomato paste, chili powder, oregano, and crushed red pepper. Cover tightly and simmer 1½ hours or until beef is tender. Add green pepper and continue cooking uncovered, 30 minutes. Sprinkle each serving with cheese and green onion slices. Serves 8 (1½ cups each).

Per serving: Cal 333; Prot 36g; Fat 16g; Carb 13g: Iron 5.7mg; Sod 731mg; Chol 102mg.

Submitted by Reba McEntire, singer, songwriter, entertainer and Oklahoman.

The Oklahoma Celebrity Cookbook

Stick-To-Your-Ribs Ribs

6½ pounds spareribs
1 onion, coarsely chopped
½ cup cider vinegar
12 black peppercorns

1 teaspoon salt
Jasmeen's Jazzi Barbecue
  Sauce

Cut ribs into serving-size pieces. Place ribs in a large Dutch oven; add water to cover. Add onion, vinegar, peppercorns, and salt. Bring to a boil; cover, reduce heat and simmer 1 hour. Drain well. Grill ribs over low coals (275°–300°) 15 minutes, turning after 8 minutes. Baste ribs generously with sauce and grill 8 minutes. Turn ribs; baste again with sauce. Grill ribs an additional 7 minutes or to desired degree of doneness.

JASMEEN'S JAZZI BARBECUE SAUCE:

1 medium onion, finely
  chopped
½ cup chopped green pepper
1 tablespoon vegetable oil
1 (24-ounce) bottle ketchup
½ cup firmly packed brown
  sugar

½ cup honey
3 tablespoons prepared
  mustard
½ cup water

Sauté onion and green pepper in oil in a large saucepan until vegetables are tender. Add ketchup, brown sugar, honey, and mustard; bring mixture to a boil. Stir in water; reduce heat and simmer, uncovered, 15 minutes.

Kitchen Klatter Keepsakes

Once known simply as Indian Territory, Oklahoma became home for the Indian tribes forced from their lands in the southeastern United States. The Cherokees, Chickasaws, Choctaws, Crees, and Seminoles are known as the Five Civilized Tribes.

Home-Made Beef Jerky

Making your own jerky may seem like a lot of fiddlin' around, but the actual working time is short; most of the time is spent sitting around waiting for the beef to dehydrate. And you'll end up with excellent preservative- and chemical-free jerky, a very decent reward.

2 pounds trimmed flank steak (lean venison or elk flank can also be used)
½ cup Worcestershire
¼ cup soy sauce
2 tablespoons liquid smoke flavoring
1½ teaspoons seasoned salt
1½ teaspoons onion salt
½ teaspoon garlic powder
½ teaspoon freshly ground pepper
Nonstick vegetable cooking spray

Freeze the flank steak until partially frozen, about 1 hour. Using a sharp knife, cut diagonally across the grain into ¼-inch-thick strips. (For chewier jerky, cut with the grain, but this is only recommended for card-carrying cowboys.)

In a large plastic bag (preferably the self-sealing kind), mix the remaining ingredients except the cooking spray. Add the sliced beef and mix well. Seal the bag and refrigerate for at least 8 hours or up to 24 hours, turning the bag occasionally so the beef strips are evenly marinated.

Remove an oven rack from the oven and lightly spray the rack with nonstick vegetable spray. Remove the strips from the marinade, shaking off excess marinade. Pat the strips dry with paper towels. Arrange the strips, close together, but not touching, on the rack. Line the bottom of the oven with aluminum foil (to catch drips).

Preheat the oven to 150°. Place the oven rack with the jerky in the oven. Bake until a cool piece of jerky (remove from the oven and let cool 5 minutes) breaks when bent, about 5 hours. Blot any surface fat with paper towels. Cool completely Store in an airtight container for up to 1 month at cool room temperature, 3 months in the refrigerator, or 6 months in the freezer. Makes about 1 pound.

National Cowboy Hall of Fame Chuck Wagon Cookbook

Mantle's Chicken Fried Steak

This recipe was one of Mickey's favorites and is the most popular at his New York restaurant, Mickey Mantle's Restaurant and Sports Bar. Developed by Executive Chef Michael Salmon, this steak is best when topped with the gravy Mickey said his Mom used when he was growing up in Oklahoma.

4 (6-ounce) ¼-inch thick,
  lightly pounded, slices of
  beef top round
2 cups of all-purpose flour
2¼ tablespoons coarse salt
2 teaspoons garlic powder

¼ teaspoon white pepper
6 large eggs
½ cup of water
Vegetable oil (½ inch deep
  in pan)

Mix flour, salt, garlic powder, and white pepper. Mix eggs and water. Beat them together. Dredge meat in flour, shake excess flour and dip into egg mixture. Place back into flour and shake off excess. Place into large frying pan with oil that is on medium high heat. Brown and turn over carefully. Brown reverse side. Place on paper towel to dab excess oil.

CREAM GRAVY:

¼ cup flour mix (flour, salt,
  garlic, and white pepper)

2 cups chicken stock
½ cup milk or heavy cream

After frying the meat, drain all but ¼ cup fat from the pan. Place pan back on medium heat and stir in flour mix until mixture resembles wet sand. Add 2 cups of well seasoned chicken stock. Add more or less stock depending upon the thickness of gravy desired. Bring to boil and reduce heat to a simmer. Cook for 8 minutes and add milk. Bring to boil. Remove and strain. Season.

Note: For creamier sauce, substitute heavy cream for milk.

The Oklahoma Celebrity Cookbook

Our Favorite Brisket

1 brisket
Garlic salt
Onion salt
Celery salt
½ bottle liquid smoke

1 onion, minced, or 2
tablespoons dry minced
onion
2½ ounces Worcestershire
Barbecue sauce

Line a baking pan (cookie sheet) with foil to seal brisket. Place brisket, fat-side-down, in the lined pan and sprinkle generously with garlic, onion, and celery salts. Add liquid smoke and minced onion. Seal foil and refrigerate overnight.

The next day, add Worcestershire and salt and pepper all over the brisket. Bake at 275° for 5–6 hours. Shred or slice meat and pour barbecue sauce over all. Serve warm or refrigerate or freeze for later use.

Note: To marinate in plastic brown-n-bags: Place brown-n-bag on cookie sheet. Sprinkle brisket with garlic, onion, and celery salts. Place fat-side-down in bag; add minced onion to bag and pour liquid smoke into bag. Close bag with a tie and marinate overnight.

The next day, open bag and add salt and pepper. Pour in Worcestershire. Close bag with a tie and puncture top of brown-n-bag by making 6 (½-inch) slits. Bake at 275° for 5–6 hours. Remove meat from brown-n-bag, slice, cover with barbecue sauce, and heat until sauce is warm. This freezes well.

Thank Heaven for Home Made Cooks

Beef Brisket

1 (5- to 8-pound) beef brisket
2 teaspoons liquid smoke
2 teaspoons Worcestershire
2 tablespoons soy sauce
2 teaspoons garlic salt

1 teaspoon onion salt
2 teaspoons celery salt
2 teaspoons pepper
1½ teaspoons salt

Put brisket on heavy foil. Mix remaining ingredients together for marinade and rub over brisket. Fold up foil and place in refrigerator overnight.

Next morning, place in 250° oven for 6–7 hours. Take out of oven. Cool slightly. Put in freezer for 2 hours. Remove from freezer. Remove all fat from marinade and brisket; drain and reserve sauce and slice brisket. Put in pan; add enough water to sauce to almost cover slices of brisket. Cover with foil or lid. Refrigerate until ready to heat and serve. Heat for 2 hours. Serve with barbecue sauce on side. This can be made the day before.

Spring Creek Club

Barbecue Beef Brisket

1 (4- to 5-pound) well-trimmed
   boneless beef brisket
1½ teaspoons salt
½ cup ketchup
¼ cup vinegar

½ cup finely chopped onion
1 tablespoon Worcestershire
1½ teaspoons liquid smoke
1 bay leaf, crumbled
¼ teaspoon pepper

Rub meat with salt. Place in an ungreased 13x9x2-inch baking dish. Stir together remaining ingredients; pour over meat. Cover tightly; bake in 325° oven for 3 hours or until tender.

Country Cooking

Claremore has been nicknamed the "Den of Antiquity" because of its large number of antique dealers.

Brisket Marinade

1 tablespoon liquid smoke	1 teaspoon onion powder
2 teaspoons celery seed	2 teaspoons black pepper
1 teaspoon garlic powder	1½ teaspoons salt
2 teaspoons Worcestershire	1 (3-pound) brisket

SAUCE:

3 tablespoons brown sugar	1 teaspoon dry mustard
3 drops Tabasco sauce	1 teaspoon soy sauce
½ cup ketchup	1 teaspoon lemon juice
Dash of nutmeg	

Mix liquid smoke, celery seed, garlic powder, Worcestershire, onion powder, black pepper, and salt together in small bowl. Stir until the ingredients reach the consistency of paste. Spread over brisket; cover and refrigerate overnight. Bake at 300° for 4 hours. Mix together sauce ingredients. Approximately 30 minutes before brisket is done, pour sauce over the brisket.

Feast in Fellowship

Brisket

1 whole brisket	1 bottle Italian dressing

Place brisket in large shallow baking pan. Pour Italian dressing over the brisket and let it marinate overnight. Next morning, place brisket in foil and bake in oven slowly at 325° for 3–4 hours or until tender.

Seems Like I Done It This A-Way II

El Reno, on Route 66, cooks up the world's largest onion-fried burger each May. But any time of the year, you can sample the town's signature sandwich at several of the town's diners.

Roast Peppered Rib Eye of Beef

5- to 6-pound boneless
  rib eye beef roast
½ cup coarsely cracked
  pepper
½ teaspoon ground
  cardamom seed
1 tablespoon tomato paste

½ teaspoon garlic powder
1 teaspoon paprika
1 cup soy sauce
¾ cup vinegar
1½ tablespoons cornstarch
  (optional)

Have fat trimmed from roast. Marinate by combining cracked pepper and cardamom seed; rub all over beef and press in with heel of hand. Place in shallow baking dish and set aside. Combine tomato paste, garlic powder, and paprika. Pour over roast. Add soy sauce and vinegar. Refrigerate overnight.

Spoon marinade over meat. Remove meat from marinade and let stand at room temperature for one hour. Wrap in foil, place in shallow pan and roast at 300° for two hours (medium rare). Open foil, ladle out and reserve drippings. Brown roast uncovered at 350° while making gravy.

GRAVY:

1 cup meat juices
1 cup water

Cornstarch mixed with ¼
  cup cold water if needed

Bring meat juices and 1 cup water to boil. If desired, add a little marinade. Serve au jus or thickened with cornstarch mixed with water. Serves 8–10.

Submitted by G.W. "Bill" Swisher, Jr., founder of the CMI Corporation and third-generation native Oklahoman.

The Oklahoma Celebrity Cookbook

Two-Step Tenderloin with a Kick

2 tablespoons Dijon mustard
1 tablespoon olive oil
1 (4-pound) beef tenderloin, trimmed
1 tablespoon freshly ground black pepper
1 tablespoon crushed dried leaf oregano

1 tablespoon crushed dried leaf thyme
1 tablespoon finely snipped chives
2 cloves garlic, minced
1 teaspoon salt

Preheat oven to 425°. Combine mustard and olive oil; brush on all sides of tenderloin. Combine pepper, oregano, thyme, chives, garlic, and salt. Pat seasoning mixture on all sides of roast. Place tenderloin on a rack in a large shallow roasting pan; let stand at room temperature for 30 minutes. Insert meat thermometer; place in oven about 45 minutes or until thermometer registers 140° for rare meat. Remove from oven; let stand for 45 minutes, then wrap and chill.

MUSTARD SAUCE:

½ cup mayonnaise
½ cup sour cream
1 tablespoon white wine vinegar

¼ cup Dijon mustard
1 tablespoon snipped chives
1 teaspoon Worcestershire

Meanwhile, make Mustard Sauce by combining mayonnaise, sour cream, mustard, vinegar, chives, and Worcestershire in a small mixing bowl. Cover and chill. Before serving meat, allow tenderloin to stand at room temperature for 2 hours. Slice roast and serve with Mustard Sauce. Yields 12 servings.

Cafe Oklahoma

Oklahoma has more horses than any other state, and there's likely a cowboy to go with every horse. Visitors can taste cowboy life (and campfire coffee) at rodeos, guest ranches, trail rides, and chuck wagon feeds.

Crowd-Pleasing Roast

Boneless roast
1 package French onion soup mix
1 can cream of mushroom soup
½ cup cooking wine (any cheap burgundy wine will do)

Place roast in a large crock pot. Combine soup and soup mix in bowl with wine. Stir until blended. Empty sauce onto top of roast. Cover and cook on high for number of hours suggested based upon size of roast.

Sequoyah's Cookin'

Tangy Ham Balls in Pineapple Sauce

1¼ pounds cured lean ham, ground
¼ pound pork, ground
1 egg
1 cup finely ground cracker crumbs
½ cup milk
¼ teaspoon pepper

Mix ingredients and form into balls about the size of a small egg. Put in 8x11-inch Pyrex pan and cover with Pineapple Sauce. Cook, uncovered, in a 300° oven about 2 hours or until done. Serve over rice. Serves 8.

PINEAPPLE SAUCE:
1 cup brown sugar
½ cup water
1 teaspoon mustard
1 small can crushed pineapple

Combine all ingredients.

Four Generations of Johnson Family Favorites

Mother's Ham Loaf

2 pounds lean pork
1 pound smoked ham
1 cup milk

1 cup dry bread crumbs
1 cup tomato purée

Grind meats; add milk and bread crumbs. Mix well and shape into loaf. Place in baking dish. Thicken purée with bread crumbs and spread over loaf. Bake at 350° for 45 minutes.

SAUCE:
1 can whole cranberry sauce
1 tablespoon horseradish

2 teaspoons grated orange
rind

Mix. Heat. Serve separately with ham.

Pow Wow Chow

Fresh Ham with Cranberry Stuffing

1 (1-pound) can whole
cranberries, drained, or
1 cup fresh
6 sprigs parsley
1 stalk celery
6 slices day-old bread

3 tablespoons orange juice
2 tablespoons sugar
1 teaspoon salt
½ teaspoon marjoram or
poultry seasoning
1 (10- to 12-pound) fresh ham

Heat oven to 500°. Make cranberry stuffing: chop cranberries, parsley and celery (use tops too). Mix cranberries, parsley, celery, and bread crumbs; add other ingredients. Mix well. Cut slit in ham; fill hollow of ham with stuffing, but don't pack it in tightly because it swells during baking. Sew opening securely; carefully cut off any rind. Cut or score fat, about ½-inch deep, into ¾-inch squares. Roast meat, uncovered, 30 minutes (this makes the little squares of fat crisp and golden); then reduce oven heat to 300°, or slow. Continue roasting, without a cover, 3½–4 hours, or until fork pierces meat easily. Serve with baked sweet potatoes and broccoli.

Recipes and Remembrances

Ham Loaf

1 pound veal (ground)
1 pound smoked ham
 (ground)
4 tablespoons ketchup
2 tablespoons minced onion
2 eggs, beaten

1 cup dry bread crumbs
1 can cream of mushroom
 soup
½ teaspoon salt
Dash of pepper

Mix in order given. Pack into greased loaf pan and bake in 350° oven for 1 hour.

Old and New

Raisin Sauce for Ham

½ cup brown sugar
½ tablespoon dry mustard
½ tablespoon flour
½ tablespoon salt
⅛ teaspoon pepper
¼ teaspoon cloves

Few grains of mace, nutmeg
 and cinnamon
¼–½ cup seedless raisins
¼ cup vinegar
1½ cups water

Mix dry ingredients. Add raisins, vinegar, and water. Cook to a syrup. Serve hot. May be reheated.

Seems Like I Done It This A-Way II

Ham Red Eye Gravy

When you fry ham, leave the "leavings" in the skillet. Take 1 teaspoon salt and sprinkle over the bottom of the skillet (less if ham is salty). A sprinkle of sugar may be added. Brown sugar and salt, then add 1 cup coffee (already made), put lid on so it won't spew on stove. Before adding coffee, make sure the fat and skillet are real hot. Pour off excess fat. Good on hot biscuits.

Seems Like I Done It This A-Way III

Ham Rolls

16 spears broccoli
16 (¼- to ⅝-inch) thick slices
  precooked boneless ham

16 slices Swiss cheese
1 (16-ounce) jar cherry
  preserves

Cook broccoli spears until crisp-tender; do not overcook. Drain; cool. Take a slice of ham; place 1 slice Swiss cheese on top. Lay 1 spear of broccoli on that; roll jelly-roll style. Continue with each slice of ham, cheese, and broccoli. Place in greased 9x13-inch pan, seam-side-down. Put in preheated 325° oven for 20–30 minutes.

While ham is baking, melt the cherry preserves in small pan. Remove ham from oven. Put 1 tablespoon of preserves on each roll. Return to oven for 10 minutes. Serves 8–10.

Spring Creek Club

Ham and Potato Bake

1½ cups cubed raw potatoes
1½ cups cooked, cubed ham
2 tablespoons chopped onion

1 (10½-ounce) can cream of
  celery soup (undiluted)
1½ cups grated cheese

Heat oven to 350°. Cube potatoes and ham in ½-inch cubes. Mix all ingredients in casserole, reserving ¾ cup of cheese. Bake covered 1 hour and 15 minutes, stirring 1 or 2 times during cooking. Remove cover and top with remaining ¾ cup cheese. Broil for just enough time to melt and brown cheese. Watch carefully. Yields 4 servings.

Thank Heaven for Home Made Cooks

Historic Fort Supply is the supply camp that was established in western Indian Territory by Lt. Col. George Custer in 1868 as a temporary facility. It was thought it would only take a few months to subdue the Indians—the post remained in use for 25 years.

One Dish Pork Chop Meal

Everybody likes this, especially men.

Salt and pepper to taste
4 (½-inch thick) pork chops
3 cups uncooked rice (can use
   instant rice and not have to
   precook rice)

2 cups tomato juice
Salt and pepper (sprinkle)
1 teaspoon sugar
1 onion
1 green pepper

Salt and pepper pork chops and sear in slightly greased skillet. Cover skillet tightly; set aside. Cook rice in boiling water until ⅓ done. Drain and pile on each pork chop. Press down slightly. Season tomato juice with salt, pepper, and sugar. Pour over chops, being very careful not to wash rice away. Cut onion and green pepper into thin rings and put over chops and rice. Bake at 350° for 40 minutes in airtight skillet. May need to add water. Good served with baked apples.

Four Generations of Johnson Family Favorites

Rabbit Stir-Fry

2 tablespoons vegetable oil
1 pound boneless rabbit meat
1 (16-ounce) package frozen
   stir-fry vegetables
¼ cup teriyaki sauce

¼ cup pineapple juice
2 tablespoons orange juice
   concentrate
1 cup pineapple tidbits

Heat 1 tablespoon oil in skillet. Add meat and cook until no longer pink. Remove meat, but keep warm. Pour 1 tablespoon oil in skillet and add frozen vegetables. Cook 1 minute. Add the teriyaki sauce, pineapple juice, and orange juice concentrate. Stir together. Cover and let cook for 4–6 minutes. Add meat and pineapple tidbits; heat thoroughly. Serve on a bed of hot rice.

Note: Can substitute chicken for rabbit meat.

Sisters Two and Family Too

Pork Forestiori

2½ pounds pork tenderloin   Cracked pepper
Dijon mustard

Coat tenderloin with mustard, then with cracked pepper. Place on broiler rack and broil on center rack of oven for 20 minutes. Remove pork from oven and slice into ½-inch thick slices. Return to oven and broil 1–2 minutes longer. Serve topped with Forestiori Sauce.

FORESTIORI SAUCE:

4 slices bacon	¼ teaspoon Worcestershire
½ cup onion, diced	½ cup dry sherry
¼ cup parsley, chopped	¼ cup brandy
4 cups mushrooms, sliced	½ cup beef broth
2 garlic cloves, crushed	¼ cup whipping cream

Cut bacon into 1-inch pieces and fry in skillet until brown. Remove bacon and pour off all but 1 tablespoon of the fat. Return the pan to medium heat and sauté onion, parsley, and mushroom until the onion is translucent. Add garlic, Worcestershire, sherry, brandy, and broth. Reduce heat and simmer 10–15 minutes. Immediately before serving, stir in cream. Pour the warm sauce over sliced pork to serve. Makes 4 servings.

Applause!

Encore Bearnaise Sauce

Essential to beef fondue.

6 green onions, minced
2 tablespoons butter
4 egg yolks
¼ cup white wine vinegar
2 teaspoons dried tarragon

¼ teaspoon dry mustard
¼ teaspoon salt
4 drops Tabasco
2 cups butter, melted

Sauté onions lightly in a little butter and put them in a blender. Add the egg yolks and spices and mix at medium speed 2 minutes. Gradually add melted butter while mixing until all is absorbed. Refrigerate. Allow to soften to serve. Yes, it holds together! Makes approximately 2 cups.

Applause!

Peach and Citrus Chutney

Peach chutney is just the thing to serve with pork chops, ham, or smoked turkey. It might even persuade a cowboy to eat lamb chops.

1 cup orange juice, preferably
   freshly squeezed
½ cup granulated sugar
½ cup raspberry or cider
   vinegar
3 large peaches, peeled,
   pitted, and coarsely
   chopped
⅓ cup dried currants
1 medium red onion, finely
   chopped

1 medium red bell pepper,
   seeded and finely chopped
⅓ cup golden raisins
2 tablespoons grated fresh
   ginger
Grated zest of 2 lemons
Grated zest of 1 large orange
1 teaspoon Madras-style
   curry powder
¼ teaspoon salt

In a large saucepan, bring the orange juice, sugar, and vinegar to a simmer over medium heat, stirring often to dissolve the sugar. Reduce the heat to low and cook for 5 minutes.

Stir in the remaining ingredients and bring to a simmer. Cook, stirring often, until thickened, about 20 minutes. Transfer to a medium bowl and cool completely. (The chutney can be prepared up to 1 week ahead, covered, and refrigerated.) Makes about 3 cups.

National Cowboy Hall of Fame Chuck Wagon Cookbook

Ranchero Sauce

Ranchero sauce is an important ingredient in Huevos Rancheros, but also hits the bull's eye when served with grilled steaks or pork chops. This recipe makes a large batch, and it freezes well.

¼ cup olive oil
1 medium onion, chopped
1 small stalk celery, chopped
1 medium green bell pepper, seeded and chopped
2 cloves garlic, minced
1 (28-ounce) can chopped tomatoes, undrained
1 (4-ounce) can chopped mild green chiles, drained

2 tablespoons Worcestershire
2 tablespoons chopped fresh parsley
2 teaspoons sweet or hot Hungarian paprika
1 teaspoon dried oregano
¼ teaspoon freshly ground pepper
½ teaspoon hot red pepper sauce, or to taste

In a medium saucepan, heat the oil over medium heat. Add the onion, celery, bell pepper, and garlic, and cook, covered, until the vegetables are lightly browned, about 10 minutes.

Add the tomatoes with their juices, green chiles, Worcestershire, parsley, paprika, oregano, and pepper and bring to a simmer. Reduce the heat to low and simmer, uncovered, until slightly thickened and the tomato juices are almost evaporated, about 30 minutes. Stir in the hot sauce. Serve the sauce hot, warm, or at room temperature. (The sauce can be prepared up to 5 days ahead, cooled, covered, and refrigerated. Reheat gently before serving.)

National Cowboy Hall of Fame Chuck Wagon Cookbook

One of the greatest athletes the world has ever known was an Indian from Oklahoma. Jim Thorpe was born on a farm near Prague to parents who were part Sac and Fox and Pottawatomie. Thorpe became an international sports hero at the 1912 Olympics in Stockholm, Sweden, where he won the pentathlon and decathlon. Thorpe also starred in football and baseball, and a 1950 Associated Press poll of the nation's sportswriters picked him as the greatest athlete of the half-century.

Cakes

Little Sahara State Park along the Cimarron River near Waynoka is made up of fine quartz sand dunes that were created over 11,000 years ago. This makes for great dune-buggy rides and races over 1,450 acres of rideable sand. And for the more adventuresome, brave the Waynoka Rattle Snake Roundup the first Sunday after Easter every year.

Seven-Up Cake

1 package lemon cake mix	1 (3-ounce) package instant
4 eggs	lemon pudding
1 (10-ounce) bottle 7-Up	1 cup oil

Mix together and bake 25 minutes in 3 cake pans at 350°. Make icing and let cool while cake is baking.

ICING:

1½ cups sugar	3 egg yolks
1 stick margarine	1 cup flaked coconut
2 tablespoons cornstarch	
1 (15-ounce) can crushed pineapple	

Mix first 5 ingredients together and boil until thick. Add 1 cup coconut. Cool and spread between layers and on top and sides of cake.

Kitchen Klatter Keepsakes

Pig Eater's Cake

1 yellow cake mix	4 eggs
1 small box instant vanilla pudding	1 small can mandarin oranges
	½ cup oil

Mix and bake cake in 9x13-inch pan as directed. Cool cake completely, then frost.

FROSTING:

1 small box instant vanilla pudding	1 small can crushed pineapple
	1 (8-ounce) carton Cool Whip

Dissolve pudding in pineapple before adding Cool Whip. Chill several hours before serving.

Seasoned with Love

Harvey Wallbanger Cake

1 package yellow cake mix
1 package instant vanilla
  pudding
½ cup oil

¼ cup vodka
¾ cup orange juice
¼ cup Galliano
4 eggs

Mix all together and beat for 4 minutes. Put in greased and lightly floured Bundt pan. Bake 45–50 minutes at 350°.

GLAZE:

1½ cups powdered sugar
1½ tablespoons Vodka

1½ tablespoons Galliano
1½ tablespoons orange juice

Mix together and pour over cake to glaze.

Dine with the Angels

Heavenly Coconut Cream Cake

1 white cake, baked as
  directed
1 can Eagle Brand Milk
1 (15-ounce) can Coco Lopez
  Cream of Coconut

1 medium container Cool
  Whip
7 ounces shredded coconut

Bake white cake in 13x9-inch pan as directed. Mix 1 can Eagle Brand Milk with cream of coconut. Pour over warm cake which has been pierced with fork. Cool in refrigerator. Frost with Cool Whip and coconut. Keep refrigerated.

Seasoned with Love

Pound Cake

1 pound butter, softened
3 cups sugar
10 eggs

1½ teaspoons vanilla
4 cups flour

Cream butter and sugar. Add eggs, one at a time, beat well after each addition, add vanilla. Gradually add 1 cup of flour at a time. Grease bottom only of angel food cake pan and pour in batter. Bake at 325° for 1 hour 15 minutes to 1 hour 30 minutes. A very good and rich cake. Delicious served with strawberries and whipped cream.

Feast in Fellowship

Burnt Caramel Cake

This was before margarine, so my mother always used fresh-churned butter. This recipe has been in our family since my childhood. I've used it many times and it's always been one of our favorites.

½ cup sugar, burnt until dark
½ cup water
1½ cups sugar
⅔ cup butter or margarine, softened
2 eggs
1 cup water
Pinch of salt
1 teaspoon vanilla
2 cups flour
2 teaspoons baking powder

In heavy pot or skillet, burn ½ cup sugar until dark. Put ½ cup boiling water in burnt sugar; let boil to a syrup (takes about 7 minutes). Cool but keep warm. Cream sugar and butter or margarine; add the beaten eggs and beat to a creamy batter. Then add water, salt, vanilla, and burnt syrup, leaving 2 tablespoons in the skillet for filling. Add the flour and baking powder; beat for 2 minutes. Bake in 2 (9-inch) greased and floured cake pans in preheated 350° oven 25–30 minutes.

FILLING:

2 tablespoons burnt sugar
2 cups sugar
3 tablespoons butter
⅔ cup milk or cream
2 tablespoons white corn syrup

Put 2 cups sugar in skillet with burnt syrup; add butter the size of a small egg, milk or light cream, and 2 tablespoons white corn syrup. Boil until it forms a soft ball in cold water; then cool and beat. Spread on cake. If icing gets too thick to spread, add a little cream or milk.

Recipes and Remembrances

Potato Cake

2 cups sugar
1 cup shortening
4 eggs
1 cup warm mashed potatoes, unseasoned
1 teaspoon soda

½ teaspoon salt
2 cups flour
4 tablespoons cocoa
1 cup buttermilk
1 teaspoon vanilla
1½ cups chopped pecans

Cream the sugar and shortening; add eggs, 1 at a time, beating well after each addition. Add potatoes. Add sifted dry ingredients alternately with buttermilk. Add vanilla and nuts. Bake in 2 or 3 layers at 350° until inserted toothpick comes out clean. May be baked in large sheet pan. Frost with caramel icing. Freezes well; is real moist.

Recipes and Remembrances

Mayonnaise Cake

2 cups flour
1 cup sugar
2 teaspoons soda
4 tablespoons cocoa

1 cup warm water
1 cup mayonnaise
1 teaspoon vanilla

Sift together the dry ingredients and add water, mayonnaise and vanilla. Mix well, put in greased and floured pan or muffin tins. Bake about 25 minutes at 350°.

FROSTING:

2 cups powdered sugar
2 tablespoons cocoa
¼ pound margarine

1 teaspoon vanilla
Enough strong black coffee to spread

Seems Like I Done It This A-Way I

Banana Pudding Cake

1 light yellow cake mix
¾ cup egg substitute
1 cup sugar
1 (15-ounce) can crushed
  pineapple
1 package whipped topping,
  prepared (with skim milk)

3 bananas
1 (4-ounce) instant vanilla
  pudding mix (regular or
  sugar-free)
½ cup Grape Nuts cereal
6 maraschino cherries

Spray a 9x13-inch cake pan with nonfat cooking spray. Preheat oven to 350°. Prepare cake according to mix directions using egg substitute. While cake is baking, mix sugar and pineapple in a saucepan; boil for 5 minutes. Remove cake from oven and prick top with a fork. Pour pineapple on top of cake. Cool completely Prepare instant pudding with skim milk as directed on package. Spread on top of cooled cake. Slice bananas and place over top of pudding. Spread prepared whipped topping over bananas. Sprinkle cereal over the top. Slice cherries in half and place on top of whipped topping. Distribute evenly over the top.

Per Serving: Fat 2g; Cal 186; 10 Cal from Fat.

Feast in Fellowship

Banana Sheet Cake

2 cups sugar
1 cup shortening
1 teaspoon vanilla
4 eggs

4 ripe bananas
2 cups flour
Salt
1 teaspoon baking soda

Cream sugar and shortening. Add remaining ingredients. Pour batter into a greased 11x16-inch jelly roll pan. Bake at 350° for 30 minutes.

FROSTING:

¼ cup margarine, softened
1 (1-pound) box powdered
  sugar

1 (8-ounce) package cream
  cheese, softened

Cream margarine and cream cheese. Add powdered sugar. Mix well. Spread on cooled cake. This will freeze either before or after frosting.

Kitchen Klatter Keepsakes

Peanut Butter Sheet Cake

2 cups flour
1 teaspoon soda
2 cups sugar
½ teaspoon salt
1½ sticks margarine
½ cup Crisco oil

½ cup chunky peanut butter
1 cup water
2 eggs, slightly beaten
1 teaspoon vanilla
½ cup buttermilk

Mix flour, soda, sugar, and salt in mixing bowl. Bring margarine, oil, peanut butter, and water to boil. Pour over dry ingredients and mix well. Add beaten eggs, vanilla, and buttermilk and mix well. Pour into 11x15x1-inch sheet pan; bake 15–18 minutes at 350°.

While cake is baking, make icing. Let cake cool 5 minutes before spreading on icing.

PEANUT BUTTER CAKE ICING:

½ cup Milnot or milk
1 cup sugar
1 teaspoon vanilla
½ cup extra crunchy peanut
  butter

½ cup miniature
  marshmallows
2 tablespoons margarine

While peanut butter cake is baking, prepare this icing. Bring Milnot, sugar, and margarine to boil and cook 2 minutes, stirring gently to keep from scorching. Remove from heat and stir in peanut butter, marshmallows, and vanilla until melted. Wait 5 minutes for cake to cool, then pour over cake and spread to cover.

Thank Heaven for Home Made Cooks

Carrot Cake with Cream Cheese Frosting

Discover all the flavor of a carrot cake in this simple recipe which contains baby food.

CAKE:

2 cups sugar
2 cups all-purpose flour
2 teaspoons baking soda
2 teaspoons cinnamon
1 teaspoon salt

1 cup vegetable oil
2 (7½-ounce) jars junior
 baby carrots
4 eggs

Heat oven to 350°. In large mixing bowl combine all cake ingredients. Beat at low speed, scraping bowl often, until well mixed, 1–2 minutes. Beat at medium speed, scraping bowl often, for 2 minutes. Pour into greased and floured 13x9-inch baking pan. Bake for 45–55 minutes or until wooden pick inserted in center comes out clean. Cool completely.

FROSTING:

½ cup margarine or butter,
 softened
1 (8-ounce) package light
 cream cheese or cream
 cheese, softened

3¾ cups powdered sugar
1 teaspoon vanilla
1 cup chopped pecans

In small mixing bowl beat margarine and cream cheese at medium speed until well blended, 1–2 minutes. Add powdered sugar and vanilla. Beat at low speed until smooth, 2–3 minutes. Spread frosting on cake. Sprinkle with pecans. Serves 15.

Per serving (serving size: ⅟₁₅ of recipe): Cal 580; Prot 6g; Carbo 74g; Fat 31g; Chol 68mg; Sod 450mg.

Sisters Two and Family Too

There are four historic national capitols within Oklahoma's borders; the Creek Council House in Okmulgee, the Cherokee capitol in Tahlequah, the Chickasaw capitol in Tishomingo, and the Choctaw capitol in Tuskahoma.

Pumpkin Roll

5 eggs
1½ cups sugar
1 cup pumpkin
1 teaspoon lemon juice
1 cup plus 2 tablespoons flour
1½ teaspoons baking
  powder

¾ teaspoon salt
¾ teaspoon nutmeg
3 teaspoons cinnamon
1½ teaspoons ginger
Powdered sugar

Beat eggs at high speed for 5 minutes. Add sugar, pumpkin, and lemon juice. Add flour, baking powder, salt, nutmeg, cinnamon, and ginger, adjusting measurements of spices to taste. Spread mixture into a greased and floured 15x10x1-inch pan. Bake for 15–20 minutes at 350°. Roll in a towel with powdered sugar and add powdered sugar on top. Leave rolled until cool. Unroll, spread with filling and re-roll.

FILLING:

2 (3-ounce) packages cream
  cheese, softened
1 cup powdered sugar

2 cups chopped pecans
½ teaspoon vanilla
4 tablespoons softened butter

Mix all ingredients together. Unroll cooled pumpkin roll; spread filling on top and re-roll.

Feast in Fellowship

Favorite Quick Fruit Cocktail Cake

1 cup sugar
2 cups flour
2 teaspoons soda
1 (16-ounce) can fruit cocktail
1 teaspoon vanilla

1 teaspoon butter flavoring
2 eggs, beaten
½ cup brown sugar
1 cup coarsely chopped
   pecans

TOPPING:
½ cup margarine
½ cup coconut

⅓ cup white sugar
½ cup brown sugar

Sift sugar, flour, and soda together. Add fruit cocktail juice and fruit, flavorings, then beaten eggs. Put in a 9x13-inch pan. Put ½ cup brown sugar and pecans on before baking. Bake at 350° for 30 minutes.

Bring topping ingredients to boil for 2 minutes. Spread on warm cake. Delicious.

Country Cooking

Apple Dump Cake

8–9 apples (2 cups cooked)
2 cups flour
2 cups sugar
1 teaspoon soda
1 teaspoon salt

1 teaspoon cinnamon
2 eggs
1 cup oil
1 cup chopped nuts

Cook apples until tender (canned may be used). Dump dry ingredients in mixing bowl and mix together. Add eggs, oil, nuts, and cooked apples. Mix. Pour into a 9x13-inch cake pan that has been greased and floured. Bake at 350° for 1 hour. A good cake and easy to make.

Seems Like I Done It This A-Way III

Oklahoma has many firsts. Among them: The first Boy Scout Troop in the United States was founded here in 1909; the first passenger plane was built here; the world's first installed parking meter was in Oklahoma City on July 16, 1935; and Oklahoma had the first flowing commercial oil well in the world (a re-creation of Nellie Johnstone #1 can be seen in Bartlesville).

Fresh Apple Cake

Wonderful for Christmas brunch.

½ cup shortening
2 cups sugar
2 eggs, beaten
2 cups flour
½ teaspoon salt
1 teaspoon soda

1 teaspoon cinnamon
1 teaspoon nutmeg
4 cups apples, peeled and
   finely chopped
1 cup dates, chopped
2 cups nuts, chopped

Preheat oven to 300°. Grease and flour 9x13-inch pan. Cream sugar and shortening. Add eggs, mixing well. Sift together flour, salt, soda, cinnamon, and nutmeg. Add to creamed ingredients. Stir in apples, dates, and nuts. Pour into prepared pan and bake 50 minutes or until brown. Serve warm with whipped cream. Makes 12–16 servings.

Applause!

Raw Apple Walnut Cake

3 cups chopped apples
2 cups sugar
1 cup chopped black walnuts
   (or pecans, or half and half)
3 eggs

1 teaspoon vanilla
1½ cups salad oil
3 cups flour
1 teaspoon cinnamon
1 teaspoon soda

Mix first 3 ingredients together and let stand. Beat together the eggs, vanilla, and salad oil. Sift together the flour, cinnamon, and soda; add to the egg mixture. Add apple mixture and beat until well mixed. The dough will be thick. Pour into a well greased and floured 13x9-inch pan, or spray with Pam. Bake in 350° oven for 45 minutes.

Note: A caramel or white icing is good with this cake.

Cooking A + Recipes

Mother's Hickory Nut Cake

Made with hickory nuts we gathered on the mountain behind Grandpa's house.

1 cup butter
4 eggs
2 cups sugar
3 cups all-purpose flour
1 teaspoon soda

2 teaspoons cream of tartar
1 cup cold water
2 cups hickory nutmeats
1 teaspoon lemon extract

Cream butter and sugar until light, add eggs one at a time and beat well. Sift flour, soda and cream of tartar together. Add alternately flour and water until thoroughly mixed. Add hickory nuts which have been dredged with some of the flour. Add extract and stir thoroughly. Pour into a 10-inch tube pan which has been lined with greased brown paper. Bake at 350° for 45–60 minutes or until tested done. Ice with boiled icing. Serves 12–14.

Cleora's Kitchens

Orange Poppy Seed Cake

Ultra lowfat—the best—wonderful.

1 package lowfat white cake mix
2 tablespoons poppy seeds
¾ cup fat-free liquid egg product
1 cup fat-free sour cream

1 (6-ounce) can frozen orange juice concentrate
⅓ cup water
2 teaspoons cinnamon
2 tablespoons sugar

Preheat oven to 350°. In large bowl, combine all ingredients except cinnamon and sugar and beat with electric mixer 2 minutes. Spray Bundt pan with nonstick cooking spray. Combine sugar and cinnamon and sprinkle evenly over inside of pan. Pour in cake batter and bake at 350° for 45 minutes. Makes 12 servings.

Grams of Fat Per Serving 3. Calories Per Serving 255.

Fat Free 2

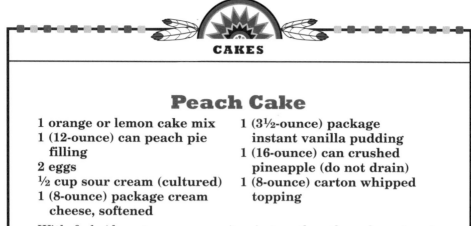

Peach Cake

1 orange or lemon cake mix
1 (12-ounce) can peach pie
  filling
2 eggs
½ cup sour cream (cultured)
1 (8-ounce) package cream
  cheese, softened

1 (3½-ounce) package
  instant vanilla pudding
1 (16-ounce) can crushed
  pineapple (do not drain)
1 (8-ounce) carton whipped
  topping

With fork (do not use a spoon), mix together the cake mix, pie filling, eggs, and sour cream. Spoon into a 10x14-inch baking dish. Bake at 350° for 30 minutes. Cool. Mix together cream cheese, instant pudding, crushed pineapple (with juice) and fold in the whipped topping. Spread on cool cake. Refrigerate until ready to serve.

Note: This is a very good cake; keeps well, but must be refrigerated.

Shattuck Community Cookbook

WIKIPEDIA.ORG

Guthrie is one of America's most charming time capsules. It was Oklahoma's territorial capital for 20 years. When the capital was moved to Oklahoma City in 1910, Guthrie was thrust into a 75-year sleep. Today there are 400 blocks of vintage architecture on the National Register of Historic Places, making it one of the nation's largest living museums.

Philbrook's Italian Cream Cake

Tulsa's beautiful Philbrook Museum reopened its restaurant with a new name and an exciting new creative menu. This delicate cream cake, a creation of their Executive Chef, Jody Walls, appears often at their Sunday brunch.

1 cup buttermilk	5 eggs, separated
1 teaspoon soda	2 cups flour, sifted
½ cup butter, softened	1 teaspoon vanilla extract
½ cup shortening	3½ ounces flaked coconut
2 cups sugar	1 cup chopped pecans

Preheat oven to 350°. Grease and flour 3 (9-inch) cake pans. Combine buttermilk and soda and set aside. Cream butter, shortening and sugar. Add egg yolks, one at a time, beating after each addition. Alternately, add buttermilk and flour, small amounts at a time. Add vanilla extract. Beat egg whites to stiff peaks; fold into batter and flour mixture. Stir in coconut and pecans. Bake for 25 minutes. Cool on racks.

ICING:

1 (8-ounce) package cream cheese, softened	1½ cups chopped pecans
1 cup butter, softened	3 teaspoons vanilla extract
8 cups confectioners' sugar, sifted	

In mixer, cream together cream cheese and butter. Add sugar slowly to spreading consistency. Add pecans and vanilla. Frost cake. Makes 12 servings.

Applause!

The Philbrook Museum of Art is truly Tulsa's unique treasure. The legacy of oilman Waite Phillips endures in this stunning Renaissance-style villa and gardens.

Cherry Chocolate Cake

1 package chocolate cake mix   1 can cherry pie filling
3 eggs

Mix cake mix, eggs, and cherry pie filling until blended. Pour into greased and floured 9x13-inch pan. Bake at 350° for 35–40 minutes. Let cool.

FROSTING:

1 cup sugar
5 tablespoons margarine
⅓ cup milk

1 (6-ounce) package
semi-sweet chocolate chips

In small pan, combine sugar, margarine, and milk. Bring to a boil, stirring constantly, and cook 1 minute. Remove from heat and stir in chocolate chips until smooth and melted. Blend well and spread on cake.

Feast in Fellowship

Chocolate Chip Cake

1 yellow cake mix
1 (4½-ounce) package
   instant chocolate pudding
1 (8-ounce) carton sour cream
¾ cup oil

3 eggs
¾ cup water
1 (6-ounce) package milk
   chocolate chips

In a large bowl, blend all ingredients except chocolate chips. Beat for 4 minutes. Fold in the chips. Pour into a well-greased and floured Bundt pan. Bake at 350° for 50 minutes. Allow cake to cool completely before removing from pan. Yields 12–16 servings.

Our Country Cookin'

Aunt Susan's Red Earth Cake

This cake is reputed to have been the favorite of the late Sam Walton.

½ cup shortening
1½ cups sugar
1 egg
4 tablespoons cocoa
1 teaspoon red food coloring
2 tablespoons strong hot
  coffee

2 cups cake flour
1 teaspoon salt
1 teaspoon soda
1 cup buttermilk
1 teaspoon vanilla

Cream the shortening and sugar until they are light and fluffy. Blend in the egg, which has been beaten until it is light and foamy. Mix the cocoa, coloring and hot coffee to make a smooth paste. Stir this into the mixture. Sift the flour and measure it, then sift it again with the salt and soda. Add a bit of the measured flour to the mixture, then alternately add buttermilk and flour, folding and beating it lightly after each addition. Add the vanilla. Turn into two 8-inch pans, 2 inches deep, lined on the bottom with buttered wax paper. Bake in a moderate oven, 375°, for 30–35 minutes.

Spiced with Wit

A Chocolate-Raspberry Cake

½ cup unsweetened cocoa
  powder
1 cup boiling water
½ cup butter
2 cups sifted all-purpose flour
2 cups sugar
1½ teaspoons baking soda

½ teaspoon salt
2 large eggs
½ cup sour cream
1 teaspoon vanilla flavoring
Raspberry liqueur
Raspberry preserves
  (seedless)

Preheat oven to 350°. Prepare a 9-inch spring-form pan by coating with a vegetable spray and dusting with a small amount of flour, or use a heart-shaped pan, or a 9-inch tube pan.

In the large bowl of an electric mixer, combine the cocoa powder with boiling water and butter. Stir until the butter is melted, and set aside to cool. Resift the flour with the sugar, baking soda, and salt. Add the flour mixture slowly to the cooled cocoa mixture, stirring constantly to avoid spattering; as the mixture

(continued)

(A Chocolate-Raspberry Cake continued)

thickens, increase speed to medium high. Stir in the eggs one at a time, incorporating each completely. Add the sour cream and vanilla flavoring. Scrape down the sides of the bowl and continue stirring until the batter is smooth. Pour into the prepared pan and bake about 45 minutes. Test for doneness with a cake tester, and if not done, bake 5–10 more minutes. Remove cake from oven and cool on a wire rack removing sides of spring-form pan.

When the cake is cooled, slice into 3 layers. Measure the depth of the cake and place toothpicks around the cake to assist in making the layers even when slicing. Brush each layer with raspberry liqueur quite thoroughly—it is best to use a feather brush. Spread the raspberry preserves or jam over the layers. Then top each layer with the Chocolate Granache as they are stacked.

CHOCOLATE GRANACHE:

9 ounces semi-sweet chocolate	**1 cup heavy cream**

Combine the semi-sweet chocolate (chips are fine) with hot cream. When heating the cream, stir constantly until hot, add the chocolate chips and blend until melted. Remove from burner and let cool, stirring occasionally. Spread over each layer as they are stacked and then frost the complete cake. Place in refrigerator until ready to serve. If fresh raspberries are available, top the cake with these luscious little berries.

Mary's Recipe Box

The Kingfisher Centennial Brick Wall near the county courthouse honors settlers who made the 1889 Land Run.

Prize Winning Johnson Special Chocolate Cake

Always won ribbons at the State Fairs. The best of the best!

2 cups sugar
½ cup butter or margarine,
  softened
2 eggs
2 cups flour
1 teaspoon baking soda
1 teaspoon salt

½ cup cocoa
½ cup sour milk or buttermilk
  (1 teaspoon lemon juice or
  vinegar in milk)
1 teaspoon vanilla
1 cup hot water

Preheat oven to 350°. Sift sugar. Beat butter or margarine until soft. Add the sugar gradually. Blend these ingredients until they are creamy. Beat in eggs. Sift flour before measuring. Resift with baking soda, salt, and cocoa. Add the flour mixture in 3 parts to the butter mixture alternately with ⅓ of sour milk or buttermilk. Lightly beat the batter after each addition until it is smooth. Add vanilla and hot water. Grease 2 (8-inch) layer cake pans with Crisco and then flour lightly. Bake the layers in a 350° oven for about 45 minutes or until done. Top with Mocha Icing.

Variation: If you want a richer cake, use ¾ cup butter instead of ½ cup and use soured cream instead of soured milk.

Hint: After taking cake pans out of oven, put on damp cloth on counter for 5 minutes. Run knife around edges and put cake pans on wire rack for 5 minutes or more before removing cakes.

AWARD WINNING MOCHA ICING:

The best chocolate icing you will ever taste!

1 box powdered sugar
½ cup cocoa
1 teaspoon vanilla
3 tablespoons cream (or milk)

3 tablespoons coffee
2 tablespoons melted butter
4 ounces Philadelphia cream
  cheese, softened

Combine powdered sugar and cocoa. Add slowly, stirring constantly, vanilla, cream, coffee, and melted butter. Add cream cheese. Mix until smooth. Use more coffee if needed to make icing the right consistency to spread.

Four Generations of Johnson Family Favorites

Lemon Chiffon Cake

2¼ cups sifted cake flour
1½ cups sugar
3 teaspoons baking powder
½ teaspoon salt
5 egg yolks
⅓ cup oil

½ cup water
2 teaspoons lemon extract
1 teaspoon vanilla
8 egg whites, stiffly beaten
½ teaspoon cream of tartar

Sift the cake flour, then sift another 3 times with the sugar, baking powder, and salt. Make well in bowl of dry ingredients and add in this order: yolks, oil, water, lemon extract, and vanilla. Beat until smooth and pour over and fold into 8 egg whites, which have been stiffly beaten with cream of tartar. Pour into an ungreased tube pan and bake at 325° for 55 minutes and 350° for 10–15 minutes. Invert pan on funnel or soft drink bottle until completely cool. Remove from pan and glaze with lemon glaze or serve with sweetened fruit or whipped cream.

Sisters Two and Family Too

Supreme Cheesecake

CRUST:

1 cup flour	½ cup butter, softened
¼ cup sugar	1 egg yolk
1 teaspoon grated lemon peel	¼ teaspoon vanilla
1 teaspoon grated orange peel	

Combine first 4 ingredients. Cut in butter till mixture is crumbly. Add egg yolk and vanilla. Blend well and pat ⅓ of dough on bottom only of 9-inch spring-form pan. (Dough is easier to handle if chilled about 90 minutes before handling.) Bake in 400° oven about 8 minutes or until light brown. Cool. Pat remaining dough 1¾ inches up sides of pan.

FILLING:

5 (8-ounce) packages cream cheese	1¾ cups sugar
¼ teaspoon vanilla	3 tablespoons flour
1½ teaspoons grated lemon peel	5 eggs
1½ teaspoons grated orange peel	2 egg yolks
	¼ cup whipping cream

Let cream cheese stand at room temperature to soften. Beat cream cheese, vanilla, and peels until creamy. Mix sugar and flour, blending well with cheese. Add eggs and yolks, one at a time, beating just to blend. Add whipping cream. Pour into pan and bake at 450° for 12 minutes. Reduce heat to 300° and bake 55 minutes. Turn oven off and leave in oven with oven door slightly open for 1 hour. Remove and cool completely on wire rack. Loosen sides with knife after ½ hour. Refrigerate at least 2 hours before removing sides and serving.

Sisters Two and Family Too

Woodward's Plains Indians and Pioneers Museum is ranked as one of the top five small museums in the nation.

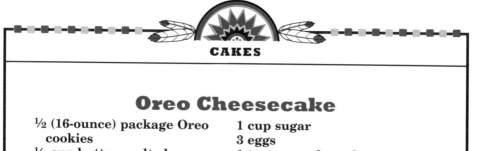

Oreo Cheesecake

½ (16-ounce) package Oreo
 cookies
¼ cup butter, melted
24 ounces cream cheese,
 softened

1 cup sugar
3 eggs
1 teaspoon almond extract
½ cup chocolate chips, melted
½ cup whipping cream

Pulverize cookies in blender. Reserve ½ cup crumbs for topping. Add melted butter to cookies in blender container. Process until moistened. Press into 9-inch spring-form pan. Beat cream cheese, sugar, eggs, and almond flavoring in mixer bowl until smooth. Pour into prepared pan. Bake at 350° for 45 minutes. Chill completely. Remove cheesecake from pan. Melt chocolate chips in whipping cream in saucepan over low heat, stirring constantly. Drizzle over cheesecake. Sprinkle with reserved cookie crumbs. Yields 8 servings.

Approx Per Serving: Cal 718; T Fat 52g; Cal from Fat 64%; Prot 11g; Carbo 55g; Fiber 1g; Chol 209mg; Sod 467mg.

The Pioneer Chef

Strawberry Sundae Cheesecake

CRUST:

½ stick margarine
 (4 tablespoons)

2 cups crushed graham
 cracker crumbs

Melt margarine in 9x13-inch pan. Add crumbs and mix well. Pat into bottom of pan.

CHEESECAKE:

2 cups water
2 (3-ounce) boxes wild
 strawberry gelatin

2 cups frozen sweetened
 strawberries (crushed) and
 juice

Heat water to boiling; add gelatin and stir till dissolved. Add frozen strawberries with juice to gelatin. Chill till set.

1 (8-ounce) package cream
 cheese, softened

⅔ cup sugar
1 large container Cool Whip

Mix until smooth. Add to gelatin mixture and mix with mixer. Fold in large container of Cool Whip. Pour over crust. Chill approximately 2 hours or till set.

Spring Creek Club

Strawberry Marbled Cheesecake

SAUCE:

1 (10-ounce) package frozen strawberries in syrup, thawed

1½ teaspoons cornstarch
Red food coloring (optional)

In blender container, combine strawberries and cornstarch; blend until smooth. In heavy saucepan, over medium heat, cook and stir until thickened. Add food coloring if desired. Reserve ⅓ cup sauce; cool. Chill remaining sauce.

1¼ cups graham cracker crumbs
¼ cup sugar
⅓ cup margarine or butter, melted
3 (8-ounce) packages cream cheese, softened

1 (14-ounce) can sweetened condensed milk (not evaporated milk)
3 eggs
¼ cup lemon juice from concentrate

Preheat oven to 300°. Combine crumbs, sugar, and margarine; press on bottom of 9-inch spring-form pan. In mixer bowl, beat cheese until fluffy. Gradually beat in sweetened condensed milk until smooth. Add eggs and lemon juice; mix well. Spoon half the batter into prepared pan. Spoon half the reserved strawberry sauce in small amounts over batter. Repeat, ending with sauce. With knife, cut through batter to marble. Bake 50 minutes or until center is set. Cool. Chill. Remove side of spring-form. Serve with chilled strawberry sauce. Refrigerate leftovers.

Watonga Cheese Festival Cookbook 17th Edition

Christmas Cake Dessert

1 package raspberry Jell-O
1 package lime Jell-O
2 packages orange Jell-O
1 pint whipping cream
1 tablespoon sugar

1 teaspoon vanilla
½ cup chopped nuts
1 small bottle maraschino
   cherries
4 cups angel food cake

Fix lime and raspberry Jell-O in separate loaf pans. Let set all night. Mix the orange Jell-O the following day and let congeal to whipping consistency. Whip orange Jell-O. Whip cream with sugar and vanilla. Whip whipping cream into orange Jell-O. Add nuts, cherries and angel food cake. Cube lime and raspberry Jell-O and fold into all the rest.

Thunderbird Cookers of AT&T

Pineapple Ice Box Cake

½ cup pineapple juice
1 package lemon gelatin
1½ cups sugar
½ pound butter, softened

4 eggs, separated
1 cup pineapple (drained)
1 cup chopped pecans
¾ pound vanilla wafers

Heat pineapple juice to boiling point. Add gelatin and stir until dissolved. Set aside to cool. Cream sugar and butter, add well-beaten egg yolks, pineapple, gelatin and nuts. Beat egg whites until stiff and fold in. Roll vanilla wafers on dough board with a rolling pin until they are crumbs. Put half the crumbs in flat pan or glass tray about 8x10 inches. Add fruit mixture. Spread last half of crumbs on top and pat down gently. Leave in ice box 24 hours.

Seems Like I Done It This A-Way I

The Cultural Center and Indian Museum in Ponca City contains a priceless collection of artifacts representing more than 30 tribes from across the United States.

Coconut Torte with Butter Sauce

½ cup butter, softened
1 cup sugar (minus 1
  tablespoon)
4 egg whites

1 (7-ounce) package moist,
  shredded coconut
1 teaspoon vanilla

Cream the butter and sugar until light and add coconut. Fold into stiffly beaten egg whites and add vanilla. Pour into shallow 9x13-inch pan. Set pan in hot water and bake in 325° oven for 45 minutes. Let cool and cut into squares.

BUTTER SAUCE:

½ cup butter, softened
1 cup sugar (minus 1
  tablespoon)
4 egg yolks

1 whole egg, beaten
1 teaspoon vanilla
1½ jiggers brandy (optional)
Dash of nutmeg

Combine butter and sugar as above and stir in egg yolks and beaten egg. Cook in double boiler until thick, stirring constantly. Strain to remove any bits of egg white. Stir in remaining ingredients. Serve over torte with your favorite ice cream. Serves 8–10 persons.

Cleora's Kitchens

On April 22, 1889, men, women and children raced across the plains to stake a homestead claim on the newly opened Indian Territory. The University of Oklahoma adopted the nickname that became associated with the settlers who arrived "sooner" than the others.

Cookies and Candies

COURTESY OF OKLAHOMA TOURISM

Nestled in the Arbuckle Mountains near Davis, Oklahoma, lies a natural treasure, Turner Falls Park. Many springs from the mountains form Honey Creek, which cascades down a seventy-seven foot fall to a natural swimming pool making the majestic Turner Falls the largest waterfall in Oklahoma.

Pecan Diamonds

Diamonds are still a girl's best friend!

½ cup butter, well chilled ½ cup ice water
1½ cups flour

Using pastry blender, cut butter into flour until mixture resembles coarse meal. Add water and toss lightly with fork. Gather dough into ball, wrap in plastic, and refrigerate 1 hour. Grease and flour 9x13-inch baking pan, not a cookie sheet. Roll dough out on lightly floured surface to about 10x14-inch rectangle. Fit into prepared pan; dough will come about half-way up sides. Pierce dough with a fork and chill. Preheat oven to 400°.

FILLING:

1½ cups light brown sugar, ⅓ cup sugar
  firmly packed 1 pound chopped pecans or
1 cup butter   pecan pieces
½ cup honey ½ cup whipping cream

Bring brown sugar, butter, honey, and sugar to boil in heavy saucepan over medium heat, stirring constantly. Boil until thick and dark, about 4 minutes, continuing to stir. Remove from heat. Stir in pecans. Blend in cream. Pour the mixture over dough in the pan. Bake in the preheated oven until edges of crust are golden, about 25 minutes. Cool completely. Cut into 1-inch strips lengthwise then horizontally to create diamond shapes. Serve at room temperature. Makes 80 diamonds.

Applause!

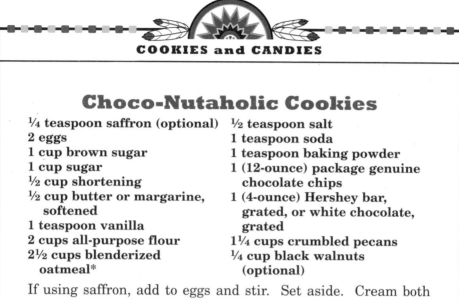

Choco-Nutaholic Cookies

¼ teaspoon saffron (optional)
2 eggs
1 cup brown sugar
1 cup sugar
½ cup shortening
½ cup butter or margarine,
  softened
1 teaspoon vanilla
2 cups all-purpose flour
2½ cups blenderized
  oatmeal*

½ teaspoon salt
1 teaspoon soda
1 teaspoon baking powder
1 (12-ounce) package genuine
  chocolate chips
1 (4-ounce) Hershey bar,
  grated, or white chocolate,
  grated
1¼ cups crumbled pecans
¼ cup black walnuts
  (optional)

If using saffron, add to eggs and stir. Set aside. Cream both sugars, shortening, butter. Add eggs and vanilla. Mix in flour, blenderized oatmeal, salt, soda, and baking powder until thoroughly moistened. Add in the chocolates and nuts. Stir thoroughly. Roll into balls and place about 2 inches apart on a greased cookie sheet. Bake for 11 minutes at 375°. Cool and eat (or eat without cooling—chocolate can burn your mouth, but fresh hot cookies may be worth the risk). This recipe makes about 4 dozen cookies unless you eat too much raw cookie dough.

*Measure oatmeal and blend in a blender until it turns to a fine powder. Food-processed oatmeal also works.

Option: If you can find hican nuts (a hickory and pecan cross), they add a special nutty flavor. Replace ¼ cup of the pecans with hicans. Also, omit the black walnuts if you can't find any.

When a Man's Fancy Turns to Cooking

The only place in the world to dig for selenite hourglass crystals is in Cherokee, gateway to the great Salt Plains. The Great Salt Plains National Wildlife Refuge is a resting stop for the elusive Whooping Crane. Bald Eagles, Golden Eagles, pelicans, herons, egrets, and Sandhill Cranes also frequent the 32,000-acre refuge as does the endangered Inland Least Tern.

White Chip Orange Cream Cookies

2¼ cups all-purpose flour
¾ teaspoon baking soda
½ teaspoon salt
1 cup butter or margarine, softened
½ cup packed light brown sugar
½ cup granulated sugar
1 egg
2–3 teaspoons grated orange peel
1 (12-ounce) package Toll House Premier White morsels

Combine flour, baking soda, and salt in small bowl. Beat butter, and sugars in large mixer bowl until creamy. Beat in egg and orange peel. Gradually beat in flour mixture. Stir in morsels. Drop dough by rounded tablespoonfuls onto ungreased baking sheets. Bake in a 350° oven for 10–12 minutes or until edges are light golden brown. Let stand for 2 minutes; remove to wire racks to cool completely.

Country Cooking

Giant Oatmeal Spice Cookies

1½ cups flour
½ teaspoon soda
½ teaspoon salt
2 teaspoons cinnamon
2 teaspoons cloves
2 teaspoons allspice
1 teaspoon ginger
1 cup soft margarine
1 cup sugar
1 cup brown sugar
2 eggs
1 teaspoon vanilla
3 cups quick-cooking oats, uncooked
1 cup chopped nuts

Combine flour, soda, salt, and spices; set aside. Combine margarine and sugars, creaming well; beat in eggs and vanilla. Add flour mixture, mixing well. Stir in oats; add nuts. Drop dough by ¼-cup measure 5 inches apart onto lightly greased cookie sheets. Bake at 375° for 12–14 minutes or until lightly browned. Cool slightly on cookie sheets; remove to wire rack or wax paper to cool completely.

Recipes and Remembrances

Cowboy Cookies

1 cup shortening
1 cup white sugar
1 cup brown sugar
2 eggs
2 cups sifted flour
½ teaspoon salt
1 teaspoon soda

½ teaspoon baking powder
1 teaspoon vanilla
1 package semi-sweet
   chocolate chips or
   butterscotch chips
2 cups rolled oats (quick)

Cream shortening and sugars. Add eggs and beat. Sift flour, salt, soda, and baking powder together and add to creamed mixture. Add vanilla, chips, and oatmeal. Drop by teaspoon on cookie sheets. Bake at 350° for 15 minutes.

Company Fare I

Potato Chip Cookies

2 cups margarine, softened
1 cup sugar
3½ cups flour

1 teaspoon vanilla extract
1 cup crushed potato chips
¼ cup confectioners' sugar

Cream margarine and sugar in mixer bowl until light and fluffy. Add flour and vanilla; mix well. Add crushed potato chips gradually, mixing well after each addition. Drop by teaspoonfuls onto ungreased cookie sheet. Bake at 350° for 15 minutes or until golden brown. Cool on wire rack. Sprinkle with confectioners' sugar. Yields 36 servings.

Approx Per Serving: Cal 168; T Fat 11g; Cal from Fat 57%; Prot 1g; Carbo 17g; Fiber <1g; Chol 0mg; Sod 127mg.

The Pioneer Chef

Apricot Brandy Cookies

These are especially good for the Christmas holidays.

½ cup sugar	1½ cups flour
⅓ cup butter, softened	1½ teaspoons soda
2 eggs, beaten	½ teaspoon salt
1 pound chopped dates	1½ tablespoons sweet milk
1 pound candied cherries	⅓ cup apricot brandy
1 pound candied pineapple	1 pound whole pecans

Cream sugar and butter. Add eggs. Flour fruits with half of the flour. Add remaining flour to egg mixture. Add soda, salt, milk, brandy, and nuts. Mix well. Drop on well-greased cookie sheet. Bake in 300° oven for about 25 minutes. When cool, store in airtight container. Keeps a long time. Rum may be substituted for the brandy.

Sisters Two and Family Too

Oatmeal Chews

1 cup butter, softened	2 cups all-purpose flour
1 cup sugar	2 teaspoons baking soda
1 cup brown sugar, firmly packed	½ teaspoon baking powder
2 eggs	1½ cups old-fashioned oats
1 teaspoon pure vanilla extract	½ cup chopped pecans
	½ cup chocolate chips
	1½ cups flaked coconut

In large bowl cream butter with both sugars. Add eggs and vanilla; mix well. In small bowl combine flour, soda, and baking powder; add to butter mixture. Stir in oats, pecans, and chocolate chips. Refrigerate one hour. Roll into walnut-size balls; roll lightly in coconut. Place on lightly buttered cookie sheet; flatten with fork. Preheat oven to 350°; bake 8 minutes. For best results, bake one sheet of cookies at a time on center rack of oven. Yields 5 dozen.

Hint: For variety, substitute raisins for the chocolate chips.

Sounds Delicious!

Peanut Butter Cookies

No flour. Easy and delicious!

1 egg
1 cup sugar
1 teaspoon baking soda

1 cup creamy or chunky
  peanut butter

Cream egg and sugar. Stir in baking soda. Fold in peanut butter. Roll into 36 balls; place on cookie sheet and crease top of balls with fork. Bake for 10 minutes at 350°.

Dine with the Angels

Peanut Kisses

1¾ cups flour
1 teaspoon soda
½ teaspoon salt
½ cup sugar
2 tablespoons milk
½ cup brown sugar

½ cup shortening
½ cup peanut butter
1 egg
1 teaspoon vanilla
48 candy kisses (Hershey's
  chocolate)

Combine all ingredients except candy kisses in large bowl. Mix at lowest speed until dough forms. Shape dough into balls using a rounded teaspoon. Place on ungreased cookie sheet. Bake at 375° for 5–6 minutes. Remove from oven and place candy kiss in center of each; return to oven for 5–6 minutes until chocolate kiss begins to brown on top. Cool on wire rack. These keep very well.

Company Fare II

Black-Eyed Susans

½ cup butter or margarine
(softened)
½ cup sugar
½ cup firmly packed brown
sugar
1 egg
1½ tablespoons warm water
1 teaspoon vanilla

1 cup peanut butter,
creamy—not crunchy
1½ cups flour
½ teaspoon salt
½ teaspoon soda
½ cup semi-sweet chocolate
chips

Combine butter and sugars, creaming until light and fluffy; add egg, warm water, vanilla, and peanut butter. Beat, mixing well. Combine dry ingredients. Add to creamed mixture, mixing well. Using a cookie press with a flower-shaped disc, press dough onto lightly greased cookie sheet. Place a chocolate chip in the center of each flower. Bake at 350° for 8 minutes or until lightly browned. Remove to wire racks and cool. Chill 30 minutes to firm up centers. Yields about 10 dozen cookies.

Court Clerk's Bar and Grill

Molasses Cookies

Spicy and old fashioned.

3½ cups all-purpose flour
2 teaspoons soda
1 teaspoon cinnamon
½ teaspoon salt
1 cup shortening

1 cup molasses
⅔ cup brown sugar, firmly
packed
1 cup thick, sour milk or
buttermilk

First grease 1 or 2 baking sheets to have handy. Sift and measure flour; add soda, cinnamon and salt. Sift again and set aside. Cream shortening. Blend in sugar gradually, then the molasses and mix well. Mix in about ⅓ of the flour, then ½ of the buttermilk; repeat; finish blending in the remaining flour. Drop rounded tablespoons on baking sheet about 1½ inches apart. Spread slightly with back of spoon.

Bake in preheated oven until lightly brown. Cool thoroughly before storing in covered container. Baking time, 12–15 minutes. Baking temperature 375°.

Seems Like I Done It This A-Way II

Ginger Strips

¾ cup shortening
1 cup sugar
1 egg, beaten
¼ cup molasses
2 cups flour
½ teaspoon salt

2 teaspoons baking soda
½ teaspoon cinnamon
¼ teaspoon ground ginger
¼ teaspoon ground cloves
2 tablespoons sugar

Cream shortening, 1 cup sugar, and egg in mixer bowl until light and fluffy. Stir in molasses. Combine flour, salt, baking soda, cinnamon, ginger, and cloves. Add to creamed mixture, beating well. Divide dough into 6 equal portions. Shape into ¼x12-inch rolls. Place on 2 cookie sheets. Brush tops with water; sprinkle with remaining 2 tablespoons sugar. Bake at 350° for 12 minutes. Cool and slice. Yields 36 servings.

Approx per serving: Cal 91; Prot 1g; Carbo 12g; Fiber <1g; T Fat 5g; 49% Cal from Fat; Chol 6mg; Sod 79mg.

Discover Oklahoma Cookin'

Landrun Brownies

2 cups crushed graham
  crackers
½ cup chopped pecans
1 (6-ounce) package
  semi-sweet chocolate chips
1 cup butterscotch chips,
  optional

1 cup shredded coconut,
  optional
1 (14-ounce) can sweetened
  condensed milk
½ cup powdered sugar,
  optional

Preheat oven to 350°. Mix together all ingredients except powdered sugar and pour into a well-greased 8x8-inch pan. Bake for 30 minutes. Remove from oven and cool 10 minutes. Cut into squares and remove from pan. Powdered sugar may be sprinkled on top if desired. Yields 10 brownies.

Cafe Oklahoma

Glazed Honey Bars

1 cup sugar
2 cups flour
½ cup cooking oil
½ teaspoon salt
½ cup honey

1 egg
1 teaspoon soda
1 teaspoon cinnamon
1 cup nuts

Mix and press in greased cookie sheet. Cook 12 minutes at 350°. While hot, glaze.

GLAZE:
1 cup powdered sugar
2 tablespoons real
  mayonnaise

½ teaspoon vanilla
1 tablespoon water

Country Cooking

Quick 'n' Chewy Crescent Bars

1 (8-ounce) can crescent
  dinner rolls
1 (14-ounce) can sweetened
  condensed milk

1 (9.9-ounce) package
  coconut almond or coconut
  pecan frosting mix
¼ cup margarine, melted

Preheat oven to 400°. Unroll crescent dough; place rectangles in ungreased 15x10-inch jelly roll pan. Gently press dough to cover bottom of pan; seal perforations. Pour condensed milk evenly over dough. Sprinkle with frosting mix. Drizzle with margarine. Bake for 12–15 minutes until golden brown. Cool. Cut into bars. Makes 3–4 dozen bars.

Company Fare II

Nanaimo Bars

These are made in 3 layers. Grease a 9-inch square pan and set aside.

CRUMB MIXTURE:

½ cup (¼ pound) unsalted
 butter
¼ cup sugar
¼ cup cocoa
1 teaspoon vanilla
1 egg

¼ teaspoon salt
1½ cups (6 ounces) graham
 cracker crumbs
¾ cup (2 ounces) flaked
 coconut
½ cup chopped pecans

In heavy saucepan, combine first 6 ingredients and cook over low heat, stirring constantly until mixture coats a spoon. Stir in crumbs, coconut, and pecans. Place in greased pan and press evenly.

FILLING:

½ cup (¼ pound) unsalted
 butter, softened
1 (3-ounce) package cream
 cheese, softened

2 tablespoons instant vanilla
 pudding
1 cup confectioners' sugar
2 tablespoons milk

Cream butter, cheese, and pudding. Beat in confectioners' sugar and milk. Spread over crumb mixture. Refrigerate 30 minutes or until pudding mixture is firm.

GLAZE:

4 squares semi-sweet
 chocolate

1 tablespoon unsalted butter

Can be made in microwave or double boiler. Melt semi-sweet chocolate with unsalted butter. Spread over pudding layer. Refrigerate until firm. Cut into 1 or 1½-inch squares. Store in refrigerator.

Thunderbird Cookers of AT&T

Held at different towns each year, the Great Western Cattle Drive in northwest Oklahoma offers an exciting vacation adventure. Seasoned cattlehands ride along with the greenhorns and city slickers in an "Old West Cattle Drive" straight out of the 1800s. Proceeds help restore historic sites in Dewey County.

Neiman-Marcus Bars

1 egg, beaten
1 yellow cake mix
½ cup butter, melted
1 (8-ounce) package cream
cheese, softened

1 pound powdered sugar
2 eggs, beaten
1 cup chopped nuts
1 cup flaked coconut

Mix first 3 ingredients well and pat into the bottom of a 9x13-inch pan. Mix remaining ingredients well and spread over cake mixture. Bake at 325° for 45 minutes.

Centennial Cookbook

Cheesecake Cookies

Absolutely fabulous!

1 cup real butter, softened
2 (3-ounce) packages cream
cheese, softened

2 cups sugar
2 cups flour
1 cup chopped pecans

Preheat oven to 350°. Cream together butter and cream cheese; add sugar, beating until light and fluffy. Add flour and beat well. Stir in pecans. Drop by teaspoonful onto ungreased cookie sheet and bake for 12 minutes. Yields 2 dozen.

Cafe Oklahoma

Chess Squares

1 box butter recipe yellow
cake mix
½ cup margarine
1 egg
1 (8-ounce) package cream
cheese, softened

1 (1-pound) box powdered
sugar
3 eggs

Combine cake mix, margarine, and egg; press into a greased and floured 9x13-inch pan. Combine remaining ingredients and pour over crust. Bake at 350° for 45 minutes. Cool and cut into squares. Yields 2 dozen squares.

Variation: Add 1 cup flaked coconut and ½ cup chopped pecans to cream cheese mixture.

Our Country Cookin'

Peppernuts

1½ cups sugar
¾ cup shortening
2 eggs
½ cup molasses
4–6 cups flour
¼ teaspoon cloves

¼ teaspoon allspice
1 teaspoon cinnamon
¾ teaspoon black pepper
1 teaspoon soda
1 teaspoon salt
½ cup sour milk

Cream shortening and sugar. Add eggs and molasses. Add the flour and spices along with the sour milk. Add enough flour so dough will not be sticky. Chill well and roll out. Cut and bake at 325° until light brown.

Home Cookin' Is a Family Affair

Coconut Macaroons

2 ounces Baker's chocolate
2 cans Baker's coconut (½ pound)

1 can Eagle Brand Milk
1 cup chopped nuts
½ cup flour

Melt chocolate in a double boiler. Add remaining ingredients. Drop from teaspoon on greased cookie sheet. Bake 20 minutes in 275° oven.

Company Fare II

Hello Dolly

¼ pound butter
1 cup graham cracker or vanilla wafer crumbs
1 (6-ounce) package chocolate chips
1 (6-ounce) package butterscotch chips

1 cup flaked coconut
1 cup chopped English walnuts
1 can Eagle Brand Milk

Melt butter in a 9x12x2-inch pan. Add each ingredient one at a time and do not stir. Bake at 325° for 20–25 minutes. Cool, cut to desired size and place on rack.

Company Fare I

Rice Krispies Marshmallow Treats

¼ cup margarine or butter
1 (10-ounce) package regular
  marshmallows or 4 cups
  miniature marshmallows

6 cups Kellogg's Rice
  Krispies

Melt margarine in large saucepan over low heat. Add marshmallows and stir until completely melted. Cook over low heat 3 minutes longer, stirring constantly. Remove from heat. Add Rice Krispies. Stir until well coated. Using buttered spatula or wax paper, press mixture evenly into buttered 13x9x2-inch pan. Cut into squares when cool. Yields 24 squares.

Variations: Stir in ¼ cup peanut butter into marshmallows before adding cereal. Or add 1 cup raisins with Rice Krispies.

Seems Like I Done It This A-Way III

Crispy Candy Bars

1 cup sugar
1 cup syrup, light, dark or
  pancake syrup
1 cup peanut butter

6 cups Rice Krispies
6 ounces chocolate chips
6 ounces butterscotch chips

In a large saucepan, combine sugar and syrup. Bring to a boil over medium heat. Remove from heat; add peanut butter. Mix well. Add Rice Krispies; stir with a spoon until cereal is well coated. Press into a well-buttered 9x13-inch pan. In a warm oven or microwave, melt together the chocolate and butterscotch chips. Stir until well blended. Spread over top of candy. Chill until topping is set. Cut in squares.

The candy does not require refrigeration after topping has hardened. You may want to cut just what will be eaten at that time.

Note: I usually serve these bars as cookies. I use about ⅔ cup each chocolate and butterscotch chips. This makes a thinner topping and requires more spreading.

Something Special Cookbook

Puppy Chow for People

1 stick margarine
1 cup peanut butter
1 (12-ounce) package
  semi-sweet chocolate chips
12 ounces Crispix cereal
3 cups powdered sugar

Melt first 3 ingredients together. Pour over cereal. Sprinkle powdered sugar over mixture. Spread out on wax paper to dry (about 5 minutes).

Sequoyah's Cookin'

Butterscotch Crunchies

1 (12-ounce) package
  butterscotch morsels
6 ounces (2 cups) chow mein
  noodles
1 cup chopped pecans

Melt butterscotch morsels in a heavy pan over a low flame. Stir gently to blend. Stir in noodles and nuts until just blended and coated. Spoon mixture by teaspoons onto wax paper. Cool completely.

Old and New

Popcorn Balls

¼ cup unpopped popcorn
2 tablespoons oil
½ cup sugar
½ cup light corn syrup
½ cup peanut butter
½ teaspoon vanilla

Pop popcorn and put in large bowl. Combine sugar and syrup into saucepan; cook, stirring constantly, until mixture comes to a full boil. Remove from heat and stir in peanut butter and vanilla. Pour over corn, mixing gently. Form into balls.

Old and New

Rocky Road Fudge Bars

2 (1-ounce) squares
unsweetened chocolate,
divided
1 cup margarine, divided
1½ cups granulated sugar
1 cup plus 2 tablespoons
all-purpose flour
1¼ cups chopped walnuts
1 teaspoon baking powder
2½ teaspoons vanilla

3 eggs
1 (8-ounce) package cream
cheese, softened
1 cup semi-sweet chocolate
chips
2 cups miniature
marshmallows
¼ cup milk
3 cups powdered sugar

Preheat oven to 350°. Spray a 13x9-inch pan with cooking spray. In medium saucepan, over medium heat, melt 1 square of the chocolate and ½ cup margarine. Remove and blend in 1 cup granulated sugar, 1 cup flour, 1 cup nuts, baking powder, 1 teaspoon vanilla and 2 eggs. Spread in pan. In a large bowl with mixer on high, blend 6 ounces of the cream cheese (reserve 2 ounces), ½ cup granulated sugar, 2 tablespoons flour, ¼ cup margarine, 1 egg, and ½ teaspoon vanilla. Spread over batter in pan. Mix together ¼ cup nuts and chocolate chips. Sprinkle over batter. Bake 25 minutes. Remove from oven and sprinkle marshmallows over top. Bake another 2 minutes.

In medium saucepan, over low heat, melt ¼ cup margarine, 1 square chocolate, 2 ounces cream cheese and ¼ cup milk. Remove from heat and add powdered sugar and remaining 1 teaspoon vanilla. Drizzle over top of marshmallows. Swirl layers together. Chill several hours before cutting.

Kitchen Klatter Keepsakes

Goodwell is the Saddle Bronc Capital of the World. It is also the home of Oklahoma Panhandle State University and the No Man's Land Historical Museum.

Baked Fudge

2 eggs
1 cup sugar
1 heaping tablespoon cocoa
½ cup butter, melted

3 level tablespoons flour
1 cup chopped pecans
½ teaspoon vanilla

Beat eggs well. Mix sugar and cocoa and add to eggs. Blend well and add melted butter, flour, nuts, and vanilla. Grease and flour 8x8-inch pan. Pour mixture in pan and put in pan of warm water. Bake at 350° for 45 minutes. When cool, refrigerate overnight. This freezes well. It may be served with whipped cream if desired.

Cookbook of Treasured Recipes

Orange Balls

½ cup margarine, softened
1 (1-pound) box powdered
  sugar
1 (6-ounce) can frozen orange
  juice concentrate, thawed
½ cup flaked coconut

½ cup chopped nuts
1 (12-ounce) box vanilla
  wafers, finely crushed
Powdered sugar, ground nuts,
  or fine coconut

Cream margarine and powdered sugar. Add orange juice, nuts and coconut gradually. Blend in crushed vanilla wafers. Form 1-inch balls and roll in powdered sugar, nuts, or coconut. Store in tin or covered container. Yields 4 dozen balls.

Our Country Cookin'

Tiger Butter

1 pound white almond bark
   coating
12 ounces (1 cup) peanut
   butter

2⅓ cups chocolate chips

Over hot water, or in the microwave, melt together almond bark and peanut butter. While melting, butter a jelly roll pan, or if you want thicker pieces of candy, use a 9x13-inch pan. Stir peanut butter mixture until well blended. Pour into prepared pan. Melt chocolate chips in the same container used to melt first mixture. Pour over the peanut butter layer. Swirl mixture together with a knife. Chill well. Cut into small squares.

Note: This candy may be made in any amount. I usually make about ¼ recipe and pour it into a small pan and cut it in chunks.

Something Special Cookbook

Chocolate Almond Bark Crunch

10–12 ounces chocolate
   almond bark
2 tablespoons peanut butter

1 cup chopped nuts
1 cup marshmallows
1½ cups Rice Krispies

Melt almond bark and peanut butter together in a large bowl. Add nuts, marshmallows, and Rice Krispies. Stir and drop by spoonfuls onto buttered foil.

Country Cooking

Cranberry Surprise

Wow! A different taste experience!

1 (1-pound) package almond bark

1 (1-pound) package fresh cranberries

Melt almond bark in microwave on low or in double boiler. Drop dry, fresh cranberries into melted bark a few at a time. Remove to wax paper, individually, and let harden. Delicious as hors d'oeuvres, candy or a snack.

Stir Ups

Peanut Butter Balls

1 stick butter or margarine
2 cups peanut butter
2 pounds powdered sugar, sifted

3 teaspoons vanilla
¼ pound paraffin
1 (6-ounce) package semi-sweet chocolate chips

Soften butter and add peanut butter. Mix well. Add sugar and vanilla. Roll into small balls and refrigerate overnight. Melt chocolate chips and paraffin in top of double boiler. Dip balls in chocolate mixture and place on wax paper.

Kitchen Klatter Keepsakes

Oklahoma is the only state in the union to have an "official" state meal. It includes: fried okra, squash, cornbread, barbecue pork, biscuits, sausage and gravy, grits, corn, strawberries, chicken fried steak, pecan pie, and black-eyed peas. This is based on popular local foods, past and present. There are no "official" recipes.

Aunt Bill's Brown Candy

This was the favorite recipe of a pioneer Oklahoman, who stood for all the big things which our job of homemaker implies.

FULL RECIPE:

6 cups white sugar, divided
2 cups cream (or whole milk)
¼ teaspoon soda
½ cup butter

1 teaspoon vanilla
4 cups broken nuts
(preferably pecans)

To begin with, let me tell you that this recipe makes more than 3 pounds of candy, so you see it is not as expensive as it may seem. You will find it much easier to manage if two of you are able to make it together, but this is not necessary, as I've made loads of it alone. The recipe halves perfectly.

1. Pour 2 cups of the sugar into a heavy aluminum or iron skillet and place it over low heat.

2. Begin stirring with a wooden spoon and keep the sugar moving so that it will not scorch. It will take about 15 minutes to completely melt all of the sugar, and at no time should it smoke or cook so fast that it turns dark. It should be about the color of light brown sugar syrup.

3. As soon as you have the sugar heating, pour the remaining 4 cups of sugar together with the 2 cups of milk or cream into a deep heavy kettle and set it over low heat to cook slowly while you are melting the sugar in the skillet.

4. As soon as the sugar is melted, begin pouring it into the kettle of boiling milk and sugar, keeping it over very low heat and stirring constantly. Now the real secret of mixing these ingredients is to pour a very fine stream from the skillet into the pan. Aunt Bill always said to pour a stream no larger than a knitting needle, while stirring across the bottom of the kettle at the same time.

5. Continue cooking and stirring until the mixture forms a firm ball (238–240°) when dropped into cold water.

6. After this test is made, turn out the fire and immediately add the soda, stirring hard as it foams up. As soon as the soda is mixed, add the butter, allowing it to melt as you stir.

(continued)

(Aunt Bill's Brown Candy continued)

7. Now set the pan of candy off the stove (but not outdoors or in a cold place) for about 20 minutes until it is lukewarm; add the vanilla and begin beating. Using a wooden spoon, beat until the mixture is thickened and heavy and takes on a dull appearance instead of a glossy sheen. Add the broken nutmeats and mix.

8. Turn into buttered tin boxes or square pans, where it can be cut into squares when cooled. This candy stays moist and delicious indefinitely. Decorate the pieces with halves of pecans and you have a most attractive candy.

Long Lost Recipes of Aunt Susan

Peanut Brittle

1 cup sugar
½ cup white corn syrup
1 cup raw peanuts
⅛ teaspoon salt

1 teaspoon butter
1 teaspoon vanilla
1 teaspoon baking soda

In 1½-quart casserole, stir together sugar, syrup, peanuts, and salt. Microwave at HIGH, 4 minutes. Stir. Microwave at HIGH, 3–5 minutes until light brown. Add butter and vanilla, blending well. Microwave at HIGH, 1–2 minutes more. Peanuts will be lightly browned and very hot. Add baking soda and gently stir until light and foamy. Pour mixture onto lightly greased cookie sheet, or unbuttered nonstick coated cookie sheet. Set to cool, ½–1 hour. When cool, break into small pieces and store in airtight container. Makes about 1 pound.

What's Cooking in Okarche?

English Toffee

2 cups sugar
2 cups butter (this is a must)
6 tablespoons water
2 teaspoons vanilla

1 (4-ounce) bar chocolate (or chocolate chips if you like dark chocolate)
1 cup chopped nuts

Combine sugar, butter, and water in heavy saucepan. Cook to 300° on candy thermometer (stirring constantly). Add vanilla and pour on buttered cookie sheet. Sprinkle chocolates on top and spread as they melt. Sprinkle nuts on top. Cool and break into pieces.

Seems Like I Done It This A-Way II

Pies and Other Desserts

LIBRARY OF CONGRESS, WASHINGTON, D.C. (c. 1930s) • INSET: WWW.TNEMEC.COM

The Oklahoma State Capitol in Oklahoma City was completed in 1917, but budget constraints forced the builders to drop plans to include a dome. The Renaissance-style dome was finally added in 2002 (inset). The Oklahoma State Capitol is the only capitol in the country with active oil rigs on its grounds and the first state capitol to be topped by a Native American figure.

Raisin Pie

It seemed we always had raisins. Mom thought they were good for our blood! When we had company we always had a raisin pie and a "poor man's pie." Every family in Otter Creek Community ate raisin pies. People got to calling um "funeral pies" because every time there was a funeral, folks took in all kinds of food—especially Raisin Pie.

1 cup raisins	1 egg, beaten
½ cups sugar	2 tablespoons grated lemon
¼ cup flour	peel
¼ teaspoon salt	3 tablespoons lemon juice
2 cups water	Pastry for 9-inch pie

Rinse raisins; drain off water. Put in top of a double boiler the sugar, flour, and salt. Add water slowly, stirring constantly. Stir in raisins. Now bring to boil over direct heat and cook 1 minute and stir fast. Take off and stir a small amount of hot mixture into the egg—I mean stir vigorously or it will cook it. Then immediately stir egg mixture into this in double boiler. Set over simmering water in bottom pan (double boiler) and cook about 5 minutes, stirring constantly. Remove from heat and stir in lemon peel and lemon juice if desired. Cool. Pour mixture in a pastry-lined 9-inch pie pan. Cover with narrow pastry strips, crisscrossed. Bake at 450° 10 minutes. Reduce heat to 350°; bake about 20 minutes longer. Makes 1 (9-inch) pie.

Seems Like I Done It This A-Way II

Sour Cream-Raisin Pie

⅔ cup raisins
Water
1½ cups thick sour cream
  (commercial)

1¼ cups sugar
2 tablespoons cornstarch
2 eggs, separated
1 pie crust, baked

Cover raisins with water; cook until water is brown. Add sour cream. Mix 1 cup sugar and cornstarch together; add to sour cream and raisins. Cook until thick, stirring constantly over medium heat.

Pour hot mixture into egg yolks; return to stove. Heat; cool. Pour into baked crust. Top with egg whites which have been beaten with remaining sugar. Bake 325° until meringue is brown.

Home Cookin' Is a Family Affair

The Best Strawberry Pie
(Diabetic)

1 (4-ounce) package
  sugar-free vanilla pie filling
  (not instant)
1 (4-ounce) package sugar-
  free strawberry Jell-O
3 cups water

4 packages artificial
  sweetener
2 teaspoons butter flavoring
2 cups sliced strawberries
1 (8-inch) graham cracker
  crust

Combine pie filling, Jell-O, water, food coloring, 2 packages of artificial sweetener, and butter flavoring in a pan. Cook until thick and clear. Cool. Fold in strawberries that have been sprinkled with 2 packages of artificial sweetener. Pour into pie shell. Top with whipped topping.

Four servings equal ½ fruit, ½ milk, 1 bread, 1½ fat, 8 optional calories, and the calories for whipped topping (optional).

United Methodist Cookbook 1993

Pineapple Pie

3 eggs
1 cup sugar
1¼ cups crushed pineapple

1 tablespoon flour
1 cup whipping cream
Baked pie shell

Beat eggs thoroughly. Add sugar, pineapple, and flour. Let cook until thick; cool. Whip cream (or use Cool Whip) and fold into mixture. Pour into baked pie shell. If desired, top with vanilla wafer crumbs.

Spring Creek Club

Mexican Plum Pie

1½–2 cups sugar
1 (30-ounce) can pitted
  purple plums
8 flour tortillas
Butter

4 teaspoons brown sugar
1 teaspoon cinnamon
¼ cup semi-sweet chocolate,
  grated
1 (8-ounce) carton sour cream

Sprinkle sugar over plums in saucepan. Let stand until sugar dissolves and juice forms. Bring plums and juices to boil and simmer until tender. While cooling, butter both sides of tortillas and arrange on large baking sheets. Combine brown sugar and cinnamon and sprinkle over tortillas. Bake at 350° for 15 minutes. (Tortillas can be turned and sprinkled with additional sugar and cinnamon halfway through baking.)

To serve, sprinkle chocolate on each tortilla. Spoon plums and sauce over chocolate. Top with dollop of sour cream. Garnish with chocolate sprinkles. Exact measurements are not a must; adjust sweetness to individual taste. Makes 8 servings.

Come Grow with Us

Granny's Apple Pie

6 or 7 tart apples
1 cup sugar
4 tablespoons all-purpose
  flour
1 teaspoon cinnamon

Dash of nutmeg
Dash of salt
Pastry for 2 crusts
2 tablespoons butter

Preheat oven to 400°. Pare apples and slice thin. Combine sugar, flour, spices, and salt; mix with apples. Line a 9-inch pie plate with pastry. Fill with apple mixture; dot with butter. Adjust top crust; sprinkle with cinnamon and sugar on top for sparkle. Be sure to cut vent holes in top crust. Bake in hot oven (400°) for 50 minutes.

Country Cooking

Sugarless Apple Pie

1 (6-ounce) can frozen,
  unsweetened apple juice,
  undiluted
2 tablespoons all-purpose
  flour

1 teaspoon cinnamon
6 cups sliced cooking apples
1 unbaked (8- or 9-inch) pie
  shell

Mix apple juice, flour, and cinnamon in saucepan. Cook until thickened. Spray pie pan with nonstick spray, and fill with sliced apples. Cover with cooked mixture. Cut vents in pie crust and fit over pie. Bake in preheated 425° oven until crust is golden.

Home Cookin' Is a Family Affair

E.W. Marland amassed a large oil empire, founding the Marland Oil Company (now Conoco, Inc.) in Ponca City. He later served as a U.S. Congressman and as Oklahoma's tenth governor, beginning in 1934. His breathtakingly beautiful 43,000-square-foot mansion, known as the "Palace on the Prairie," was modeled after the Davanzatti Palace in Florence, Italy. It is open to the public.

Mrs. Croman's Rhubarb Pie

PIE CRUST:

2 level cups flour, sifted
Pinch of salt
2 level ⅓ cups Crisco

Lump of butter (little over 1 tablespoon)
⅓ cup cold water

Mix flour and salt; add Crisco and butter; mix with pastry blender till corn meal consistency. Then add water. Very little more, if needed.

PIE:

2 cups or more rhubarb, cut up
1½ cups sugar

2 tablespoons flour
Pinch of salt

Mix 1 cup sugar with rhubarb and put flour and salt with the other ½ cup sugar. Mix well. Put in bottom crust. Put in a little water to get sugar out of bowl. Need juice anyway! Dot rhubarb with butter. Put top crust on. Dampen edges with water and perforate top well around edges. Sprinkle crust with sugar and you have a pie that will melt in your mouth. Bake at 350° until brown or about 45 minutes, depending on oven.

Seems Like I Done It This A-Way I

The Pioneer Woman is a bronze statue of a young, heroic, sun-bonneted pioneer mother, protectively leading her son by the hand. Courage, determination, and humility are in her face; a bible is in her hand. In 1927, twelve of the leading sculptors in the world were commissioned by E.W. Marland to submit three-foot high models of a pioneer woman. Bryant Baker's submission was selected, and the finished 12,000-pound, 17-foot-high bronze statue was erected in 1930 at a cost of $300,000. It is the third largest bronze statue in the world, and stands on a quarter section of land near Ponca City.

Peanut Butter Pie

CRUST:

½ cup margarine, softened   ½ cup chopped pecans
1 cup flour

Mix margarine, flour, and pecans until coarse crumbs appear. Press in 9-inch pie pan. Bake 15 minutes at 350°. Cool.

FILLING:

1 (3-ounce) package cream   ½ cup creamy peanut butter
  cheese, softened   2 cups Cool Whip
1 cup powdered sugar

Mix cream cheese, powdered sugar, and peanut butter until creamy. Add 1 cup Cool Whip at a time; fold in gently. Drizzle with Chocolate Sauce.

CHOCOLATE SAUCE:

¾ cup sugar   ¼ teaspoon salt
½ cup white syrup   ½ cup Milnot or milk
2 tablespoons butter   1 tablespoon vanilla
2 ounces unsweetened
  chocolate

Mix all ingredients, except vanilla. Cook over low heat 10–15 minutes until thick. Cool; drizzle over filling.

Spring Creek Club

Dreamy High Pumpkin Pie

1 tablespoon gelatin
¼ cup cold water
3 eggs separated
1 cup sugar
1½ cups canned pumpkin
⅓ cup milk
½ teaspoon salt

½ teaspoon pumpkin pie
  spice
1½ cups heavy cream
1 (10-inch) pie shell, baked
¾ cup moist shredded
  coconut, toasted

Soften gelatin in cold water. Beat egg yolks until thick and lemon colored; add ½ cup sugar and mix. Add pumpkin, milk, salt, and spice. Cook in double boiler until thick, stirring constantly (about 10 minutes). Add gelatin; stir until thoroughly dissolved; cool. Beat egg whites stiff; add remaining ½ cup sugar. Gradually beat until stiff peaks will stand up; fold into cooled pumpkin mixture. Beat ½ cup cream stiff; fold into mixture. Spoon lightly into baked pie shell. Chill several hours or overnight. When ready to serve, spread 1 cup of cream, whipped, on top of pie. Sprinkle toasted coconut on top to decorate. Serves 6 or 8.

Feast in Fellowship

Orange Chiffon Pie

4 egg yolks, beaten
¼ teaspoon salt
1 tablespoon lemon juice
½ cup orange juice
½ cup sugar
1 teaspoon orange rind

1 package gelatin in ½ cup
  cold water
4 egg whites
½ cup sugar
1 (9-inch) pie crust, baked
Whipped cream

Cook first 5 ingredients in double boiler until it thickens. Add gelatin and orange rind. Cool till almost congealed; fold in egg whites beaten with ½ cup sugar. Place in cool baked crust. Refrigerate. Top with whipped cream and grated rind.

Pow Wow Chow

Coconut Pie

1 cup sugar
⅓ cup flour
3 egg yolks
Pinch of salt
2 cups milk

4 tablespoons margarine or
    butter
1 teaspoon vanilla
1 cup coconut

Mix sugar, flour, salt; add milk and place in double boiler. Cook until smooth. Add a little of mixture to beaten egg yolks. Stir and slowly add egg mixture to milk mixture. Cook about 5 minutes. Remove from fire. Add butter and vanilla. Stir well. Add coconut.

MERINGUE:

3 egg whites
6 tablespoons sugar

¼ teaspoon cream of tartar

Combine. Beat until stiff. Place on cooled pie filling. Be sure to seal edges. Brown meringue slowly, 250°.

Seems Like I Done It This A-Way II

Macadamia Nut Cream Pie

1⅓ cups milk
¾ cup sugar
½ cup macadamia nuts,
    chopped
Dash of salt
1 teaspoon vanilla

1 egg
5 teaspoons cornstarch
2 egg whites
1 baked (9-inch) pie shell
1 cup heavy cream, whipped

In saucepan, combine 1 cup milk, ¼ cup sugar, ¼ cup nuts, salt, and vanilla; scald. Blend remaining ⅓ cup milk with whole egg and cornstarch. Stir some of the hot mixture thoroughly into egg mixture; return all to saucepan. Cook 5 minutes more, stirring constantly, until mixture thickens. Cool 1 hour.

Beat egg whites until soft peaks form. Gradually add the remaining ½ cup sugar, beating until stiff. Fold carefully into cooled mixture. Pour into baked pie shell; chill. Top with sweetened whipped cream and remaining ¼ cup nuts.

Thunderbird Cookers of AT&T

Oklahoma Pecan Pie

On the outskirts of Vinita, the Little Cabin Creek Pecan Orchard Gift Shop makes a mouthwatering stop. Don and Michel Gray own forty acres of pecan trees that have supplied three generations of Highway 66 travelers. This is one of their favorite recipes.

3 eggs, lightly beaten	1 teaspoon vanilla
1 cup sugar	1 cup pecan halves or pieces
1 cup light corn syrup	1 unbaked (9-inch) pie shell
1 tablespoon melted butter	

Beat eggs, add sugar, corn syrup, and butter and mix together until well blended. Stir in vanilla and pecans. Pour mixture into pie shell and bake in a preheated 350° oven for 45–55 minutes or until knife inserted halfway between center and edge comes out clean. Cool well on wire rack. Serve plain or with whipped cream. Makes 6–8 slices.

The Route 66 Cookbook

Jell-O Pudding Pecan Pie

1 (3¼-ounce) package vanilla instant pudding	1 egg, slightly beaten
1 cup white corn syrup	1 cup chopped pecans
¾ cup evaporated milk	1 (8-inch) unbaked pie shell

Blend pudding with corn syrup. Add milk and egg, then add pecans. Pour into pie shell. Bake at 375° until firm, about 40 minutes.

Old and New

Most of the numerous federal and state highways that connect northwest Oklahoma were built along homestead section lines, and are ruler straight.

Honey Pecan Pie

No, this is not pecan pie made by Honey or for Honey; the pie has honey in it. For a traditional pecan pie, use corn syrup in place of the honey.

4 eggs, slightly beaten	1 cup sugar
½ cup honey	¼ teaspoon salt
½ cup light corn syrup	1 teaspoon vanilla or bourbon
⅓ cup butter or margarine, melted	1¼ cups pecans

Combine the first 7 ingredients and mix well, but not to the point that it is frothy. Add pecans and stir until the pecans are coated. Pour into an uncooked pastry shell and bake in a pre-heated oven at 350° for approximately 55 minutes.

PASTRY SHELL:

1¼ cups flour	2 tablespoons cold water
½ teaspoon salt	
½ cup shortening or margarine	

Mix flour and salt. Using a pastry blender, cut shortening into the flour; mix until it resembles coarse meal. Add water, stirring with a fork or spoon until thoroughly moistened. Form a ball with the dough and roll out on floured wax paper. Place the dough in a 9-inch pie plate and prepare the edges to your liking. Use extreme care not to put any holes in the dough, or the filling will run under the crust.

When a Man's Fancy Turns to Cooking

Black Forest Pie

1 package Pillsbury
  refrigerated pie crusts
¾ cup sugar
⅓ cup cocoa
2 tablespoons flour
¼ cup margarine
⅓ cup milk

2 eggs, beaten
1 (21-ounce) can cherry pie
  filling
1 (9-ounce) carton Cool Whip
1 (1-ounce) square
  unsweetened chocolate,
  coarsely grated

Prepare 1 pie crust according to directions for filled pie. Heat oven to 350°. In medium saucepan, combine sugar, cocoa, and 2 tablespoons flour. Add margarine and milk. Cook until mixture begins to boil, stirring constantly. Remove from heat. Add small amount of hot mix to eggs, then slowly stir egg mix into pan. Fold in ½ can pie filling. Reserve the rest of the filling for topping. Pour chocolate mix into pie-crust-lined pan. Bake at 350° for 35–45 minutes or until center is set but still shiny. Cool. Chill 1 hour.

Combine 2 cups of Cool Whip and grated chocolate; spread over chilled pie. Top with remaining pie filling and Cool Whip. Chill at least ½ hour before serving.

Thunderbird Cookers of AT&T

Cocoa Cream Pie

⅓ cup cocoa
1¼ cups sugar
¼ teaspoon salt
⅓ cup cornstarch
3 cups milk

3 tablespoons butter or
  margarine
1½ teaspoons vanilla
1 (9-inch) pie shell, baked
Cool Whip

Combine cocoa, sugar, salt, and cornstarch in medium saucepan. Gradually blend milk and dry ingredients, stirring until smooth. Cook, over medium heat, stirring constantly until filling boils, 1 minute. Remove from heat; blend in butter and vanilla. Pour into pie crust. Carefully press plastic wrap onto pie filling. Cool. Chill 3 or 4 hours or overnight. When ready to serve, remove film and garnish with Cool Whip.

Feeding Our Flock

Chocolate Pie

2½ cups milk
1 cup sugar
6 tablespoons flour
½ teaspoon salt
2 egg yolks, slightly beaten
1 teaspoon vanilla

2 squares Baker's
unsweetened chocolate
2 tablespoons butter
Baked pie shell
Whipped cream

Heat milk. Meanwhile, mix together in blender, sugar, flour, salt, yolks, and vanilla. Add just enough milk to make a smooth paste. Stir into milk and cook till thick. Remove from heat and add chocolate and butter. This fills a 9- to 10-inch pie shell. Top with whipped cream.

Here's What's Cookin' at Zion

Chocolate Cobbler

3 cups sugar
2 tablespoons cocoa
(rounded)
2 cups water
½ stick margarine
1 cup flour

1 tablespoon baking powder
(rounded)
½ teaspoon salt
1 cup milk
½ teaspoon vanilla

Mix 2 cups sugar and cocoa in saucepan; add water and margarine. Bring to boil on low heat stirring often; pour in 9x13x2-inch pan. Mix last cup sugar, flour, baking powder, salt, milk, and vanilla. Pour batter onto cocoa mixture; (drizzle from side to side, do not stir). Bake at 400° until batter is well done (about 15–20 minutes). Cool for about ½ hour before serving.

100 Years of Cooking

The city of Guymon is the Hub City of the Panhandle. It is situated on top of the Guymon-Hugoton Gas Field which has the largest deposit of natural gas reserves in the world.

Fresh Peach Cobbler

CRUST:

2 cups sifted flour
1 teaspoon salt
1 teaspoon baking powder
¼ teaspoon soda

½ cup shortening
½ cup buttermilk (if sweet
  milk is used, omit soda)

Sift flour, salt, baking powder, and soda into mixing bowl. Cut shortening in with fork or knife until it is like coarse crumbs. Add milk and stir all together until dough is damp-through-out. Divide dough into 2 parts. Roll out half to size of baking dish to be used. Line bottom of baking dish (1½-quart size) with pastry. Sprinkle with sugar and put into oven to prebake at 400° for 10–12 minutes.

FRUIT FILLING:

6 cups sliced peaches
1½ cups sugar
½ lemon, juice only

2 tablespoons cornstarch
2 or 3 tablespoons butter
Sprinkling of cinnamon

Pare, slice and measure peaches. Place peaches in bowl, pour lemon juice over them, and add sugar and cornstarch. Let set for an hour or more. They will form their own juice. Do not add water. Pour peaches and any juice into prebaked crust. Dot with butter. Roll out other half of dough and cut into strips. Cross the strips over the top and sprinkle with a little sugar and cinnamon. Bake in preheated oven 400° for 25 minutes.

Seems Like I Done It This A-Way I

WIKIPEDIA.ORG

Once America was blanketed with an ocean of grass; the 35,000-acre Tallgrass Prairie Preserve near Pawhuska still offers a rare glimpse of that mystic landscape. You can hear the silence...where buffalo graze and wildflowers bloom extravagantly. The visitor's center is a vintage cowboy bunkhouse.

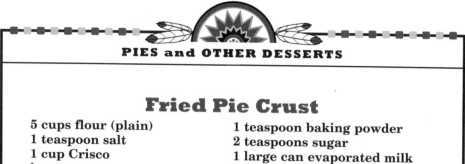
Fried Pie Crust

5 cups flour (plain)
1 teaspoon salt
1 cup Crisco
l egg

1 teaspoon baking powder
2 teaspoons sugar
1 large can evaporated milk

Sift dry ingredients, cut in shortening and add milk. Mix well. Add eggs and gently mix. Put in icebox and chill. Roll and cut dough in saucer-size cutouts. Fill with fruit filling on one side. Fold other side over. Press edges together with fork. Fry in hot grease until brown.

Seems Like I Done It This A-Way II

Pie Crust Mix

5 pounds plus 1½ cups flour	4½ teaspoons salt
4½ tablespoons sugar	3 pounds Crisco

In a very large bowl, combine flour, sugar and salt. Add shortening; using your hands, mix until well blended and small particles remain. Mix may now be placed in an airtight container and stored on the shelf for many months.

PIE CRUST:

4 cups Pie Crust Mix	1 egg
2 tablespoons vinegar	

To make 3 large crusts or 4 smaller ones, measure out 4 cups mix, packed tightly in cup. Place mix in a large bowl. Measure 2 tablespoons vinegar in a ½ cup measuring cup. Fill cup with water; pour mixture into a small bowl. Add 1 egg to the water; mix well with a fork. Add egg mixture to crust mixture; stir with a fork until well blended. Cover; chill. This pie crust will keep in the refrigerator 3 days or in the freezer several months.

20 PIE CRUSTS:

To make up all of the mix into dough, measure 9 tablespoons vinegar into 1 cup measuring cup. Fill cup with water. Pour into a medium bowl. Add 1¼ cups additional water (a total of 2¼ cups water and vinegar), and 4 eggs. Mix well with a whisk. Pour into the pie crust mix; stir with a large spoon until well blended. Chill dough before rolling. This amount of dough makes 17–20 crusts, depending on size. I usually make up the whole amount of dough and shape it into balls, using the amount of dough required for 1 crust. Wrap individually in plastic wrap and place in large plastic bag and freeze.

After the pie crust mix has been made into dough and chilled, it may be rolled out and fitted into the desired pans. I flute the edges and stack them, with plastic wrap between each crust. The stack needs to be wrapped well in foil to freeze. These crusts keep many months in the freezer.

Something Special Cookbook

Cathy Kelley's Cherry Pie Tarts

⅔ cup warm milk
1 package dry yeast
1 cup shortening
3 cups flour

2 tablespoons sugar
1 teaspoon salt
1 can cherry pie filling

GLAZE:

½–¾ cup powdered sugar   2–3 tablespoons warm water

Warm the milk; add yeast. Stir until dissolved. Cut shortening into flour, sugar, and salt; add milk and yeast. Mix well. Divide dough in half. Roll out flat on floured board to fit cookie sheet (with sides). Spread pie filling evenly onto dough. Roll out second part of dough; place on top. Crimp or flute edges. Bake at 375° for 20–25 minutes or until light brown. Let cool. Add glaze and cut into squares.

Recipes and Remembrances

Pear Tart

A dessert to impress!

PÂTÉ SUCRÉE:

1¾ cups flour
10 tablespoons plus 2
  teaspoons unsalted butter,
  well chilled

¼ cup sugar
2 egg yolks
¼ teaspoon water
4 drops vanilla

Combine flour, butter, and sugar in processor and mix using on and off turns until mixture resembles coarse meal, about 45 seconds. Add yolks, water, vanilla, and continue mixing until dough is crumbly. Work into a ball. Flatten into a disc and freeze 30 minutes. (Dough can be prepared ahead and frozen for several months.)

FILLING:

1 cup plus 3 tablespoons
  sugar
6 tablespoons flour
3 eggs
¾ cup butter, melted

2 Bartlett pears, peeled,
  cored, and quartered
  lengthwise
Powdered sugar

Combine sugar, flour, and eggs and whisk until smooth. Whisk butter into sugar mixture and set aside. Roll out dough on floured surface to ⅛-inch thick. Press into an 11-inch tart pan with removable bottom. Place in refrigerator.

Cut pears crosswise ⅛-inch thick and gently open into a fan shape. Arrange pears in crust in flower petal pattern. Pour filling into tart shell over pears. Bake in preheated 375° oven 35–40 minutes until crust and filling are brown. Sprinkle with powdered sugar. Serves 8–10.

Gourmet Our Way

Alabaster Caverns near Freedom is known as the world's largest commercially-operated gypsum cave.

Pears Melba

3 cups water
1 (3-inch) cinnamon stick
1 teaspoon pure vanilla
extract
1½ tablespoons fresh lemon
juice, divided
1 (1x3-inch) piece lemon rind
4 large fresh pears, stems
intact, peeled, halved and
cored

1 tablespoon cornstarch
10 ounces frozen raspberries,
thawed, drained (reserve
juice)
1 cup lowfat cottage cheese
2 teaspoons sugar
Mint leaves

In large skillet combine water, cinnamon stick, vanilla, 1 table-spoon lemon juice, and rind. Bring water to high simmer; add pears and poach, covered, 10 minutes. (Can be prepared up to this point, covered and chilled overnight.) Add cornstarch to reserved raspberry juice; heat until slightly thickened. Add berries; cool.

Purée cottage cheese, reserved lemon juice, and sugar until smooth and creamy. Matching halves, fill each pear half with 2 tablespoons cheese mixture; stand upright on plate and press halves together. Level bottom, if necessary, by cutting off thin slice. Spoon 2 tablespoons raspberry sauce over each pear. Place mint leaf at each stem. May be chilled several hours. Yields 4 servings.

Nutritional information per serving: 148 calories.

Hint: If fresh pears are not available, canned pear halves can be sub-stituted.

Sounds Delicious!

Apricot Ecstasy

2½ cups canned apricots
1¾ cups sugar
¾ cup shortening
2 cups flour

1 teaspoon salt
½ teaspoon soda
1½ cups chopped coconut
½ cup chopped nuts

Cook together for 5 minutes the apricots and ¾ cup of the sugar. Cream together rest of sugar and shortening. Add flour, salt, and soda. Add coconut and nuts. Press 3½ cups crumb mixture into well-greased oblong pan. Bake for 10 minutes at 400°. Spread hot apricot mixture over crust. Sprinkle remaining crumbs over top and bake at 325° for 25 minutes. Cut into squares and top with Cool Whip or ice cream.

United Methodist Cookbook 1993

Lemon Fluff

A delightful dessert.

1½ cups finely crushed
   graham cracker or vanilla
   wafer crumbs

⅓ cup chopped pecans
6 tablespoons butter

Combine vanilla wafer crumbs, pecans, and butter. Reserve ¼ cup crumb mixture and press remainder into 10x6x1½-inch baking dish. Chill.

FILLING:

2 (3-ounce) packages lemon
   gelatin
1¼ cups boiling water
½ cup whipped cream

1 (3¼-ounce) package
   instant lemon pudding mix
1 pint lemon sherbet
Pinch of salt

Dissolve gelatin in boiling water; cool to lukewarm. Whip cream until soft peaks form. Set aside. Add dry pudding mix to gelatin and mix. Add softened sherbet and beat at low speed on mixer until thick. Add pinch of salt. Fold in cream. Turn into baking dish and sprinkle remaining crumbs on top. Chill at least one hour. This dessert can be made a day ahead and it keeps nicely in the refrigerator.

Company Fare II

Banana Split Cake

CRUST:

3 cups graham cracker crumbs

1½ sticks butter, softened
3 tablespoons sugar

Mix together and pat into a 9x13-inch pan. Freeze.

FILLING:

1 (8-ounce) package cream cheese, softened
1 stick butter, softened

2 cups powdered sugar
4–6 tablespoons milk

Whip together; spread over crust.

TOPPING:

4 bananas, sliced
1 large can crushed pineapple, drained

Cool Whip (large)
Nuts (on top)

Layer over filling in order listed. Refrigerate.

100 Years of Cooking

Make Ahead Casadda Dessert

1 pound cake (homemade or boxed)
1 teaspoon amaretto liqueur, per slice (about 12)
2 (6-ounce) packages instant vanilla pudding

2 cans canned fruit cocktail, drained
1 (12-ounce) carton Cool Whip
1 jar red sugar sparkles (used in cake decorating)

Slice the pound cake into as many pieces as needed. Place them in a serving dish. Drizzle 1 teaspoon amaretto liqueur over each slice of pound cake. Let the cake set while you make the pudding mix according to the package directions. Fold in the drained fruit, mixing thoroughly. Spoon the pudding and fruit mixture over the pound cake and set in the refrigerator until you are ready to serve.

Before serving, frost with Cool Whip. Cut the dessert into servings. Sprinkle each piece with the sparkly sugar. This recipe serves 12.

Gourmet: The Quick and Easy Way

Angel Filling Supreme

1 angel food cake	½ cup bourbon
½ pound butter, softened	2 half pints whipping cream
1 pound powdered sugar	Toasted almonds
4 egg yolks	

Split angel food cake in 3 layers. Cream butter and powdered sugar with electric mixer. Add egg yolks one at a time, beating after each addition. Gradually add bourbon. Spread filling between layers and over top of cake. Ice cake with whipped cream. Sprinkle with toasted almonds. Allow to stand in refrigerator several hours.

May be used with ladyfingers, alternating layers and cutting into squares to serve.

Pow Wow Chow

Fantastic Layered Dessert

1 cup flour	1 (3-ounce) package vanilla
½ cup margarine, softened	instant pudding
1½ cups chopped nuts	3½ cups milk, divided
1 (8-ounce) package cream	1 (3-ounce) package
cheese, softened	chocolate instant pudding
1 cup powdered sugar	1 small Hershey bar, grated
1 (9-ounce) carton whipped	
topping	

Combine flour, margarine and ½ cup nuts; mix until crumbly. Press into a 13x9x2-inch pan. Bake at 350° for 15 minutes. Cool.

Combine cream cheese and sugar. Add 1 cup whipped topping. Spread over crust. Prepare vanilla pudding mix as directed on label, using 1¾ cups milk. Pour over second layer; chill until set. Prepare chocolate pudding mix, using 1¾ cups milk, pour over third layer. Chill until set. Top with remaining whipped topping, remaining nuts and grated Hershey bar. Chill several hours.

What's Cooking in Okarche?

Twinkie Treat

2 boxes or 24 Twinkies snack
cakes
1 large box strawberry Jell-O
1 large package instant
vanilla pudding

1 can strawberry pie filling
1 medium-size container
whipped topping
½ cup chopped pecans

Place all the Twinkies in a 9x13-inch pan (may have to squeeze them to fit). Mix Jell-O according to directions on package. Pour over Twinkies. Prepare pudding mix as directed on package. Pour over Jell-O. Spread pie filling over pudding. Top with whipped topping and sprinkle nuts over all. Chill at least 2 hours before serving. Even better to refrigerate overnight. This is an easy, but delicious dessert. Your friends will think you have spent hours on this luscious treat

Centennial Cookbook

Chocolate Nut Torte to Diet For

4 squares semi-sweet
chocolate
1¾ cups pecans
2 tablespoons plus ½ cup
sugar
¼ cup unsalted butter at
room temperature

3 large eggs at room
temperature
1 tablespoon Grand Marnier
or rum

Generously grease 8-inch round cake pan, then cut a circle of wax paper to fit the bottom of the pan. Then grease the paper. Melt the chocolate in the top of a double boiler. Set aside. Place nuts and 2 tablespoons of the sugar in a food processor. Pulse on and off until the nuts are ground. Remove to a bowl. Process butter and ½ cup sugar until blended. Add chocolate and process until smooth. Add eggs and Grand Marnier or rum and mix. Add nuts, pulsing once or twice. Pour into the cake pan and bake in preheated 375° oven 25 minutes. Cake will be soft when removed but will firm as it cools. Cool 20 minutes on wire rack. Invert the cake onto the rack, remove paper, and cool completely.

Note: Unglazed torte can be kept tightly covered at room temperature for up to 2 days, or frozen in tightly wrapped foil.

GLAZE AND GARNISH:

22 pecan halves
6 tablespoons unsalted butter

6 squares semi-sweet
chocolate

Bake pecan halves on baking sheet at 460° for 10–15 minutes, stirring occasionally. Melt the butter and chocolate . Stir until smooth. Dip end of each pecan into the chocolate and put on wax paper to dry. Set the rest of the glaze aside to thicken slightly. It should be soft enough to pour, but thick enough to coat the cake. Holding the cake on the rack over a sink or wax paper, pour the glaze onto the middle of the cake and tilt the cake so that the glaze runs evenly down all sides and covers them completely. A knife dipped in hot water will smooth sides if necessary. Put the pecans in a circle on the top of the torte around the edge. (May be held overnight uncovered at room temperature.) Serves 8.

Gourmet Our Way

Cherry-Berries on a Cloud

The meringue crust is an unusual twist. Delightful! Everyone wants this recipe.

6 egg whites	1 teaspoon vanilla
½ teaspoon cream of tartar	2 cups whipping cream,
¼ teaspoon salt	whipped
1¾ cups sugar	2 cups miniature
6 ounces cream cheese,	marshmallows
softened	Cherry-Berry Topping
1 cup sugar	

Heat oven to 250°. Grease 13x9x2-inch pan. Beat egg whites, cream of tartar, and salt until frothy. Gradually beat in 1¾ cups sugar. Beat until very stiff and glossy, about 15 minutes. Spread in prepared pan. Bake 60 minutes. Turn off oven and leave meringue in until cool, about 12 hours or overnight. Mix cream cheese with 1 cup sugar and vanilla. Gently fold in whipped cream and marshmallows. Spread over meringue; refrigerate 12 hours or overnight. Cut into serving pieces and top with Cherry-Berry Topping. Makes 10–12 servings.

CHERRY-BERRY TOPPING:

1 (1-pound, 5-ounce) can	2 cups sliced fresh
cherry pie filling	strawberries or 1 (1-pound)
1 teaspoon lemon juice	package frozen, thawed

Stir cherry pie filling and lemon juice into sliced fresh strawberries or frozen strawberries (thawed).

Four Generations of Johnson Family Favorites

Elegant Daiquiri Soufflé

A beautiful dessert!

½ cup light rum
2 tablespoons unflavored
  gelatin
10 eggs, separated
2 cups sugar, divided
½ cup lemon juice
½ cup lime juice
Grated rind of 2 lemons and 2
  limes

⅛ teaspoon salt
3 cups whipping cream,
  divided
Crystallized violets (optional)
1 (2-ounce) package pistachio
  nuts, finely chopped

Cut a piece of aluminum foil to fit around a 1½-quart soufflé dish, allowing a 1-inch overlap. Fold the paper in half and wrap around the dish with the foil extending 5 inches above the rim of the dish to form a collar. Set aside.

Combine light rum and gelatin. Let stand 5 minutes. Mean while, beat the egg yolks until light and fluffy. Gradually add 1 cup of the sugar, beating constantly until thick and lemon colored. Combine the yolk mix with the fruit juices, grated rind and salt in a 2½-quart saucepan. Cook over low heat, stirring constantly until thickened (about 12 minutes). Remove from the heat and add the gelatin mixture, stirring until dissolved. Allow to cool.

In a large chilled mixer bowl, beat the egg whites until stiff peaks form, gradually adding ½ cup of the sugar. Beat 2 cups of the whipping cream with ¼ cup of the sugar until stiff peaks form. Fold the whipping cream and egg whites into the cooled yolk mix and pour into the soufflé dish. Chill until firm. Souffle may be frozen.

Remove the collar and gently pat crushed nuts on the exposed sides of the soufflé. Whip the remaining 1 cup of cream with ¼ cup sugar until stiff peaks form. Spoon in mounds on top of the soufflé or fill a pastry bag and decorate the top with rosettes and petals. Garnish with crystallized violets and twisted slices of lime if desired. Soufflé may be frozen. Makes 12 servings.

Applause!

Tulips Through the Snow

Strawberries look like tulips pushing up through snow.

½ cup butter
1 cup boiling water
1 cup all-purpose flour
2 tablespoons cocoa powder

2 tablespoons sugar
¼ teaspoon salt
4 eggs

In medium saucepan, melt butter in boiling water. Meanwhile, stir together flour, cocoa powder, sugar, and salt. Add to pan; stir vigorously. Cook and stir until mixture forms ball and follows spoon. Remove from heat; cool 10 minutes.

Add eggs one at a time, beating well after each addition. Using pastry bag with large star tip (⅝-inch opening), pipe batter into 24 spirals 1¾ inches in diameter onto greased baking sheet. (Use about 2 tablespoons batter for each.)

In preheated 400° oven, bake 20–25 minutes or until puffed. Remove from oven. Cool on wire rack. Cut off tops and set aside. Remove soft dough from inside and discard. Set aside. Reduce oven temperature to 350°.

CHEESECAKE FILLING:

16 ounces cream cheese,
  softened
½ cup plus 2 tablespoons
  sugar, divided
1 cup whipping cream
24 large ripe strawberries,
  hulled

1 egg
½ teaspoon pure almond
  extract, divided

Beat cream cheese, ½ cup sugar, egg, and ¼ teaspoon almond extract just until smooth. Fill bottoms of puffs with mixture. Place on ungreased baking sheet. Bake 15 minutes or until cheese mixture is set. Chill. Beat whipped cream to soft peaks. Add remaining 2 tablespoons sugar and ¼ teaspoon almond extract; beat to stiff peaks. Partially quarter strawberries from pointed end to stem end (do not cut through stem end).

Using pastry bag with same tip, pipe cream into strawberries. Place berries on top of filled puffs. Place reserved tops on berries, angling slightly. Sprinkle with confectioners' sugar (snow). Yields 24 pieces.

Sounds Delicious!

Frozen Chocolate Crunch

This is a delicious and impressive dessert. Can be made days in advance.

8 ounces sweet German
    chocolate or milk chocolate
⅓ cup light corn syrup
2 cups whipping cream,
    divided

1½ cups crushed chocolate
    Oreo cookies
1 cup coarsely chopped
    English walnuts

In a double boiler pan, combine chocolate and corn syrup. Stir occasionally until chocolate melts. Remove from heat. Stir in ½ cup of the cream until blended. Refrigerate 25–30 minutes or until cool. Stir in cookies and walnuts.

In a small bowl, with mixer at medium speed, beat remaining 1½ cups cream until soft peaks form. Gently fold in chocolate mixture just until combined. Spread mixture into a 9-inch glass baking dish and freeze 4–6 hours or until firm. Cut into squares to serve.

Note: You can pour this mixture into 12 individual dessert dishes and freeze. You can garnish with chocolate shaves, nuts, or whipped cream if desired. This will store, covered, in freezer for up to 1 month. Before serving, let set at room temperature several minutes.

Shattuck Community Cookbook

Butterfinger Dessert

Very good.

2 cups graham cracker
  crumbs
1 cup saltine cracker crumbs
½ cup margarine, melted
2 small packages instant
  vanilla pudding

2 cups milk
2 cups vanilla ice cream
5 Butterfinger candy bars,
  crushed
2 cups Cool Whip

Combine cracker crumbs and margarine. Press ¾ of mixture into a 9x13-inch pan. Combine pudding and milk. Beat 1 minute and add ice cream. Beat until smooth. Pour over crumbs and refrigerate 1 hour. Do not freeze. Spread with Cool Whip. Combine remaining crumbs with the Butterfingers and sprinkle over Cool Whip.

Home Cookin' Is a Family Affair

Caramel Ice Cream in Freezer

2½ cups sugar
¼ teaspoon salt
3 quarts milk

1 pint cream
4 eggs
2 tablespoons vanilla

Mix 2 cups sugar, salt, 2 quarts milk and cream. Beat eggs and add to 1 quart milk. Scald the egg mixture to a boiling point. Caramelize ½ cup sugar in iron skillet and cook until brown. Add this to the scalded milk mixture. Add sugar and milk mixture to scalded mixture. Cool. Add vanilla. If any more milk is needed to fill 1 gallon freezer container, fill to within 1½ inches of top. Cover. Pack with ice and freeze.

Seems Like I Done It This A-Way II

Having gained world-wide recognition from Merle Haggard's song, Muskogee, nestled in the rolling hills of Green County on the west bank of the Arkansas River, is one of Oklahoma's most recognized cities. The Five Civilized Tribes Museum is located there.

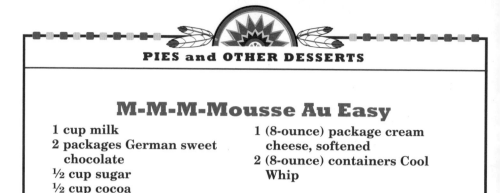

M-M-M-Mousse Au Easy

1 cup milk
2 packages German sweet
  chocolate
½ cup sugar
½ cup cocoa

1 (8-ounce) package cream
  cheese, softened
2 (8-ounce) containers Cool
  Whip

Combine in small saucepan over medium heat milk, chocolate, sugar, and cocoa. (If you stir the sugar and cocoa together, it will dissolve more quickly.) When the chocolate is melted, this mixture should be combined with the cream cheese in a large mixing bowl. Beat this well and scrape bottom and sides of mixing bowl a few times to be sure all lumps are dissolved. When this mixture looks like a rich chocolate syrup, add the Cool Whip and mix well. Do not over beat, but scrape bottom and sides of bowl to make sure your mousse is well-blended.

Serving Ideas: Put in clear glass bowl and garnish with whipped cream and chocolate shavings.

Double Chocolate Pie: Put in a chocolate cookie crumb crust and keep in freezer until one hour before serving.

Optional: For an elegant spur-of-the-moment trick, garnish with real whipped cream and a candied violet.

Stir Ups

Pam's Special Banana Pudding

5 cups milk
3 small boxes instant vanilla
  pudding
1 (8-ounce) carton sour cream

1 (12-ounce) container Cool
  Whip
Vanilla wafers
5 bananas, sliced

Mix milk with puddings. Add sour cream and ½ the Cool Whip into mixture. Layer in bowl, first vanilla wafers; second, pudding mixture; third, banana layer. Keep on layering, then top with remaining Cool Whip.

Sequoyah's Cookin'

German Chocolate Pudding

1 (4-ounce) bar German's
Sweet Chocolate
¼ pound butter
3 eggs, separated
1 cup powdered sugar

1 teaspoon vanilla
1 pint whipping cream,
whipped
1 (10-ounce) box vanilla
wafers

Melt chocolate and butter together. Add chocolate mixture to beaten egg yolks; then add ⅔ cup powdered sugar and vanilla. Chill, then fold in whipped cream. Beat egg whites until they begin to stand in peaks. Add remaining ⅓ cup sugar into egg whites and fold into chocolate mixture. Grind vanilla wafers and line 9x9-inch deep dish with part of chocolate mixture over crumbs, then add another layer of crumbs. Repeat until all the mixture is used. Remainder of crumbs go on top. Refrigerate 24 hours.

Court Clerk's Bar and Grill

Date Pudding

1 pound dates
1 tablespoon butter
1½ cups boiling water
2 eggs
1⅓ cups flour
1½ cups sugar

1 teaspoon soda
1 teaspoon baking powder
Pinch of salt
1 cup chopped nuts
1 teaspoon vanilla

Cut dates in bowl and add butter. Pour water over this. When cool, add eggs. Sift flour, sugar, soda, baking powder, and salt. Mix in with dates. Add nuts and vanilla. Bake in 325° oven for 1 hour. Top with whipped cream.

Thank Heaven for Home Made Cooks

At Rogers State College in Claremore, the Lynn Riggs Memorial honors the author of *Green Grow the Lilacs* on which the musical "Oklahoma!" is based.

Date Pecan Pudding

2 eggs	1 cup solidly packed bread
1½ cups milk	crumbs
1 teaspoon baking powder	1 cup flaked coconut
1 cup sugar	1 cup chopped dates
1 cup chopped pecans	1 tablespoon butter, melted

Beat the first 3 ingredients together. Add the other ingredients except butter. Mix well and add melted butter. Pour mixture in a buttered pan or spoon into individual paper cups. Bake at 350° for 45 minutes, or less for cup cakes. Top with whipped cream or with frosting.

Cookbook of Treasured Recipes

Effie Romberger's Old-Fashioned Rice Pudding

I still hunger for mother's rice pudding!

1 cup uncooked rice	1 teaspoon salt
6 eggs	½ cup milk
1 cup sugar	1 stick butter (only)
1 teaspoon nutmeg	

Cook rice. Beat eggs; add sugar, nutmeg, salt, milk, and cooked rice. Pour into 2-quart baking dish in which 1 stick butter has been melted. Bake at 400° about 30 minutes. Do not over-cook. Center should be a little shaky.

GRANDMOTHER ROMBERGER'S LEMON SAUCE:
This is good over bread pudding, rice pudding, or leftover crumbled cake.

3 tablespoons cornstarch	1 tablespoon butter
½ cup water	1 egg, beaten
¾ cup sugar	Yellow food coloring (if
⅛ teaspoon salt	desired)
⅓ cup lemon juice	

Mix cornstarch with water. In saucepan, mix sugar, salt, lemon juice, butter, and egg. Add cornstarch mixture. Stir and cook slowly until thick. Makes 1 cup.

Four Generations of Johnson Family Favorites

Bride's Bread Pudding

Your next family favorite!

1 (10-ounce) loaf stale French
  bread
2 tablespoons water
2¼ cups evaporated milk
7 eggs, beaten
1 can Eagle Brand Milk

½ cup sugar
½ cup raisins
1 (8-ounce) can pineapple,
  crushed
2 tablespoons vanilla extract
¼ cup butter, melted

Preheat oven to 350°. Lightly coat 9x12-inch baking dish with cooking spray. Tear bread into pieces and sprinkle lightly with water. Blend in all other ingredients. Prepare a large pan of water and place on middle rack in oven. Fill baking dish with pudding and place in water pan. Bake for 1 hour or until set. Serve warm with Bourbon Sauce.

BOURBON SAUCE:

1 cup butter, softened
2 cups super fine granulated
  sugar

Nutmeg to taste
½ cup bourbon

Using an electric mixer, combine sugar and butter until light and fluffy. Add nutmeg and bourbon, beating until smooth. Sugar should be completely dissolved. Place a small scoop of sauce on top of warm pudding and serve immediately. Makes 8 servings.

Applause!

French Silk Pie

CRUST:

1 cup flour
1 cup finely chopped pecans

½ cup margarine, melted

Combine flour, nuts, and margarine until crumbly. Press into a large pie plate. Bake for 15 minutes at 375°.

PIE:

1 cup margarine, softened
1½ cups sugar
4 squares unsweetened chocolate, melted and cooled

2 teaspoons vanilla
4 eggs
8 ounces whipped topping

Beat with mixer the margarine and sugar until fluffy and smooth. Blend in melted chocolate and vanilla. Beat in eggs one at a time, beating 5 minutes after each egg. Turn into cooled pie shell. Chill several hours. Garnish with whipped topping and shaved chocolate (if desired).

Country Cooking

WIKIPEDIA.ORG

On September 16, 1893, the starting gun signaled the opening of 6,400,000 acres of the Cherokee Outlet territory where 40,000 claims of 160 acres each were offered. Over 100,000 settlers participated in the Land Run.

Catalog of
Contributing Cookbooks

Established in 1892, Mohawk Lodge Indian Store on Route 66 in Clinton was the first trading post in Indian Territory. It opened in 1892 as an outlet for Cheyenne women to sell their handmade goods. The store still buys, sells, and trades authentic Indian crafts and artifacts across the same counter used in 1892, and displays original photos and other museum-worthy treasures.

Catalog of
Contributing Cookbooks

Fifty-nine cookbooks from all regions of Oklahoma have contributed recipes to this collection. The contributing cookbooks range from large Junior League editions to modest church cookbooks from small communities. Each cookbook has contributed a sampling of their most popular recipes, capturing the flavor of the state. The BEST OF THE BEST STATE COOKBOOK SERIES' goal is to *Preserve America's Food Heritage*. Since many of the contributing cookbooks have gone out of print, the BEST OF THE BEST COOKBOOKS serve to preserve a sampling of those wonderful family recipes that might have otherwise been lost.

APPLAUSE! OKLAHOMA'S BEST
PERFORMING RECIPES
Oklahoma City Orchestra League
Oklahoma City, OK

CAFE OKLAHOMA
Junior Service League of Midwest
City, OK

CENTENNIAL COOKBOOK
First Christian Church CWF
Seiling, OK

CLEORA'S KITCHENS
by Cleora Butler
Council Oak Books
Tulsa, OK

COME GROW WITH US
United Methodist Women
Sayre, OK

COMPANY FARE
Presbyterian Women
First Presbyterian Church
Bartlesville, OK

COMPANY FARE II
Presbyterian Women
First Presbyterian Church
Bartlesville, OK

COOKBOOK OF TREASURED
RECIPES
St. Antony's Orthodox Christian
Church
Tulsa, OK

COOKING A+ RECIPES FROM
ST. MARY'S CATHOLIC SCHOOL
St. Mary's Catholic School
Ponca City, OK

COUNTRY COOKING
Port Country Cousins
Sentinel, OK

COURT CLERIC'S BAR AND
GRILL
Tulsa County Court Clerk's Office
Tulsa, OK

DINE WITH THE ANGELS
St. Michael's Catholic Youth
Henryetta, OK

DISCOVER OKLAHOMA
COOKIN'
Oklahoma 4-H Foundation, Inc.
Stillwater, OK

FAT FREE & ULTRA LOWFAT RECIPES
by Doris Cross
Prima Publishing • Rocklin, CA

FAT FREE 2
by Doris Cross • Prima Publishing
Rocklin, CA

FEAST IN FELLOWSHIP
First United Methodist Women
Altus, OK

FEEDING OUR FLOCK
Fort Supply United Methodist
Fort Supply, OK

15 MINUTE STORAGE MEALS
by Jayne Benkendorf
Ludwig Publishing
Edmond, OK

FOUR GENERATIONS OF JOHNSON FAMILY FAVORITES
by Ruth Johnson
Oklahoma City, OK

GOURMET OUR WAY
Cascia Hall Preparatory School
Tulsa, OK

GOURMET: THE QUICK AND EASY WAY
by Diana Allen
Enid, OK

HEALTHY AMERICA
by Mimi Rippee
Enid, OK

HELEN'S SOUTHWEST SPECIALTIES
by Helen L. Krause
Kellyville, OK

HERE'S WHAT'S COOKIN' AT ZION
Zion Amish Mennonite Church
Thomas, OK

HOME COOKIN' IS A FAMILY AFFAIR
by Emily Swisher
Sayre, OK

THE HOMEPLACE COOKBOOK: HERBAL COOKERY MADE EASY
Homeplace
Stillwater, OK

KITCHEN KLATTER KEEP-SAKES
Kiwash Electric Cooperative
Cordell, OK

LONG LOST RECIPES OF AUNT SUSAN
M-PRESS
Hot Springs Village, AR

MARY'S RECIPE BOX
by Mary Gubser
Council Oak Books
Tulsa, OK

NATIONAL COWBOY HALL OF FAME CHUCK WAGON COOKBOOK
by B. Byron Price
Oklahoma City, OK

THE OKLAHOMA CELEBRITY COOKBOOK
Neighbors Executive Coffee
Oklahoma City, OK

OKLAHOMA COOKIN'
Barnard Elementary School
Tecumseh, OK

OLD AND NEW
Abell F.C.E. Club
Guthrie, OK

100 YEARS OF COOKING
Oologah United Methodist Church
Oologah, OK

OUR COUNTRY COOKIN'
Junior Social Workers of
Chickasha, OK

THE PIONEER CHEF
Oklahoma Pioneers of America
Bethany, OK

POW WOW CHOW
The Five Civilized Tribes Museum
Muskogee, OK

QUICK BREADS, SOUPS AND
STEWS
by Mary Gubser
Council Oak Books
Tulsa, OK

RECIPES & REMEMBRANCES
Northfork Electric Cooperative
Sayre, OK

THE ROUTE 66 COOKBOOK
by Marian Clark
Council Oak Books
Tulsa, OK

SEASONED WITH LOVE
Faith United Methodist Women
Woodward, OK

SEEMS LIKE I DONE IT
THIS-A-WAY
by Cleo Stiles Bryan
Tahlequah, OK

SEEMS LIKE I DONE IT
THIS-A-WAY II
by Cleo Stiles Bryan
Tahlequah, OK

SEEMS LIKE I DONE IT
THIS-A-WAY III
by Cleo Stiles Bryan
Tahlequah, OK

SEQUOYAH'S COOKIN'
Sequoyah Schools PTO
Claremore, OK

SHATTUCK COMMUNITY
COOKBOOK
Shattuck Chamber of Commerce
Shattuck, OK

SISTERS TWO AND FAMILY TOO
by Nancy Barth and Sue Hergert
Beaver County, OK
and Ashland, KS

SOMETHING SPECIAL
COOKBOOK
by Areline Bolerjack
Enid, OK

SOONER SAMPLER
Junior League of Norman
Norman, OK

SOUNDS DELICIOUS!
Volunteer Council of the Tulsa
Philharmonic Society
Tulsa, OK

SPICED WITH WIT
M-PRESS
Hot Springs Village, AR

SPRING CREEK CLUB
Deer Creek, OK

STIR-UPS
Junior Welfare League of Enid
Enid, OK

THANK HEAVEN FOR HOME
MADE COOKS
Dover Christian Women's
Fellowship
Dover, OK

THUNDERBIRD COOKERS OF
AT&T
Telephone Pioneers—Thunderbird
Chapter 94
Oklahoma City, OK

UNITED METHODIST COOK-
BOOK 1993
United Methodist Women
Elk City, OK

WATONGA CHEESE FESTIVAL
COOKBOOK 17TH EDITION
Watonga Chamber of Commerce
Watonga, OK

WHAT'S COOKING IN
OKARCHE?
Apron Annies F.C.E.
Okarche, OK

WHEN A MAN'S FANCY TURNS
TO COOKING
by G. Wesley Rice
Pecan Quest Publications
Ponca City, OK

Oklahoma Timeline

Presented below is a brief chronology of historical Oklahoma events.

1803: The United States acquired most of Oklahoma in the Louisiana Purchase.

1830s–1840s: The Cherokee, Chickasaw, Choctaw, Creek and Seminole (called the Five Civilized Tribes) are encouraged and then forced to relocate from their native lands (by the US government) into Oklahoma, known then as the Indian Territory. Thousands of native Americans lost their lives on the bloody marches to Oklahoma.

1834: Set aside as Indian Territory

1842: Remaining Seminole Indians (from Florida) move to Oklahoma.

1845: Western Panhandle region became US territory with the annexation of Texas.

1860s: After the Civil War, because the Indians had sided with the Confederacy, they faced ruin and forfeiture of their lands.

1870s: An additional 25 tribes were moved to Oklahoma to reside on federal lands.

1889:
- Land in Indian Territory was opened to white settlement by land runs, lotteries, and auctions. The territory was split in half, and the western half became Oklahoma Territory.
- The first land run was held April 22nd. At exactly noon, a cannon boom signaled the start of the run which opened the Unassigned Lands for settlement.

1890: Region was divided into Indian Territory and Oklahoma Territory.

1891: The Sac and Fox, Pottawatomie-Shawnee Lands, located just east of the original run site, were opened.

1892: The Cheyenne and Arapaho lands in western Oklahoma were opened.

1893: The largest and most spectacular run in northern Oklahoma, the Cherokee Strip, was held.

1895: The Kickapoo Land Run was held in central Oklahoma.

1907: Indian Territory and Oklahoma Territory were combined to make a new state, Oklahoma—the 46th state to join the Union.

1930s: Oklahoma part of the Dust Bowl

1937: Route 66, which is also known as "The Mother Road," was paved end to end.

1990: Oklahoma's Native American population is the largest in the nation—252,420.

1995: Terrorist bomb blows up the Murrah Federal Building in downtown Oklahoma City, killing 168 people, and injuring hundreds more.

Index

GWEN MCKEE

Founded in 1955 in Oklahoma City, the National Cowboy & Western Heritage Museum is America's premier institution of Western history, art, and culture. The Museum collections focus on preserving and interpreting the heritage of the American West. Here Barbara and Gwen pose next to "Welcome Sundown," a bronze sculpture of a weary cowboy, part of the museum's permanent collection.

A

Almond Crusted Oven Pancakes 46
Angel Filling Supreme 242
Annie's Mexicorn Dip 14
Appetizers: *see also* Dips
  Blender Salsa 15
  Chutney Cream Cheese Ball 16
  Curry Chicken Spread 14
  Fun Veggies 18
  Grandma Amy's Meatballs 19
  Holiday Cheese Roll 16
  Pankey's Easy Hors D'Oeuvres 17
  Pepperoni Cheese Ball 17
  Ranch Seasoned Bagel Chips 18
  Salmon Party Log 21
  Sausage Balls 20
  Sausage-Cheese Balls 20
  Savory Stuffed Mushrooms 21
  Sooner Salsa 15
  Suzanne's Crab Appetizer 22
  Swedish Pecans 19
  Tortilla Wagon Wheels 17
Apples:
  Apple Dump Cake 184
  Fresh Apple Cake 185
  Granny's Apple Pie 225
  Raw Apple Walnut Cake 185
  Sugarless Apple Pie 225
  Sweet Potato Apple Salad 77
Apricot:
  Apricot Brandy Cookies 204
  Apricot Date Loaf 36
  Apricot Ecstasy 240
  Apricot Nibble Bread 37
Asparagus:
  Chicken Asparagus Casserole 133
  Escalloped Asparagus 111
Aunt Bill's Brown Candy 218
Aunt Susan's Red Earth Cake 190
Aztec Casserole 133

B

Baked Beans, Cotton Eyed Joe's 127
Baked Eggs in Herbed Cheese Sauce 45
Baked Fudge 215
Baked Herbed Tomatoes 109
Bananas:
  Banana Oat Pancakes 47
  Banana Pudding Cake 180
  Banana Sheet Cake 180
  Banana Split Cake 241
  Pam's Special Banana Pudding 250
Barbecue Beef Brisket 163
Barbecued Meatballs 153

Bart Conner's Eggplant Parmigiana 115
Basil Tomato Tart 108
Beans:
  Black Beans and Rice Soup 58
  Calico Beans 128
  Chuck Wagon Bean Hot Pot 59
  Cotton Eyed Joe's Baked Beans 127
  Crazy Beans 126
  Green Beans Supreme 125
  Italian Green Beans 125
  Southwestern Pinto Beans 126
  Sweet and Tangy Beans 127
Bearnaise Sauce, Encore 173
Beef: *see also* Brisket, Chilis
  Barbecued Meatballs 153
  Beef and Potato Casserole 149
  Bierocks 152
  Company Casserole 149
  Crowd-Pleasing Roast 167
  Ground Beef Casserole 148
  Home-Made Beef Jerky 160
  Mantle's Chicken Fried Steak 161
  Mexicali Meat Loaves 155
  Opal's Meat Loaf 155
  Poor Man Steak 154
  Roast Peppered Rib Eye of Beef 165
  Rock Cafe Old Fashioned Greasy
    Hamburger 153
  Russian Sauerkraut 156
  Sloppy Joes 151
  Spaghetti Sauce with Meat Balls 89
  Spoon Meat Loaf 154
  Steve's Favorite Mexican Casserole 148
  Taco Salad Casserole 150
  Two-Step Tenderloin with a Kick 166
Berry Best Muffins, The 41
Best Strawberry Pie, The 223
Better Meal Sandwich 51
Beverages:
  Herbal Tea 23
  Lemon Lime Punch 23
  Orange Mint 24
  Slush Punch 24
Bierocks 152
Biscuits:
  Biscuits 29
  Herb Biscuits 30
  Hot Pull-Apart Biscuits 31
  Mile-High Biscuits 29
  Pinch Cake 30
Black Beans and Rice Soup 58
Black Forest Pie 232
Black-Eyed Susans 206
Blender Salsa 15
Blueberry Salad, Mom's 79

Bran Muffins 39
Breakfast: *see also* Coffeecake, Eggs,
  Pancakes, Waffles
  Cheese Grits Casserole 42
  Ready-To-Eat Breakfast Cereal 52
Breads: *see also* Biscuits, Muffins, Rolls
  Apricot Date Loaf 36
  Apricot Nibble Bread 37
  Bride's Bread Pudding 253
  Broccoli Bread 26
  Cheese Popovers 39
  Cinnamon Bread 37
  Cream Cheese Braid 33
  Creamy Corn Bread Salad 69
  Jalapeño Corn Bread 26
  Kolaches 34
  Oatmeal Bread 38
  Pumpkin Cheese Bread 34
  Southern Spoon Bread 27
  Speedy Rolls and Bread 28
  Squaw Bread 27
  Strawberry Bread 36
  White Bread 27
Bride's Bread Pudding 253
Brisket:
  Barbecue Beef Brisket 163
  Beef Brisket 163
  Brisket 164
  Brisket Marinade 164
  Our Favorite Brisket 162
Broccoli:
  Broccoli Balls 102
  Broccoli Bread 26
  Broccoli-Corn Bake 104
  Cheesy Broccoli Casserole 103
Brownies and Bar Cookies:
  Chess Squares 210
  Glazed Honey Bars 208
  Hello Dolly 211
  Landrun Brownies 207
  Nanaimo Bars 209
  Neiman-Marcus Bars 210
  Pecan Diamonds 200
  Quick 'n' Chewy Crescent Bars 208
  Rice Krispies Marshmallow Treats 212
Burnt Caramel Cake 178
Butch's Rancher's Omelette 43
Butterfinger Dessert 249
Butterscotch Crunchies 213

C

Cabbage:
  Herman's Slaw 72
  Red Cabbage with Wine 111
Caesar Salad 72

Cakes: *see also* Cheesecakes, Coffeecakes
  A Chocolate-Raspberry Cake 190
  Apple Dump Cake 184
  Aunt Susan's Red Earth Cake 190
  Banana Pudding Cake 180
  Banana Sheet Cake 180
  Banana Split Cake 241
  Burnt Caramel Cake 178
  Carrot Cake 182
  Cherry Chocolate Cake 189
  Chocolate Chip Cake 189
  Christmas Cake Dessert 197
  Favorite Quick Fruit Cocktail Cake 184
  Fresh Apple Cake 185
  Harvey Wallbanger Cake 177
  Heavenly Coconut Cream Cake 177
  Lemon Chiffon Cake 193
  Mayonnaise Cake 179
  Mother's Hickory Nut Cake 186
  Orange Poppy Seed Cake 186
  Peach Cake 187
  Peanut Butter Sheet Cake 181
  Philbrook's Italian Cream Cake 188
  Pig Eater's Cake 176
  Pinch Cake 30
  Pineapple Ice Box Cake 197
  Potato Cake 179
  Pound Cake 177
  Prize Winning Johnson Special
    Chocolate Cake 192
  Pumpkin Roll 183
  Raw Apple Walnut Cake 185
  Seven-Up Cake 176
Calico Beans 128
Calzones 88
Candies: *see also* Fudge
  Aunt Bill's Brown Candy 218
  Butterscotch Crunchies 213
  Chocolate Almond Bark Crunch 216
  Cranberry Surprise 217
  Crispy Candy Bars 212
  English Toffee 220
  Orange Balls 215
  Peanut Butter Balls 217
  Peanut Brittle 220
  Popcorn Balls 213
  Puppy Chow for People 213
  Hello Dolly 211
  Rice Krispies Marshmallow Treats 212
  Tiger Butter 216
Caramel Ice Cream in Freezer 249
Carrots:
  Carrot Cake with Cream Cheese
    Frosting 182
  Company Carrots 100

INDEX

Copper Pennies 100
Creamy Carrot Soup 60
Honey-Dijon Carrots 100
Casserole, Company 149
Cathy Kelley's Cherry Pie Tarts 237
Cauliflower Salad 76
Cavattini 84
Caviar Dip, Oklahoma 12
Cheese:
Baked Eggs in Herbed Cheese Sauce 45
Cheese Corn Bake 104
Cheese Grits Casserole 42
Cheese Popovers 39
Chutney Cream Cheese Ball 16
Holiday Cheese Roll 16
Onion Cheese Pie 93
Pepperoni Cheese Ball 17
Pumpkin Cheese Bread 34
Sausage-Cheese Balls 20
Cheesecakes:
Cheesecake Cookies 210
Oreo Cheesecake 195
Strawberry Marbled Cheesecake 196
Strawberry Sundae Cheesecake 195
Supreme Cheesecake 194
Cheesy Broccoli Casserole 103
Cherries:
Cathy Kelley's Cherry Pie Tarts 237
Cherry Chocolate Cake 189
Cherry-Berries on a Cloud 245
Chess Squares 210
Chicken:
Aztec Casserole 133
Chicken and Pasta-Stuffed Tomatoes 65
Chicken Asparagus Casserole 133
Chicken Cannelloni 134
Chicken Chowder 54
Chicken Enchilada Bake 141
Chicken Enchiladas with Sour Cream 140
Chicken Fricassee with Dumplings 137
Chicken Lasagna 86
Chicken Mexican Salad, Hot 65
Chicken Quiche in Lemon Pastry Shell 90
Chicken Salad with Cranberry Dressing 64
Chicken Spaghetti 144
Chicken Tetrazzini 141, 142
Chicken Tomato Pasta Soup, Spicy 55
Chicken Vegetable Gumbo 54
Chicken Waikiki Beach 143
Colby's Cheesy Chicken 131
Cotillion Chicken Salad 64

Crispy Herb Chicken 139
Curry Chicken Spread 14
Homemade Shake & Bake 135
Honey Dijon Oven Chicken 130
Hot Chicken Mexican Salad 65
Marinated Chicken Breasts 130
Mexican Chicken 132
Miss Bonnie's Fried Chicken 136
Mother's Chunky Chicken and Strip Dumplings 138
Peachy Chicken Casserole 131
Ro-Tel Chicken Casserole 132
Route 66 Diner Philly Chicken 139
Spicy Chicken Tomato Pasta Soup 55
Terry's White Chili 58
White Chili 144
Chile Corn Casserole 106
Chilis:
Concession Chili 156
Herbal Chili 157
Hot 'n' Spicy Chunky Beef Chili 158
Hot Chili Mexican Salad 70
Terry's White Chili 58
White Chili 144
Choco-Nutaholic Cookies 201
Chocolate:
Cherry Chocolate Cake 189
Chocolate Almond Bark Crunch 216
Chocolate Chip Cake 189
Chocolate Cobbler 233
Chocolate Nut Torte to Diet For 244
Chocolate Pie 233
Chocolate-Raspberry Cake, A 190
Frozen Chocolate Crunch 248
German Chocolate Pudding 251
Prize Winning Johnson Special Chocolate Cake 192
Chowders:
Chicken Chowder 54
Crab and Corn Chowder 61
Low-Fat Clam Chowder 62
Potato Bacon Chowder 61
Christmas Cake Dessert 197
Chuck Wagon Bean Hot Pot 59
Chutney Cream Cheese Ball 16
Chutney, Peach and Citrus 173
Cinnamon Bread 37
Cleo's Pizza 92
Cobbler, Chocolate 233
Cobbler, Fresh Peach 234
Cocoa Cream Pie 232
Coconut:
Coconut Macaroons 211
Coconut Pie 229

Coconut Torte with Butter Sauce 198
Heavenly Coconut Cream Cake 177
Coffeecake, Raspberry Cream Cheese 31
Coffee Cake, Sour Cream 32
Colby's Cheesy Chicken 131
Company Carrots 100
Company Casserole 149
Company Scalloped Potatoes 120
Concession Chili 156
Confetti Turketti 87
Cookies: *see also* Brownies and Bar
  Cookies
  Apricot Brandy Cookies 204
  Black-Eyed Susans 206
  Cheesecake Cookies 210
  Choco-Nutaholic Cookies 201
  Coconut Macaroons 211
  Cowboy Cookies 203
  Giant Oatmeal Spice Cookies 202
  Ginger Strips 207
  Molasses Cookies 206
  Oatmeal Chews 204
  Peanut Butter Cookies 205
  Peanut Kisses 205
  Peppernuts 211
  Potato Chip Cookies 203
  White Chip Orange Cream Cookies 202
Copper Pennies 100
Corn:
  Broccoli-Corn Bake 104
  Cheese Corn Bake 104
  Cheese Grits Casserole 42
  Chile Corn Casserole 106
  Crab and Corn Chowder 61
  Creamy Corn Bread Salad 69
  Fried Corn 105
  Jalapeño Corn Bread 26
  Jalapeño Corn Pudding 105
Cotillion Chicken Salad 64
Cotton Eyed Joe's Baked Beans 127
Cowboy Cookies 203
Cowboy Potato and Vegetable Bake 120
Crab:
  Crab and Corn Chowder 61
  Crab Appetizer, Suzanne's 22
Cranberries:
  Cranberry Orange Salad 80
  Cranberry Sauce 146
  Cranberry Surprise 217
  Fresh Ham with Cranberry Stuffing
  168
Crazy Beans 126
Cream Cheese Braid 33
Creamy Carrot Soup 60

Creamy Corn Bread Salad 69
Creamy Potato Soup 60
Crescent Bars, Quick 'n Chewy 208
Crisp Buttery Waffles 48
Crispy Candy Bars 212
Crispy Herb Chicken 139
Crock Pot Pizza 92
Crowd-Pleasing Roast 167
Crystalline Pickles 98
Cucumber Salad 78
Curry Chicken Spread 14

D

Daiquiri Soufflé, Elegant 246
Date Pecan Pudding 252
Date Pudding 251
Delicious Rice 97
Desserts: *see specific dessert*
Dips:
  Annie's Mexicorn Dip 14
  Layered Dip 12
  Oklahoma Caviar Dip 12
  Pumpkin Dip 13
  Shrimp Dip 14
  Too Easy Tamale Dip 13
  Vegetable Dip 13
Dreamy High Pumpkin Pie 228
Dressing, French 82
Dressing, Ranch 82

E

Easy No-Knead Refrigerator Rolls 28
Effie Romberger's Old-Fashioned Rice
  Pudding 252
Eggplant:
  Bart Conner's Eggplant Parmigiana
  115
  Eggplant Parmigiana 114
  Eggplant—Chick Pea Dinner 114
Eggs:
  Baked Eggs in Herbed Cheese Sauce 45
  Butch's Rancher's Omelette 43
  Eggs À La Buckingham 44
  Panhandle Casserole 42
  Pankey's Easy Hors D'Oeuvres 17
  Squash with Eggs 110
  Volunteer Egg and Sausage Casserole 43
Eight (8) Bean Soup 59
Elegant Daiquiri Souffl6 246
Elegante Squash 110
Encore Bearnaise Sauce 173
English Toffee 220
Escalloped Asparagus 111
Everyday Waffle 47

F

Fantastic Layered Dessert 242
Fast Fettuccine 91
Favorite Quick Fruit Cocktail Cake 184
Fettuccine, Fast 91
French Dressing 82
French Silk Pie 254
Fresh Apple Cake 185
Fresh Ham with Cranberry Stuffing 168
Fresh Peach Cobbler 234
Fried Chicken, Miss Bonnie's 136
Fried Corn 105
Fried Green Tomatoes 107
Fried Pie Crust 235
Frosted Salad 79
Frozen Chocolate Crunch 248
Fruit: *see also specific fruit*
  Favorite Quick Fruit Cocktail Cake 184
  Fruit Salad with Cardamom 77
Fudge, Baked 215
Fudge Bars, Rocky Road 214
Fun Veggies 18

G

Garden Goulash 109
German Chocolate Pudding 251
Giant Oatmeal Spice Cookies 202
Ginger Strips 207
Glazed Honey Bars 208
Gourmet Potatoes 119
Grandma Amy's Meatballs 19
Granny's Apple Pie 225
Gravy, Ham Red Eye 169
Green Beans Supreme 125
Grilled Green Tomatoes 107
Ground Beef Casserole 148
Gumbo, Chicken Vegetable 54

H

Ham:
  Fresh Ham with Cranberry Stuffing
    168
  Ham and Potato Bake 170
  Ham Delicacy 98
  Ham Loaf 169
  Ham Red Eye Gravy 169
  Ham Rolls 170
  Ham-Pecan-Blue Cheese Pasta Salad
    67
  Hot Ham Sandwich 51
  Mother's Ham Loaf 168
  Raisin Sauce for Ham 169
  Tangy Ham Balls in Pineapple Sauce
    167

Hamburger, Rock Cafe Old Fashioned
    Greasy 153
Harvey Wallbanger Cake 177
Heavenly Coconut Cream Cake 177
Heavenly Jam 50
Hello Dolly 211
Herb Biscuits 30
Herbal Chili 157
Herbal Tea 23
Herman's Slaw 72
Hickory Nut Cake, Mother's 186
Holiday Cheese Roll 16
Home-Made Beef Jerky 160
Homemade Shake & Bake 135
Hominy Casserole 106
Honey-Dijon Carrots 100
Honey Dijon Oven Chicken 130
Honey Pecan Pie 231
Hot 'n' Spicy Chunky Beef Chili 158
Hot Chicken Mexican Salad 65
Hot Chili Mexican Salad 70
Hot Ham Sandwich 51
Hot Pull-Apart Biscuits 31

I

Ice Box Peach Jam 50
Indian Tacos 84
Italian Green Beans 125

J

J.J.'s Pepper Relish 98
Jalapeño Corn Bread 26
Jalapeño Corn Pudding 105
Jam, Heavenly 50
Jam, Ice Box Peach 50
Jell-O Flavored Syrups 49
Jell-O Pudding Pecan Pie 230
Jelly, Oklahoma Sandplum 49

K

Kolaches 34
Kugulas 117

L

Landrun Brownies 207
Laredo Potato 118
Lasagna, Chicken 86
Lasagna, Mexican 87
Layered Dip 12
Lebanese Tabouleh Salad 69
Lemons:
  Lemon Chiffon Cake 193
  Lemon Fluff 240
  Lemon-Lime Punch 23

Linda's Sweet Potato Casserole 121
Low-Fat Clam Chowder 62

M

M-M-M-Mouse Au Easy 250
Macadamia Nut Cream Pie 229
Make Ahead Casadda Dessert 241
Mantle's Chicken Fried Steak 161
Marinated Chicken Breasts 130
Mayonnaise Cake 179
Meat Loaf, Opal's 155
Meatballs, Barbecued 153
Meatballs, Grandma Amy's 19
Meats: see Beef, Ham, Pork, Rabbit,
  Sausage
Mexicali Meat Loaves 155
Mexican Casserole, Steve's Favorite 148
Mexican Chicken 132
Mexican Lasagna 87
Mexican Plum Pie 224
Mile-High Biscuits 29
Miss Bonnie's Fried Chicken 136
Molasses Cookies 206
Molly's Landing Marinated Mushrooms
  112
Mom's Blueberry Salad 79
Mother's Chunky Chicken and Strip
  Dumplings 138
Mother's Ham Loaf 168
Mother's Hickory Nut Cake 186
Mrs. Croman's Rhubarb Pie 226
Muffins:
  "Berry-Best" Muffins, The 41
  Bran Muffins 39
  Orange Streusel Muffins 40
  Tumbleweeds 40
Mushrooms:
  Molly's Landing Marinated Mushrooms
    112
  Mushroom Salad 76
  Savory Stuffed Mushrooms 21
My Favorite Potatoes 119
My Sister's Pear Preserves 50

N

Nanaimo Bars 209
Neiman-Marcus Bars 210

O

Oatmeal Bread 38
Oatmeal Chews 204
Oklahoma Caviar Dip 12
Oklahoma Pecan Pie 230
Oklahoma Sandplum Jelly 49

Okra Creole Style 110
Omelette, Butch's Rancher's 43
One Dish Pork Chop Meal 171
Onion Cheese Pie 93
Onions, Stuffed Baked 113
Opal's Meat Loaf 155
Oranges:
  Cranberry Orange Salad 80
  Orange Balls 215
  Orange Chiffon Pie 228
  Orange Mint 24
  Orange Poppy Seed Cake 186
  Orange Rice 94
  Orange Streusel Muffins 40
  White Chip Orange Cream Cookies 202
Oreo Cheesecake 195
Our Favorite Brisket 162

P

Pam's Special Banana Pudding 250
Pancakes:
  Almond Crusted Oven Pancakes 46
  Banana Oat Pancakes 47
  Potato Pancakes 116
Panhandle Casserole 42
Pankey's Easy Hors D'Oeuvres 17
Pasta: see also Lasagna
  Calzones 88
  Cavattini 84
  Chicken and Pasta-Stuffed Tomatoes 65
  Chicken Quiche in Lemon Pastry Shell
    90
  Chicken Spaghetti 144
  Confetti Turketti 87
  Fast Fettuccine 91
  Ham Delicacy 98
  Pasta Salad 66
  Ramen Noodle Salad 71
  Shanghai Shrimp and Pasta Salad 66
  Spaghetti Sauce with Meat Balls 89
  Wood Chuck 88
  Zucchini and Basil Pasta Salad 68
Peaches:
  Fresh Peach Cobbler 234
  Ice Box Peach Jam 50
  Peach and Citrus Chutney 173
  Peach Cake 187
  Peachy Chicken Casserole 131
Peanut Brittle 220
Peanut Butter:
  Peanut Butter Balls 217
  Peanut Butter Cookies 205
  Peanut Butter Pie 227
  Peanut Butter Sheet Cake 181

Peanut Kisses 205
Pears:
My Sister's Pear Preserves 50
Pear Tart 238
Pears Melba 239
Pecans:
Date Pecan Pudding 252
Ham-Pecan-Blue Cheese Pasta Salad 67
Honey Pecan Pie 231
Jell-O Pudding Pecan Pie 230
Oklahoma Pecan Pie 230
Pecan Diamonds 200
Swedish Pecans 19
Pepper Relish, J J's 98
Peppernuts 211
Pepperoni Cheese Ball 17
Philbrook's Italian Cream Cake 188
Pickles, Crystalline 98
Pie Crust: *see* Pies
Pies:
Black Forest Pie 232
Cathy Kelley's Cherry Pie Tarts 237
Chocolate Nut Torte to Diet For 244
Chocolate Pie 233
Cocoa Cream Pie 232
Coconut Pie 229
Dreamy High Pumpkin Pie 228
French Silk Pie 254
Fried Pie Crust 235
Granny's Apple Pie 225
Honey Pecan Pie 231
Jell-O Pudding Pecan Pie 230
Macadamia Nut Cream Pie 229
Mexican Plum Pie 224
Mrs. Croman's Rhubarb Pie 225
Oklahoma Pecan Pie 230
Onion Cheese Pie 93
Orange Chiffon Pie 228
Peanut Butter Pie 227
Pie Crust Mix 236
Pineapple Pie 224
Raisin Pie 222
Sugarless Apple Pie 225
Sour Cream-Raisin Pie 223
The Best Strawberry Pie 223
Turkey Vegetable Pot Pie 145
Pig Eater's Cake 176
Pinch Cake 30
Pineapple:
Pineapple Ice Box Cake 197
Pineapple Pie 224
Tangy Ham Balls in Pineapple Sauce 167

Pizza, Cleo's 92
Pizza, Crock Pot 92
Plum Pie, Mexican 224
Poor Man Steak 154
Popcorn Balls 213
Pork: *see also* Ham, Sausage
Crowd-Pleasing Roast 167
One Dish Pork Chop Meal 171
Pork Forestiori 172
Stick-To-Your-Ribs Ribs 159
Potatoes: *see also* Sweet Potatoes
Beef and Potato Casserole 149
Company Scalloped Potatoes 120
Cowboy Potato and Vegetable Bake 120
Creamy Potato Soup 60
Gourmet Potatoes 119
Ham and Potato Bake 170
Kugulas 117
Laredo Potato 118
My Favorite Potatoes 119
Potato Bacon Chowder 61
Potato Cake 179
Potato Chip Cookies 203
Potato Pancakes 116
Prairie Schooners 118
Summer Potato Salad 76
Poultry: *see* Chicken, Turkey
Pound Cake 177
Prairie Schooners 118
Preserves, My Sister's Pear 50
Prize Winning Johnson Special Chocolate Cake 192
Pudding:
Banana Pudding Cake 180
Bride's Bread Pudding 253
Date Pecan Pudding 252
Date Pudding 251
Effie Romberger's Old-Fashioned Rice Pudding 252
German Chocolate Pudding 251
Jalapeño Corn Pudding 105
Jell-O Pudding Pecan Pie 230
Pam's Special Banana Pudding 250
Pumpkin:
Dreamy High Pumpkin Pie 228
Pumpkin Cheese Bread 34
Pumpkin Dip 13
Pumpkin Roll 183
Punch: *see* Beverages
Puppy Chow for People 213

Q

Quick Salad 81
Quick 'n' Chewy Crescent Bars 208

R

Rabbit Stir-Fry 171
Raisin Pie 222
Raisin Sauce for Ham 169
Ramen Noodle Salad 71
Ranch Dressing 82
Ranch Seasoned Bagel Chips 18
Ranchero Sauce 174
Raspberry Chocolate Cake, A 190
Raspberry Cream Cheese Coffeecake 31
Raw Apple Walnut Cake 185
Ready-To-Eat Breakfast Cereal 52
Red Cabbage with Wine 111
Relish, J.J.'s Pepper 98
Rhubarb Pie, Mrs. Croman's 226
Ribbon Salad 80
Ribs, Stick-To-Your-Ribs 159
Rice:
    Black Beans and Rice Soup 58
    Delicious Rice 97
    Effie Romberger's Old-Fashioned Rice
        Pudding 252
    Orange Rice 94
    Rice Almondine 95
    Wild Rice Bake 95
    Wild Rice Baron 94
Roast Peppered Rib Eye of Beef 165
Roast, Crowd-Pleasing 167
Rock Cafe Old Fashioned Greasy
    Hamburger 153
Rocky Road Fudge Bars 214
Rolls:
    Easy No-Knead Refrigerator Rolls 28
    Ham Rolls 170
    Speedy Rolls and Bread 28
Ro-Tel Chicken Casserole 132
Route 66 Diner Philly Chicken 139
Russian Borscht 56
Russian Sauerkraut 156

S

Salads:
    7-Up Salad 81
    Caesar Salad 72
    Cauliflower Salad 76
    Chicken and Pasta-Stuffed Tomatoes 65
    Chicken Salad with Cranberry Dressing
        64
    Cotillion Chicken Salad 64
    Cranberry Orange Salad 80
    Creamy Corn Bread Salad 69
    Cucumber Salad 78
    Frosted Salad 79
    Fruit Salad with Cardamom 77
    Ham-Pecan-Blue Cheese Pasta Salad 67
    Herman's Slaw 72
    Hot Chicken Mexican Salad 65
    Hot Chili Mexican Salad 70
    Lebanese Tabouleh Salad 69
    Mom's Blueberry Salad 79
    Mushroom Salad 76
    Pasta Salad 66
    Quick Salad 81
    Ramen Noodle Salad 71
    Ribbon Salad 80
    Shanghai Shrimp and Pasta Salad 66
    Shoe Peg Salad 75
    Sour Cream Spinach Salad 74
    Spinach Salad 73
    Summer Potato Salad 76
    Summer Tomato Salad with Brie 74
    Sweet Potato Apple Salad 77
    Taco Salad Casserole 150
    Waldorf Salad 78
    Zucchini and Basil Pasta Salad 68
    Zucchini-Artichoke Salad 75
Salmon Party Log 21
Salmon Patties 97
Sandplum Jelly, Oklahoma 49
Sandwiches:
    Better Meal Sandwich 51
    Hot Ham Sandwich 51
    Stromboli 51
Santa Fe Taco Soup 56
Sauces:
    Cranberry Sauce 146
    Encore Bearnaise Sauce 173
    Raisin Sauce for Ham 169
    Ranchero Sauce 174
    Tarter Sauce 97
Sausage:
    Panhandle Casserole 42
    Sausage Balls 20
    Sausage-Cheese Balls 20
    Volunteer Egg and Sausage Casserole 43
Savory Stuffed Mushrooms 21
Sensational Spinach and Zucchini Pie 101
Seven-Up Cake 176
Seven-Up Salad 81
Shanghai Shrimp and Pasta Salad 66
Shoe Peg Salad 75
Shrimp Dip 14
Shrimp and Pasta Salad, Shanghai 66
Simply Southwest 96
Slaw, Herman's 72
Sloppy Joes 151
Slush Punch 24
Sooner Salsa 15

INDEX

Soups: *see also* Chowders
  8 Bean Soup 59
  Black Beans and Rice Soup 58
  Chicken Vegetable Gumbo 54
  Chuck Wagon Bean Hot Pot 59
  Creamy Carrot Soup 60
  Creamy Potato Soup 60
  Russian Borscht 56
  Santa Fe Taco Soup 56
  Spicy Chicken Tomato Pasta Soup 55
  Taco Soup 57
Sour Cream Coffee Cake 32
Sour Cream Spinach Salad 74
Sour Cream-Raisin Pie 223
Southern Spoon Bread 27
Southwestern Pinto Beans 126
Spaghetti Sauce with Meat Balls 89
Speedy Rolls and Bread 28
Spicy Chicken Tomato Pasta Soup 55
Spinach:
  Sensational Spinach and Zucchini Pie 101
  Sour Cream Spinach Salad 74
  Spinach Cups 102
  Spinach Salad 73
Spoon Meat Loaf 154
Squash, Elegante 110
Squash with Eggs 110
Squaw Bread 27
Steve's Favorite Mexican Casserole 148
Stick-To-Your-Ribs Ribs 159
Strawberries:
  Best Strawberry Pie, The 223
  Strawberry Bread 36
  Strawberry Marbled Cheesecake 196
  Strawberry Sundae Cheesecake 195
Stromboli 51
Stuffed Baked Onions 113
Sugarless Apple Pie 225
Summer Potato Salad 76
Summer Tomato Salad with Brie 74
Summer Vegetable Casserole 121
Supreme Cheesecake 194
Suzanne's Crab Appetizer 22
Swedish Pecans 19
Sweet and Tangy Beans 127
Sweet Potato Apple Salad 77
Sweet Potato Casserole, Linda's 121

T

Taco Salad Casserole 150
Tacos, Indian 84
Taco Soup 57
Taco Soup, Santa Fe 56

Tangy Ham Balls in Pineapple Sauce 167
Tart, Pear 238
Tartar Sauce 97
Terrific Tortilla Torte 85
Terry's White Chili 58
Tiger Butter 216
Tomatoes:
  Baked Herbed Tomatoes 109
  Basil Tomato Tart 108
  Fried Green Tomatoes 107
  Grilled Green Tomatoes 107
  Spicy Chicken Tomato Pasta Soup 55
  Summer Tomato Salad with Brie 74
Too Easy Tamale Dip 13
Torte, Terrific Tortilla 85
Torte with Butter Sauce, Coconut 198
Tortilla Wagonwheels 17
Tulips Through the Snow 247
Tumbleweeds 40
Turkey Croquettes 146
Turkey Vegetable Pot Pie 145
Twinkie Treat 243
Two-Step Tenderloin with a Kick 166

V

Vegetables: *see also specific vegetable*
  Garden Goulash 110
  Summer Vegetable Casserole 121
  Vegetable Casserole 124
  Vegetable Dip 13
  Vegetable Medley 123
  Vegetable Patties 122
Volunteer Egg and Sausage Casserole 43

W

Waffle, Everyday 47
Waffles, Crisp Buttery 48
Waldorf Salad 78
White Bread 27
White Chili 144
White Chip Orange Cream Cookies 202
Wild Rice Bake 95
Wild Rice Baron 94
Wood Chuck 88

Z

Zucchini:
  Sensational Spinach and Zucchini Pie 101
  Zucchini and Basil Pasta Salad 68
  Zucchini-Artichoke Salad 75

Collect the Series!
Best of the Best State Cookbook Series

Cookbook collectors love this Series! The forty-two cookbooks, covering all fifty states (see next page for listing), contain over 15,000 of the most popular local and regional recipes collected from approximately 3,000 of the leading cookbooks from these states. The Series not only captures the flavor of America, but saves a lot of shelf space.

To assist individuals who wish to collect the Series, we are offering a **Collect the Series Discount Coupon Booklet.** With the Booklet you get:

Collect the Series!
BEST OF THE BEST STATE COOKBOOK SERIES
With this Special *Collect the Series* Discount Coupon Booklet

OVER 3 MILLION STATE COOKBOOKS SOLD! *continued inside . . .*

- 25% discount off the list price ($16.95 minus 25% = $12.70 per copy)
- With a single order of five copies, you receive a sixth copy free. A single order of ten cookbooks, gets two free copies, etc.
- Only $4.00 shipping cost for any number of books ordered (within contiguous United States).

Call **1-800-343-1583** to order a free, no-obligation Discount Coupon Booklet. A free catalog of all QRP cookbooks is also available on request.

Recipe Hall of Fame Cookbook Collection
is also included in the **Collect the Series Discount Coupon Booklet.**

| 304 pages • $19.95 | 304 pages • $19.95 | 304 pages • $19.95 | 240 pages • $16.95 |

The four cookbooks in this collection consist of over 1,200 of the most exceptional recipes collected from the entire BEST OF THE BEST STATE COOKBOOK SERIES.
The Hall of Fame Collection can be bought as a four-cookbook set for $40.00.
This is a 48% discount off the total individual cost of $76.80.

QUAIL RIDGE PRESS
P. O. Box 123 • Brandon, MS 39043 • 1-800-343-1583
E-mail: info@quailridge.com • www.quailridge.com

BEST OF THE BEST STATE COOKBOOK SERIES

ALABAMA

ALASKA

ARIZONA

ARKANSAS

BIG SKY
Includes Montana, Wyoming

CALIFORNIA

COLORADO

FLORIDA

GEORGIA

GREAT PLAINS
Includes North Dakota, South Dakota, Nebraska, and Kansas

HAWAII

IDAHO

ILLINOIS

INDIANA

IOWA

KENTUCKY

LOUISIANA

LOUISIANA II

MICHIGAN

MID-ATLANTIC
Includes Maryland, Delaware, New Jersey, and Washington, D.C.

MINNESOTA

MISSISSIPPI

MISSOURI

NEVADA

NEW ENGLAND
Includes Rhode Island, Connecticut, Massachusetts, Vermont, New Hampshire, and Maine

NEW MEXICO

NEW YORK

NO. CAROLINA

OHIO

OKLAHOMA

OREGON

PENNSYLVANIA

SO. CAROLINA

TENNESSEE

TEXAS

TEXAS II

UTAH

VIRGINIA

VIRGINIA II

WASHINGTON

WEST VIRGINIA

WISCONSIN

All BEST OF THE BEST COOKBOOKS are 6x9 inches, are comb-bound, contain over 300 recipes, and total 264–352 pages. Each contains illustrations, photographs, an index, and a list of contributing cookbooks, a special feature that cookbook collectors enjoy. Scattered throughout the cookbooks are short quips that provide interesting information about each state, including historical facts and major attractions along with amusing trivia. Retail price per copy $16.95.

To order by credit card, call toll-free **1-800-343-1583**, visit **www.quailridge.com**, or use the Order Form below.
